Chronicle of an Islander

Edwin B. Athearn

Chronicle of an Islander

by
Edwin B. Athearn

MARTHA'S VINEYARD STORIES

ISBN # 1-883154-01-4

Edwin B. Athearn

This Martha's Vineyard series of events in the form of a book is dedicated to

My wonderful mother, Jean MacLeod Athearn and to my immediate family members and relations, along with all members of the Athearn clan wherever they happen to be located.

Shown above with author and Son, Edwin B. Athearn, 1947.

Foreword

The purpose of producing this autobiography is partly to relive youthful experiences and also for the hopeful reason that this collection of anecdotes will provide some historic value. I have made an effort to record this variety of events in a sort of orderly squence. The memories are clear and the experiences true, but variations in timing are to be expected. My boyhood pal, David Dorn, now living in Marathon, Florida, a surviving contemporary, provided me copies of his diaries of our daily Menemsha Creek activities during the mid-1920's. Remembering and writing about Martha's Vineyard has proved to be a pleasurable experience. May this reminiscing generate entertainment for all potential readers.

Edwin B. Athearn

The Charles W. Morgan at sea south of the Azores.
Note masthead lookouts on watch
for spouting whales. (Thar she blows!)
My grandfather, Edwin W. Athearn, made four
voyages on this whaleship. Average voyage was four years.
This famous whaleship is enshrined and on exhibit
at Mystic Seaport, Connecticut.

Introduction

The Athearn Family Historic Origin

In Volume II of The History of Martha's Vineyard, Charles E. Banks mentions the name of Simon Athearn, the recorded originator of the Athearn clan on Martha's Vineyard Island (p. 28).

According to his ancient gravestone in the West Tisbury cemetery, he was born in 1643 and lived until 1715. He was married at a young age and raised nine children: four boys and five girls.

Simon Athearn's own origin is something of a mystery. The prevailing theory is that he came to the island in the employ of Nicholas Butler and settled in the village of Edgartown.

In the course of his life, Simon was noted for his active opposition to Governor Thomas Mayhew. However, during all those turbulent years he managed to acquire an impressive acreage of land in many mid island areas. Much of that property which included large points of land, was ideally located along the shorefront of the Great Ponds. In terms of real estate, Simon was considered a rather wealthy citizen. His ambitions and land acquisitions required many legal battles in the court.

He was considered to be one of Tisbury's great citizens and a man of considerable influence. It is quite evident that the lifetime of Simon Athearn was an era of special historical significance.

Notable among the newer generation of Athearns are Jim and Debbie, who are the successful proprietors of the Morning Glory Farm in Edgartown. One of their children is a boy who is blessed with the name Simon.

Perhaps this is an example of heredity influencing destiny.

Table of Contents

Chapter 1

Memories of a Young Islander

Memories are the origin of this story. A boxful of old diaries I recently discovered in storage provided the incentive. Some of these daily notations dated from the nineteen twenties and the thirties.

My birthplace, in the village of West Tisbury, is located several hundred yards south of Edgartown Road on a side road known as New Lane. The old house and the neighboring Baxter house remain liveable today.

A dual-rut wagon road extended through the woods about a mile to the farm of George and Daisy Manter. The farm bordered Town Cove, where the Manters had a sizeable workshop combined with a boathouse. An old lapstrake double-ended sailboat owned by a neighbor, Charlie Foote, lay bottom-up on the grass outside the boathouse for years. My fascination with boats began there. More about that later. Another of my early fascinations was with Barbara Foote, who rode leisurely around town on her palomino pony. She was a summer girl who never became aware that I was in love with her!

A pyramid of young Athearns. Left to right: Clifton Athearn (on top); Louise Athearn and Leonard Athearn (middle row); Ed Athearn, Elmer "Mike" Athearn and Lawrence "Tad" Athearn (bottom row).

The Harry Athearn family lived about a mile east of us in a heavily wooded area reached by a narrow wagon road. Cousins Elmer, Leonard, Clifton and Louise Athearn were our nearest playmates. They had cleared an area in their backyard brush and built a miniature village, complete with houses, stores and a system of roads. The real fun, though, was playing with their collection of miniature cars and trucks, small cast-iron models about six inches long, complete with rubber tires, which provided us many hours of amusement. Their mother always kept us supplied with her special homemade molasses cookies.

Our nearest neighbors were Dionis and Sidney Riggs, artistic people who lived in the Capt. Cleaveland house (originally an Athearn homestead), a big two-story building located on a large tract of land that formed the eastern corner of New Lane and Edgartown Road. Sidney favored knickers, a style of breeches that were popular in those days.

Creating blockprints, I believe was his special talent. Somehow, I never did get to know their daughter Cynthia.

Dionis Coffin Riggs recently celebrated her 95th birthday. She continues to be active and writes a weekly column of West Tisbury news for the Vineyard Gazette. She was among many prominent citizens included in a social gathering of entertainment for President Bill Clinton and family during his highly publicized Martha's Vineyard vacation of 1993.

Automobiles were, of course, a novelty in those days. Another neighbor, Dexter Athearn, a carpenter by trade, owned a big Buick touring car. The springtime thaws and rains changed New Lane into a muddy, deeply-rutted trail. Tough going for heavy, underpowered cars. Never could understand why he didn't leave the Buick parked on the grass by the highway, then walk in the short distance to the house on a path close to New Lane.

When I was about ten, someone gave me a small wooden wheelbarrow. It was fun to dash around the yard with it. Cousin Dexter, watching my antics one day, came over and said to me, "Your wheelbarrow needs a motor." He had with him a big old alarm clock. He separated the inner works from the case and fastened the mechanism to the front panel of the wheelbarrow. If we wound the alarm spring (the bell had been removed) the hammer would make an impressive sort of noisy vibration. I ran along the road at full speed until the motor stopped. The clock mechanism was only a noisemaker and not used in any way to propel the wheelbarrow. A quick rewind and away we went some more. An early start for mechanized travel!

Chapter 2

Young Fishermen

One day at age 12 in 1925 a neighbor, Jimmy Mayhew, gave me a ride home from school in his Model T Ford Roadster. It was April and we were just about to start a week of school vacation. Jimmy asked, "How would you like to ride up to Menemsha tomorrow and help me to bail herring out of a fish trap?"

I said, "Wow! What time do we go?"

At dawn the next day we were on the way to Menemsha Creek by way of the North Road. The trap crew was waiting at the town landing. We boarded a beamy powerboat, and towing three big dorys, we followed a winding channel into Menemsha Pond. We went across the pond and came upon a string of weirs along the Gay Head shoreline.

By mid-morning, using dip nets, the boats were all deeply loaded with the species of herring known as "alewives". The outgoing tide quickly carried us the length of the creek and on out into Menemsha Bight, where a fleet of five big Gloucester schooners, known as "Halibuters", lay at anchor.

One of the vessels that I remember clearly was the *ORETHA B. SPINNEY*. Several years later she would be bought by a Hollywood movie producer, renamed *WE'RE HERE* and used in MGM's version of the classic sea story, Kipling's *Captain's Courageous*, with

Capt. Percy Tilton, 1925. World War I veteran, owner of boat LOIS T. (now TURMOIL) looking for lobster pot buoys off Gay Head. Percy kept his package of Lucky Strike cigarettes under his cap where they would stay dry!

great actors such as Lionel Barrymore and Spencer Tracy. Quite a realistic production, I recall.

Each vessel carried ten double dorys on deck, for catching halibut with their hook and line tub trawl gear. Two men worked in each dory when they were on the fishing grounds. We knew they needed herring to use as bait.

We went alongside the nearest vessel, where two boatloads of fish were transferred in canvas baskets quickly hoisted by the schooner crew. The herring were salted in the fish hold pens. Two days of that intensive work provided the vessels with all the bait they needed. Then, one by one, they sailed out of Vineyard Sound on their way to the Grand Banks, a thousand miles eastward. It was a beautiful sight that any real sailor would long remember.

Because of my work with the herring project, one of the men, Percy Tilton, offered me a job as deckhand on his lobster boat for the coming summer season for five dollars a week and room and board at his Chilmark house. Just a year earlier, at age eleven, I had earned my first dollar by mowing a neighbor's yard with a man-sized reel push-mower. My mother had framed the one dollar bill and displayed it on a wall in the kitchen. The school year ended early in June and the new era began right away when I thumbed a ride to Chilmark with my baggage. My bedroom would be in the attic of the Tilton house.

Soon after sunrise, on my first day, we arrived at the "Creek" in Percy's big Buick. The *LOIS T's* deck was stacked with lobster traps. Once underway, we proceeded past Lobsterville and Dogfish Bar to the Campbell and Flanders fish weir off the Gay Head shoreline. The weir crew hauled the trap netting into a work boat known as the "bathtub". Both ends of the boat were rounded so that the crew could move around easily inside the trap structure.

We filled our three barrels with a mixture of fish to be used as lobster bait. Right away I was told to fill bait bags, net bags that would be tied inside each lobster trap. By the time we had gone out around the dangerous ledge known as Devil's Bridge off the colorful Gay Head cliffs and encountered an impressive groundswell, I had become seasick, an embarrassing predicament. However, we continued to bait and set the deckload of pots. After that we hauled, baited and reset a string of fifty big, soggy, round-top pots while the tide was relatively slack and the orange-colored wooden buoys were visible. Each pot produced an average of three or four legal-sized lobsters, which we'd drop through a small hatch into the wet well, a compartment full of seawater to keep lobsters and fish alive. We'd trap some big conger eels too, along with plenty of scup and sea bass. "Short" lobsters by the dozen had to be tossed overboard. Female lobsters, loaded with their tiny black eggs, also had to be returned to their natural element. Sensible conservation.

Then we ate lunch, a couple of dry sandwiches out of a small cardboard box, while we went along over to East Bend, a cove on the north side of Noman's Land, a small island, to haul five pots that Percy had set in there. Each pot was solid full of lobsters and fish. "Usually these pots are emptied by poachers before I can get here," Percy said. "It's a popular overnight anchorage."

It was late in the day when we finally returned to our Menemsha Creek pier. We soon learned that Carleton Mayhew and his son, Ben, in their boat *CARRIE V* had brought in a swordfish, the first one of the summer season. Excitement!

Percy said, "Tomorrow we will be hauling gear off Noman's, so we had better keep a lookout for fins." The *LOIS T* was rigged for swordfishing with a long stand and pulpit out over the bow and harpoon poles, darts, buoy lines and kegs.

Early next morning we stopped at a roadside spring to refill the water jugs before boarding the boat. Again, we picked up lobster bait at the Gay Head fish trap. Percy explained that fresh bait was more productive than salt bait. He went on to say that by midsummer, sand fleas would devour the fresh bait overnight, and that then we'd need salt bait, mostly skates.

We hauled and set four 25 pot strings that day to the moans of the Noman's sea buoy known as the "Hooter". The buoy emitted a series of mournful groans as it rose and fell in the ocean swell. However, whenever the fog rolled in, it was a pleasure to hear that moaning aid to navigation!

We'd sighted sharks during the day, no swordfish, but we had about 800 pounds of lobsters in the live well. On the way homeward I found a dry spot on the forward deck, stretched out and slept for an hour or so. It had been a busy day for a twelve-year-old kid!

Chapter 3

A Summer on the Sea

The following day a brisk sou'wester provided a fair wind to Woods Hole and Sam Cahoon's seafood market. We hoisted four crates of live lobsters that we'd secured under the pier and covered them with wet burlap. Two hours later we tied up in Woods Hole where we found that another Menemsha fisherman, Dan Larsen, and his oldest boy, Bjorn, had arrived there ahead of us.

When I stepped ashore I was on Mainland, U.S.A. for the first time! It was exciting to be off-island. A steam locomotive huffed and puffed on the tracks near the steamboat wharf. People and traffic, hustle and bustle. Eating an ice cream cone, double-scooped. A holiday with an entirely new atmosphere! A different world entirely!

The summer fishing campaign became a routine of lobstering and swordfishing on alternate days. We tried to haul and reset the traps off Gay Head before doing likewise with the gear south of Noman's Land. A long dawn-to-dusk day saw us back to the house for supper by about ten P.M., upstairs to bed by eleven o'clock and shaken awake again by three A.M. Then over to the creek and we'd be underway again for a day of swordfishing offshore southward from Noman's, a plodding seven or eight hour cruise.

Usually, on swordfishing trips, we had another crew member along, either Norman West or Herb Flanders. My job was mostly steering a compass course. The two other crewmen stood aloft on the masthead spreader keeping a sharp lookout for fins. Sharks of many species were plentiful. When a swordfish appeared, I would hear a shout as Percy Tilton slid down the headstay into the pulpit, where he'd grab the harpoon pole. He would then point the pole in the direction that he wanted me to steer the boat. The trick was to maneuver the boat so we'd have the bright sunlight behind us and could approach the fish "head-on". Underwater visibility was important in the event that the fish settled, which would make an accurate strike difficult.

By mid-afternoon as we headed toward Noman's, we'd feel a moderate southwest breeze, a smoky sou'wester. But in those days, it was wood smoke from numerous inland forest fires that gave it its nickname, not the big city smog so common nowadays.

On a good day, we would have three swordfish on deck, more often, though, we'd land only one or two. Some days the fish were wild and would disappear in a flash. We'd see an occasional breecher in the distance, leaping high out of the water and coming down with a big splash.

In the course of the day, we would wander in all directions. On the way home, we'd go by "dead reckoning". Returning toward land in the smoky atmosphere, we would glimpse dim sandy cliffs. Unless we could see the Hooter, we couldn't be sure whether we were seeing the south side of Noman's or the cliffs known as the Yellow Hills on the ocean side of Martha's Vineyard.

When visibility was limited, we depended on the sounding lead. We knew that the water depth south of the Vineyard increased by about a fathom to the mile all the way out to fifty miles or more. In thick fog, if we could not locate the Noman's Hooter, we would head to the north and try to find the hooter at the mouth of Vineyard Sound. We usually could get a bearing on our location by stopping the engine to listen for the deep-voiced fog horn broadcasting from the Vineyard lightship, anchored at the entrance to Buzzards Bay, southwest of Cuttyhunk Island. When we came into the lee of Gay Head, the fog would quickly thin out and the shoreline would become visible. Fish buyers waited for us at the Menemsha town landing to bid on the day's catch of swordfish.

Prohibition had brought with it an aura of mystery about the activities of "rum-runners". Out around Noman's, in the late afternoon, we would often see one of these large, gray, streamlined craft headed offshore in a rush. Sometimes one of the 75 foot Coast Guard patrol boats were cruising in the vicinity and would fire a few shots from their "One Pounder" at the disappearing rum-runner. The "rummies" were clever though; they'd create a dense black smoke screen by piping dirty drain oil into the flaming hot manifolds of their powerful converted aircraft engines.

One day while hunting for our pot buoys in a thick fog about fifteen miles southeast of Noman's, we came upon an anchored Mother Ship, a huge former Gloucester fishing schooner, the *ARETHUSA*, outside the twelve-mile limit. Her deck was loaded with boxes and burlap sacks. Two of the crew were stationed up on the foremast spreaders with rifles, ready to discourage hijackers! We had heard stories about this vessel and her legendary Capt., Bill McCoy, whose supply came from St. Pierre and Nassau by alternate voyages. He handled only top-grade liquor, a product which had become widely known as "The Real McCoy". (Hence, the origin of that commonly used expression.) We eased in close enough to trade a bushel of lobsters for a six bottle package of Haig & Haig Scotch whiskey. We had met the real Bill McCoy—a big man with a booming voice and a bushy brown beard.

Sometime toward the end of August, we made ready for a longer swordfishing trip to an area about 40 miles southeast of Noman's, near the edge of the Steamer Track. It would be a three-day expedition provided we had good weather. This time both Herb Flanders and Norman West went along with Percy and me. Three men and a boy, who would turn 13 during a swordfishing trip somewhere south of Noman's Land.

At two A.M. we set out under bright starlight and a light southerly breeze. Off Gay Head we encountered a sizeable ground swell. By the time we arrived at the Noman's Hooter, we suddenly became enveloped in what a Newfoundlander might describe as a "dungeon of thick fog". We continued on a southeasterly compass course. Percy said, "This fog will burn off when the sun comes up." It didn't. We chugged along in dense fog and an ocean swell that was like a roller coaster. There was talk about what to do next. By mid-morning we decided to go no further offshore. Instead we steered to the westward toward Block Island in hope that the fog would lighten enough so that swordfish fins would be visible.

We saw numerous sharks and some big schools of mackerel, but only one swordfish. It was on the surface "milling" — playfully going around in circles. The big fish vanished as we turned in that direction.

After that disappointment, and with the continued low visibility. We decided that it was time to head for home. We steered in a northerly direction and used the sounding lead occasionally. A dark shadow directly ahead proved to be a drifting 75 foot Coast Guard patrol boat, the first and only boat that we encountered all day. We drew closer to the wallowing vessel.

We hailed them with a shout — "What direction is the Noman's Hooter buoy?" The reply was not reassuring: "We have been drifting for about twenty-four hours. We don't know where anything is!"

However, the Coastie skipper promptly proceeded to get underway as we headed north. It was immediately apparent that they were trying to keep us in sight, but their slowest speed was much faster than we were going, so they had to steer in a zig-zag pattern in order to stay astern while attempting to follow us somewhere. Such maneuvers created an imminent danger of collision as the nearly unmanageable Coast Guard craft came rushing toward us on the slope of a big swell!

Suddenly the fog cleared. A mixture of rain and hail followed by rumbling thunder and brilliant lightning changed the atmosphere. A weird darkness descended and we felt an eerie sense of impending disaster. Jagged bolts of lightning darted all around us. Percy shouted, "Keep away from the mast!" He was aft trying to steer the boat by means of the stubby tiller that extended inboard through a curving slot in the stern rail. A puff of wind introduced a more threatening gust from the northeast. Instantly, a blast of wind out of the east struck us, butt-end first. We'd run into a full-fledged hurricane!

LOIS T (Now TURMOIL) decorated with Christmas lights at Parkers Boatyard (Photo courtesy of CAPE COD LIFE)

For a while, the terrific force of the wind flattened the swells and created a smother of salty spume. The wind pressure swung clockwise around to the southwest. We bobbed around like a cork. Soon, however, the sky brightened with the last rays of sunset. The worst of it lasted only about an hour. With our visibility quickly improving, we caught a glimpse of the flashing Gay Head lighthouse. An inspiring sight! The boys in the Coast Guard 75-footer likewise saw the light from their distant position, having lost sight of us during the height of the tempest. They were headed at full speed toward their home base at Woods Hole. When at last we chugged into the channel at our Menemsha home port, quite a reception of people waved flashlights from the jetties. Still others helped us with dock lines at the pier. Our adventure was the talk of the town for several days.

By the way, that able 28 foot lobster boat, *LOIS T*, is in use today. She was repaired and maintained by "Razz" Parker, rechristened *TURMOIL*, and is now the workboat at the Parker Boatyard on Red Brook Harbor in the village of Cataumet near Buzzards Bay.

TURMOIL - a stern view at Parker's Boatyard pier. Friend Shirley Christophers standing on the pier, ready to go for a boatride.

Chapter 4

A Farm Boy's Adventures

Early in September of that year, 1925, it became time to return home to West Tisbury and get ready for school. After such a busy summer it was a pleasure to resume a normal way of life again.

My parents refused to allow me to go fishing the following year because I had been subjected to long hours of hard work and near starvation. Instead, my occupation became farming, thanks to Capt. Ellsworth West. After a long seafaring career as a Master on ships operating between West Coast ports and Alaska, he retired at 72, and had recently returned to his farm on Middle Road in the hills of Chilmark. Upon arrival home, he promptly married my cousin Elsie Athearn, who was about half his age. She soon became pregnant and ultimately produced a baby daughter. Capt. West was a tall, thin man with a bushy white mustache. He had enormous energy which he put to good use from dawn to dark. He also had a most complete vocabulary of swear words, which he could employ so vociferously that they could be heard a mile away against the wind!

There were cows to be milked and acres of corn and other crops to be hoed or weeded on the Capt.'s farm. The hayfields were the most fun. Instead of a horse, Capt. West preferred to use his 4 cylinder Buick touring car to tow the mowing machine and, when the hay was dry, the hay rake. It was my pleasure to drive the car in low gear while he rode the machinery. We kept busy all through the summer. The pay was $2.00 per day.

Saturday and Sunday were vacation days, time for sailing on West Tisbury Great Pond in that tired old, lap-strake double-ender that our generous neighbor, Charlie Foot, had presented to me. I rounded up a crew of three lively boys, the brothers Dodd, to help with repairs to the ancient 18 foot sloop. One of our projects was to apply hot roofing tar to the open seams. We made such a mess that we had to spread the gooey tar over the entire hull. That was a regretable mistake that we slowly learned to tolerate.

We managed to roll the boat over, and with borrowed planking and rollers, made a successful launching. It was hilarious! She got away from us on the downward slope and hit the water with a huge splash, promptly filled with water and sank. We decided to let her soak for a few days in hopes that the seams would tighten up. Then we stepped the mast and rigged the boom, gaff and baggy old canvas sail. The wooden centerboard was stuck and we could not budge it while the boat was aground.

We cast off anyway and hoisted the sail after an hour of bailing with buckets. Three of our four-man crew bailed continuously while the other handled the tiller and sheet rope. Town Cove, being long and narrow, required short tacks. Without the centerboard, we made impressive leeway, finally reaching Little Sandy Point, where we rested with the boat aground. We spent another peaceful interlude at Great Sandy Point after many long tacks against the prevailing southwest breeze. Eventually we emerged into the roomy expanse of Great Pond.

After a long tack to the eastward, with drinking water and sandwiches consumed, we swung off and took a fair wind back to our berth on the boathouse beach. It had been a good cruise with plenty of exercise.

Sometime later that summer we made an expedition to South Beach. Great Pond had recently been reopened to the ocean, and as we neared the shore, the outgoing current carried us toward the wide channel. We were suddenly in danger of being swept through the breakers; indeed, we were in danger of being shipwrecked. Fortunately, the water shallowed so that three of us could jump toward the shore with the bow line. With the aid of the sail and one of the Dodd boys at the tiller, we managed to drag the heavy, half-sunk boat along the beach and out of the swiftly moving tide until we could go aground safely, where we bailed out the sloop.

When the Dodd boys reached home that night they told their parents about our adventure. Mrs. Dodd, who was my teacher at West Tisbury School, gave me a lecture by telephone and made it clear that her boys were never to sail with me again! That ended our sail-training season. On July 21st we celebrated my fourteenth birthday by hauling the boat back up to her previous resting place, with George Manter and his horse providing the pulling power.

The month of August that year, 1926, was hot and sultry. Commuting to and from Capt. West's farm on a heavy bicycle was a dusty ride. Hoeing seemingly endless rows of corn and chopping clustered weeds was the ultimate in boredom. On the way home a quick swim in the cool water of the Mill Pond was a refreshing way to rinse off a layer of dust.

After doing weekend chores around home, I'd spend my spare time having fun around town with kids of my age. Everett Whiting, Bobby Shultz and Tony Campbell, along with the Athearn boys, always played competitive games. In the late afternoon Johnny Whiting would appear in front of the store, later known as Alley's, (now a name that is world famous as a result of a recent complete renovation and front page newspaper stories) driving a large black Kissel sedan. A bunch of us would already be there, waiting for a ride to South Beach and a swim in the surf. Some of us had to stand on the running boards and hold on as best we could. It was a fast, wild ride. Somehow, by good fortune, in spite of the bumpy winding roads, we never had an accident.

At that time, 1926, Alley's Store was known as Sanderson's, a name related to the Mayhew family, the original owners of the store. Charlie Turner was the owner and proprietor during my youthful era. Albion Alley, a genial character who served as manager and did most of the work as he took care of incoming customers while chomping on a sizeable cigar. Eventually, Albion became established as owner of the thriving business. It proved to be a successful family operated general store and Post Office. Their slogan was "Dealers in almost everything!" David Correlus handled freight supplies and drove the Ford delivery truck all around the area taking grocery orders to the more distant customers. It was fun to ride along with David occasionally as a spare time helper. He had a comical point of view. The store was headquarters for the townspeople while serving as a club where local characters of all ages gathered to socialize and tell stories.

The West Tisbury Annual Fair, held in August, however, was the main event of our summer. Farm products were exhibited inside the building with all sorts of animals outside, while athletic events took place around the fairgrounds. Crowds of people all over the place made the fair the high point of the summer.

Chapter 5

The Simple Life

Early in September it was time to go to school again. A fence separated the fairgrounds from the Academy, as the three-story school was known. Here, students in grades one through eight, the "grammar school," attended. High school students commuted by bus to Vineyard Haven. Jenkinson, the bus driver, picked up Gay Head and Chilmark students before stopping for us West Tisbury scholars. There had to be some lively moments during that daily bus ride. The usual deviltry prevailed in spite of dire threats from the driver.

The winters back then were long and cold. Prevailing northwest winds brought low temperatures. Northeast storms of gale force usually left behind one or two feet of snow and drifts several feet deep. Horse-drawn snowplows could make only a narrow path along the edge of the roads. The highways had to be shoveled out. All the available men and boys were put to work, with the main roads being cleared first. Five or six of us working side by side could clear about a mile of roadway in eight hours. Deep snow had to be shaped into blocks about two feet square and thrown over to the roadside pile. All that exercise in very cold, fresh air garnered us fifty cents an hour, or an average of four dollars for a day's work.

Houses along or near the highway were usually snowed in. Two or three of us would volunteer to clear a path to their doors. Usually we would earn a bowl of soup or a cup of coffee as a reward for our efforts. Sometimes, housewives treated us to molasses cookies or even pie or cake..

Once the roads became passable, our next job was to clear the snow that covered the ice on Whiting's "Parsonage Pond." Nearly all the younger people in town liked to go skating. We played hockey, too.

When it was extremely cold and windy, the Whitings' huge barn provided many of us with an indoor playground. We played hide and seek up in the haymows. The storage bins contained a variety of tasty apples.

In general, it was a simple way of life. Real pleasures—such as reading an adventurous book or playing disc records on the turntable of the family Victrola, compensated for an abundance of hard physical work. The backyard woodpile, for instance, with its several cords of oak, presented a program of daily and, sometimes, nightly (via kerosene lantern illumination) drudgery. We had two woodstoves in the house, the kitchen cookstove and the "parlor" heater. Both required continuous feeding and the sawhorse and bucksaw required all my spare time and energy. The goal was to cut and split enough wood to last or supply the two stoves for a period of about twenty-four hours. One of the family would volunteer to get up and feed both stoves at least once during the night. A cast-iron hand pump supplied water at the kitchen sink from a well deep beneath the house. The outhouse was only about a hundred feet from the water supply. We didn't know enough to be concerned.

A new opportunity was presented to us, the Frederick B. Athearn family, when an old farm house in Eastville was being redesigned for use as a hospital. The location, near the Vineyard Haven-Oak Bluffs town line, overlooked Vineyard Haven harbor to the west and Lagoon Pond and the bridge to the south. Beatrice Gifford, a nearby West Tisbury neighbor, had been chosen as the head nurse for the new hospital. It was her influence that ushered in the new era of our existence. Mother was to be the hospital's cook, father its maintenance man. A new apartment-like layout on the ground floor of the barn behind the hospital was to become our new living quarters. The barn was a drafty building with, of course, two woodstoves that somehow managed to counteract the chill of winter winds.

From our new home, my brother, Lawrence "Tad" Athearn, a few neighboring kids and I had to walk two miles through the fields and woods to the Oak Bluffs School. Snowstorms seldom interfered with the school routine except during severe weather conditions, when we might be allowed to leave for home early in the afternoon.

I had a homemade cart with big wheels upon which I rigged with a square sail. On it, we'd sail at a fast clip across the Lagoon Bridge all the way to Vineyard Haven. After furling the sail, we would usually hail a truck for a ride back to Eastville. A scooter was the next novelty. My left shoe wore out quickly. Eventually we acquired a bicycle — luxury transportation!.

After two years at the very busy ten-room hospital, my folks decided to move to Vineyard Haven, where they became housekeepers for Mr. Edward C. Lord, whose house at Owens Park provided a nice view of the harbor.

Chapter 6

The Busy Harbor

In those days Vineyard Haven's harbor was a busy scene, a holdover place for coastwise shipping. Cargo schooners waited there for a favorable wind. Likewise, tugs and barges waited for northeast winds to moderate.

Sometimes a dozen or more ocean-going tugs bunched around the Steamboat Wharf, three or four abreast on both sides and across the outer end. Powerful vessels with huge triple expansion steam engines, these tugs could tow three and often four barges heavily laden with coal usually from Philadelphia or Baltimore to Boston or Portland, Maine. When the ferry steamer was due, the tugs would cast off and jog around the outer harbor until the ferry departed. The tugs would then return to the wharf like a flock of huge seabirds recovering from a disturbance. A three-day northeaster would create a large fleet of coasting schooners, mostly two-masters, such as the *MOONLIGHT*, but also including three, four, occasionally even five or six-masters. These were State of Maine or Nova Scotia vessels loaded with lumber for New York or Philly, where they'd be loaded with coal for the return voyage. At times, the entire harbor was crowded with vessels.

One of the more notable casualties during the era of big schooners was the six master — *RUTH E. MERRILL.*

At daylight on the morning of January 24, 1924, a glance revealed the masthead spreaders and six topmasts of a sunken schooner in the main channel outside of Vineyard Haven harbor.

The submerged six master proved to be the *RUTH E. MERRILL* with a cargo of 5,000 tons of hard coal originally destined for Portland, Maine.

There were rumors that the schooner had collided with a steam powered freighter, but we have no evidence of that being true.

A phone call to Mrs. Egan, librarian at the Vineyard Gazette, provided information that is more useful. After loading the capacity cargo of coal at Norfolk, Virginia, the big schooner had sailed into a wild Northeast gale of long duration. By the time that the vessel reached the shelter of Vineyard Sound, she was in a sinking condition. It is probable that the pump intake strainers had become clogged with coal dust. Finally, with the schooner anchored, the thirteen man crew abandoned the sinking ship in the yawl boat and rowed to a safe landing at Woods Hole Harbor.

My memory indicates that the salvage firm of Merritt-Chapman & Scot based at New London, Connecticut, appeared at the scene of the wreck. They managed to salvage the masts and rigging. Ample charges of dynamite were used to destroy the hull thereby eliminating a menace to navigation. It seems to me that much of the cargo of coal was salvaged by a system of air lift equipment that was controlled by "hard hat" divers working in periods of slack tide. Our native deep sea diver, Dave Curney may have been one of the salvage crew. On another occasion I can recall working with Dave as one of the deck crew on one of the many attempts to salvage the military cargo of the sunken steamer *PORT HUNTER* located off East Chop on Hedge Fence Shoal. Two men were required to crank the wheels of Dave's air supply pump while a third man communicated with Dave by prearranged yanks on his rope life-line. Adventurous activities.

Incoming coal barges with cargo consigned to the Crowell Yard were unloaded on the south side of the town wharf by mast and boom, with a hoisting cable attached to a big scoop bucket. The bucket, filled with coal by two very active shovelers, was yanked out of the hatch by a front-driven winch powered by a noisy tractor secured to the wharf planking. From daylight to dusk the tractor operator alternately varied the engine speed while the Model T Ford dump trucks rumbled to and from the coalyard. Unloading was a monotonous process that could last as long as ten days. When the cavernous hold was finally empty, the barge sat high out of the water. When the barge departed, a man with a skiff and a bullrake could scavenge plenty of spilled coal: a precious resource in those days of economic depression. Many a kitchen cookstove was adapted to use coal as fuel when it was available.

The Lehigh Valley Line tugs were notably big and powerful. The Star Line tugs, *MARS, VENUS* and *JUPITER*, competed equally in the coastwise towing trade. The *MARS* in particular, with Capt. Jack Kendrick in charge, became famous for towing barges in nearly impossible weather.

In the schooner fleet, Capt. Alton Colbert in the husky two-master *ANNA SOPHIA*, the only schooner with a pilot house, was a legendary driver. The *ANNA SOPHIA* was built in Stockton Springs, Maine around World War I. The vessel was built specifically to carry huge 500 lb. blocks of granite from Maine ports to New York. The masts were further apart than normal, a feature that had something to do with hoisting the heavy granite blocks during loading and unloading. The yawl boat, carried on davits over the stern, was powered with a Model T Ford engine.

Near the end of the coaster era, the *ANNA SOPHIA*, overloaded as usual, was caught in a howling, freezing nor'wester. Capt. Colbert managed to work into the lee of the Cape Cod shore off Chatham. The vessel, plastered with tons of salty ice, was on the verge of sinking. The deck was underwater. With the schooner anchored, the yawl boat was lowered and the vessel abandoned. The engine would not start, but with the use of two pairs of oars, they landed on the beach in front of a Coast Guard station. After being provided with a complete dinner at mid-day, Capt. Colbert used the station telescope to view his heavily laden vessel, which looked like a schooner-rigged iceberg. She wallowed slowly on the prevailing swells, barely afloat. Station Capt. Cahoon called for volunteers to join Capt. Colbert and his men to go out in an effort to save the *ANNA SOPHIA*.

The station lifeboat was launched and the yawl boat was pushed afloat. Five men in each boat, armed with iron bars, wooden clubs and shovels, arrived alongside. Ice in the rigging was dislodged first. Then the rails and deck were cleared. Tons and tons of salty, slushy ice went overboard. Once the scuppers were opened, seawater a foot deep quickly drained away. Three hours of intense work made the difference. Freeboard had increased by nearly two feet.

Capt. Cahoon returned to the station with his men. He promptly called Coast Guard Headquarters, whence the cutter *ACUSHNET* was dispatched to the scene. Portable pumps were hoisted aboard the schooner and a towing hawser was secured. Several hours later the two ships reached the safety of Vineyard Haven. About a week later the sturdy schooner sailed away and arrived safely at a Brooklyn pier to unload its enormous tonnage of block granite.

Several years later, when the era of the coasting schooners was nearly over (they were replaced by coastwise steamships), the *ANNA SOPHIA* was seen at anchor on the eastern side of Vineyard Haven Harbor. She looked so lonesome, the only schooner in sight. We soon learned that she had been sold to a new owner in Brazil near the Amazon River. The following morning she sailed with a fair tide, out of our realm and into another career.

The schooner *LUCY EVELYN* was also one of our favorite visitors. About twice a year she docked on the south side of the steamboat wharf to unload a cargo of spruce and fir lumber. She was a huge three-master with an upper and lower hold known in the trade as "tween decks," or a "double-decker." Although both holds were packed full of lumber, she also carried an uncommonly high deckload, which shortened the sail area of the foresail and mainsail.

Most of the lumber cargo was unloaded at the Tilton Lumberyard, a neighbor of the Crowell Coal Company, where between fishing trips I worked as a lumber stacker. Donald Tilton provided us workers with an innovation of the Roosevelt Administration's soon to be known as Social Security, a great idea born in the Depression year of 1937. I received a neat card with a personal I.D. number. Today a sizable percentage of elder citizens depend upon their monthly Social Security dividends for economic survival. Hail to Roosevelt!

The schooner *LUCY EVELYN*, toward the end of her era, sailed from Rockland, Maine with a full cargo of northern Maine potatoes destined for Hamilton, Bermuda. Capt. Wilkinson, an expert coastwise navigator, was somewhat limited, however, in his knowledge of celestial navigation. Gulf Stream currents and a buffeting series of gales put him astray. After three weeks of zigzag and triangular courses, the island of Bermuda still eluded them. Food and water grew short. For several days the crew of seven was obliged to live on a diet of potatoes. The cook presented a variety of choices: baked, boiled or fried, with or without the skins. By that time, the spud cargo had begun to grow sprouts.

Finally an ocean steamship came within hailing distance. Food and water were transferred by one of the ship's lifeboats. Capt. Wilkinson was informed of his latitude and longitude and provided with direct compass course toward Bermuda. The *LUCY EVELYN* was nearly 300 miles east of the island! After reaching Bermuda, she discharged the potatoes and took on a load of Bermuda onions, which also served as ballast. The return voyage was an uneventful pleasure cruise with favorable currents and fair winds.

Near the end of her cargo-carrying career, during a raging northeast storm, the *LUCY EVELYN* was anchored in Vineyard Haven Harbor where she dragged her anchors and was driven into the breakwater and badly damaged. Soon, sufficiently repaired, she was towed to New Jersey, where she was put on display as a tourist attraction and ended her seafaring life. I was at sea on an oil tanker and would not learn of the *LUCY EVELYN* shipwreck until many months later.

The coasting schooner era produced many spectacular events. One bright windy winter morning, I was surprised to look across the harbor from Eastville beyond the West Chop lighthouse to see a huge four-masted schooner high and dry on the beach, after a northwest gale the previous night. A phone call brought nearby neighbor Charlie Williams, his daughter Dorothy and son Woodrow in their open Model T Ford to pick me up for the drafty ride via Vineyard Haven out to West Chop. There we came upon the colossal schooner *AUGUSTA G. HILTON* with the hailing port Rockland, Maine on her transom. She sat upright nearly parallel to the shoreline, close to the original West Chop Pier. At low tide we could walk all the way out to the four-master. A new vessel being delivered to Philadelphia in ballast, she was refloated undamaged and resumed her voyage.

Chapter 7

Odd Jobs Ashore

During that busy era of coastwise vessels, a ship chandlery store stood on the western shore of Vineyard Haven Harbor near the present yacht club. The proprietor was Edward C. Lord, our landlord at his Owen's Park house and the owner of a shoe store on Main Street adjacent to the post office. His hobby was the salvaging of vessel anchors. He owned a small auxiliary schooner, the *HERMAN L. ROGERS*, which was moored behind the breakwater near the flashing beacon. In his spare time he would round up a crew and, with the help of a hired power boat, tow a sweep cable along the harbor bottom until he'd snagged an anchor, usually immediately after a long northeast storm when a few schooners and barges had parted from one of their two anchors. The salvaged kedge anchors were kept on the deck of Lord's schooner until he sold them, quite often to the anchor's original owner. Anchor salvage proved to be a profitable occupation.

A waterfront landmark — generally known as the Seaman's Bethel — was attended to capacity by visiting sailors. It stood on the corner near the Steamboat Wharf, bordering the beach. The state-owned ferry system now owns the vacant building and is threatening to move or demolish the historic Bethel. (Update:The famous old building was saved. It was moved on planking and rollers to a new location uptown to be used as a recreation place adjacent to the Veteran's Building.)

However, back in the "good old days" Austin Tower, the chaplain, with his Bethel boat *MADISON EDWARDS*, served the anchored fleet as a shuttle for the crew members. It was exciting for me and many other volunteers to become deckhands. We handled fenders and helped crewmen to get aboard and later return safely to their vessels. On shore there were religious services, after which the Bethel people provided each man with a ditty bag containing woolen socks and mittens and some special goodies such as cookies and candy.

The *MADISON EDWARDS* had just refueled over at the Texaco pier at dusk one day. When Austin pressed the engine starter button, an instant fiery explosion rocked the boat! Austin was blown out of the pilot house, scorched but fortunately uninjured. The boat was soon repaired and put back in service.

Back in those days the ferry steamers did not handle much bulk. They had side-opening sliding doors that provided access to the forward freight deck. The *NOBSKA* is now

*The **S/S NOBSKA** was built by the Bath Iron Works in Bath, Maine in 1925 for the New England Steamship Company and named for the point of land on the southeastern tip of Woods Hole. She was designed with seaworthiness in mind to withstand severe weather conditions and was powered by an engine that represents marine reciprocating steam power at its zenith. In style, accoutrements and performance she is a classic and only remaining example of a pure 19th-and early 20th-century American coastal steamboat. Printed with permission of Lockhead Collection, Steamship Historical Society of America.*

the lone survivor of that era—a floating museum, now urgently in need of a complete renovation. Only products that could be rolled aboard on dollies towed by a battery-powered tractor were transported, mostly groceries, cartons of canned products or anything readily handled from trucks arriving at the Woods Hole wharf. Once the loaded dollies were safely located on the freight deck, the mate in charge of loading would wave the waiting fifteen or twenty cars up the ramp to be fitted snugly into the limited available space. It was usually a tight squeeze. Unloading at the island wharf required plenty of manipulation.

Most of the cars were disembarked in reverse. At high tide the unloading ramp was set at a steep angle. This was no place for a timid driver. The loaded dollies arrived on the wharf after the cars were out of the way. Horse-drawn "drays", low-slung platform wagons driven by Al Luce and Manuel Silvia, hustled to unload the dollies, and promptly delivered the variety of products to Main Street stores, generally the A&P and the First National. Cronig's & Bangs' Market ("the LITTLE store with the BIG business") used their own trucks.

One of my numerous shore jobs was as an employee of Paul Bangs. His Vineyard Haven store was opposite the post office on Main Street. He also operated stores in Oak Bluffs and Chilmark. To complete the picture, he maintained a store on the remote island of Cuttyhunk. My primary occupation was as a truck driver from 7 AM to 6 PM, Monday thru Friday, and until 10 PM on Saturday: seventy hours a week, Sundays off, and a daily half-hour lunch break. Sometimes. The pay: $8.50 per week! Hard times.

My first responsibility was to deliver customers' orders door-to-door. Customers phoned in for their daily food supplies, which store clerks packed in cartons. Delivering those occupied the AM. Then a load of rubbish to the town dump. By mid-PM it was time to pick up the daily freight at the wharf, then unload the truck at the warehouse located behind the store. (The other Bangs-operated stores had their own trucks and drivers.) In order to keep occupied completely, I'd find continual work in the warehouse. Heavy barrels, boxes and big chunks of meat had to be moved and refrigerated. Potatoes, one hundred pounds of them in burlap bags, had to be repackaged into half-peck and peck-sized brown paper bags, ready for delivery to customers the next morning. Never a dull moment!

Another Bangs enterprise was the up-island supply wagon — a big heavy-duty, van-type Dodge truck with rear-opening doors — a store-on-wheels crammed with grocery supplies. The back end of the truck was the meat market. The driver, Rex Weeks, was a natural salesman, although somewhat handicapped because he was clubfooted.

By 8 AM, five days a week, the truck was loaded with meat and supplies and on the road. Rex's helper stood on the driver's side running board and held onto the extended rear-view mirror because the rider's seat was piled high with paper bags and saleable products. The helper's job was quite an experience, especially in cold winter weather. Stops were made at the houses of regular customers in North Tisbury, West Tisbury, along the South Road to Chilmark, then over to Menemsha before returning via the North Road to the Vineyard Haven Store. The helper's job was to run to the door of each customer, get the order, return to the truck for Rex to put it together, then deliver it. With the day's business completed, there would be room for the helper to ride inside the truck, to recover from being nearly frozen all day, since the supply of materials had vanished from the rider's seat during the course of the day's trading. Only on two or three occasions was I called upon to replace the regular helper, but the memory lingers clearly. My routine truck-driving job seemed easy by comparison.

Before leaving the employment of Bang's Market, another Bang's worker, John Coutino, who had replaced Rex Weeks on the up-island meat wagon, rode along with me in my delivery truck over to West Chop on an errand. Because it was late in the day John asked, "How about you giving me a ride home?" He lived at the other end of town on Edgartown Road. We bowled along at a speedy rate until we reached the intersection of Franklin and Center Streets, a blind corner. At that moment a Ford "Woody" station wagon, doing about 40 MPH, hit us broadside. The velocity of the collision forced my truck sideways and wrapped us around a huge fieldstone structure on the diagonal corner.

When the dust settled, I was amazed to see that John had been popped out of the open window and was sitting on the grass with a stunned look on his face, bruised but fortunately uninjured. The truck, a total wreck, was shaped like an hourglass! Blood trickled from a cut on my forehead caused by being bounced up into the rear view mirror. The town truck crew had to break the door hinges in order for me to get out.

The investigation of that accident clearly favored the Bang's truck. We had what is known as the right-of-way. The insurance company totalled the old truck and provided Paul Bangs with a brand new Model B Ford delivery wagon. The employees involved were considered lucky survivors!

After being employed by Paul Bangs through the winter months, I decided to return to commercial fishing. When I spoke to Bangs about it, he advised that fishing was a poor-paying gamble and that if I would stay on the job through the summer, he would raise my pay to ten dollars a week. Double the work for an additional one dollar and fifty cents. "No, thanks" was my answer. However, I did agree to operate his boat *MILDRED*, which I recently had delivered from New Bedford (a separate chapter will follow) as a freight-carrier for the Cuttyhunk store, once a week, usually on Sunday, as the cargo was loaded on Saturday. Food supplies were stored in the cabin. Coal in canvas bags went into the hold, along with bags of cement. A truckload of lumber was stacked on deck. Upon its arrival at Cuttyhunk most of the cargo was hoisted by power-winch up onto the wharf, often at low tide. My pay for the round-trip, was ten dollars. A week's pay in one day!

While waiting for a chance to go fishing, I managed to get in on a Roosevelt W.P.A. project. The job was to construct a new sidewalk from Main Street down to the Seaman's Bethel at the Steamboat Wharf.

The village of Vineyard Haven, having been built on the slope of a hill, had a water drainage problem. When rain fell heavily or when snow melted, the flow of water from the higher streets funnelled into Union Street, creating a river that overflowed the sidewalk. With funds available from the Federal Works Progress Administration (WPA) the sidewalk became a priority project. LeRoy Luce worked with me and the regular town road crew to dig a trench, into which large oblong chunks of granite were placed in order to form a curb. Truckloads of sand and gravel were dumped and spread behind the granite so that by the time that new hardtop paving was in place, the new sidewalk was a foot higher than the old one.

87' Motor Sailer, NORTHERN LIGHTS en route to Halifax, Nova Scotia from Gloucester—June 1948, with delivery crew.

Chapter 8

The EBEN A. THACHER

In those days the heavy bulky freight that arrived by railroad in Woods Hole was transported to Vineyard Haven by the cargo vessel *EBEN A. THACHER*. Former schooner Capt. Henry Stevensen, a Danish Master Mariner, was a resident of Vineyard Haven. Capt. Armindo Pinto became skipper of the *THACHER* as Capt. Stevensen gradually retired. He had a husky four-man crew that seemed to thrive on hard work.

Stevenson's original *E. A. THACHER* was a beamy boat about 57 feet in length. The engine and pilothouse were aft. The cargo winch and mast were directly in front of the wheelhouse. The boom was rigged forward over the main hatch. Stevenson had foreseen the need for a boat to provide a supply of water to the everchanging fleet of vessels in the harbor. To that end, the hold was lined with cypress sheathing, making it a huge watertight tank. The transfer pump was on deck and the suction hose had a foot valve and screen to filter out coal dust and other dirt in the bottom of the hold.

The *THACHER* had a special berth on the north side of the wharf on the inshore end at an angle toward the northwest. Cargoes of cement, lumber and big timbers were common. Railroad boxcars and flat cars rode on tracks that extended out on the Woods Hole wharf.

On one occasion I was called upon to fill in for one of the regular crew. We unloaded a boxcar loaded with bagged cement. We lifted the hundred-pound bags and placed them on a slippery, chute sloping into the cargo hold. Two of us worked in the boxcar, the other two in the hold. We changed ends about once an hour. Piling those clumsy bags (a few broken or torn) was the ultimate in heavy, sweaty, dusty, "jackass work"! Unloading at the Vineyard end consisted of piling six bags of cement on a pallet, which was then hoisted to a waiting truck on the wharf. One trip was enough for me!

Soon after that experience, Capt. Pinto took on a huge deckload of iron piping, twenty-foot lengths, two feet in diameter. Too long to go into the hold, the pipes had to be stacked high on deck. There was a strong southwest breeze blowing with a sizeable swell in Vineyard Sound. Rounding the channel bell buoy the *THACHER* made a long roll to leeward. Pinto tried to steer to windward, but turning increased the problem. Suddenly the top-heavy vessel rolled completely over, sinking instantly. Capt. Pinto and his crew barely had time to jump overboard. Fortunately they were all promptly rescued by a vessel that happened to be nearby at the time. Two of the crew, Wilbur Jerrod, a seagoing Indian, and a husky man by the name of Claudina Paiva described the adventure, but the identities of the rescuers remain a mystery. A New Bedford marine contractor salvaged the *THATCHER* and most of the pipe cargo. The old vessel was sold to a Boston company, renamed *UNO* and was used for years to carry supplies out to ships anchored in Boston Harbor.

The old freight boat was soon replaced by a new *EBEN A. THACHER*. Erford Burt, a son-in-law of Capt. Stevensen and a Vineyard master boatbuilder, designed the new craft.

It was a handsome vessel that was powered by a big slow-turning Wolverine diesel engine. The new 65 foot freighter was similar in layout to the original, with white oak frames and hard pine planking. The cargo hold was built with watertight bulkheads and was useable as a water carrier. The builder was the Major Casey Shipyard at Fairhaven. As the years went by, such vessels would be replaced by double-ended ferries, onto which heavy cargoes were rolled aboard on huge trailer trucks. When the era of the *EBEN A. THACHER* came to an end, the fine vessel was sold to a Connecticut oyster company for a new career as an oyster-dredger and freighter. It's probably still in use today.

Chapter 9

A Voyage With Capt. Zeb

The local cargo schooner *ALICE S. WENTWORTH,* sailed by the famous character Capt. Zeb Tilton, kept quite busy with freight from more distant ports, like a load of bricks from Greenport, Long Island, or a full load of road oil, known as liquid asphalt, in fifty gallon drums, which were trucked and unloaded in a sandpit on a side road near the top of Tashmoo Hill. (More about that later.) Between trips, the *WENTWORTH* was anchored in just about the same location that the Douglas schooner *SHENANDOAH* occupies today. Tom Tilton, Zeb's nephew, sailed as mate in the *WENTWORTH* for many years. That two-man team did the work of a four-man crew!

Capt. Zeb, a huge man, was widely known for his great feats of strength. They are enumerated in a book entitled *ZEB — A Celebrated Schooner Life*, wonderfully written and illustrated by Polly Burroughs of Edgartown, and published by The Chatham Press, Inc. (Riverside, Connecticut 1972. ISBN 85699-050-7). It's the sort of a book that you can read and enjoyed more than once.

During a mid-winter school holiday, it was my special pleasure to sail with Zeb from Vineyard Haven to Nantucket. A deckload of 105 tons of soft coal loaded in New Bedford was to be discharged at the Island Service Company at its Nantucket wharf. With both foresail and mainsail reefed for the strong nor'wester (we also had a fair tide), we arrived at the destination in a record sailing time of four hours!

Unloading it was hard dusty work; we shoveled the coal into a scoop, which was hoisted by a tractor and dumped into a waiting truck, the same system as unloading a coal barge at Vineyard Haven except that it was performed on deck instead of deep in a cargo hold. When the day's work was done, and we had rinsed off coal dust from hands and faces, we enjoyed a hearty supper. A big pot of beef stew or a boiled dinner of corned beef and cabbage always simmered on the coal burning cabin stove. Additional ingredients were added whenever it was necessary to maintain an ample supply. Nantucket marine characters came aboard to visit each evening, each one an entertainer with seafaring yarns of all sorts. One fellow, Wallace Long, an accordion player, led many a sing-along. He was also an authority on coasting schooners, their history and adventures. It was a competition between him and Capt. Zeb as to who was the better informed. The whole performance would have made a great video recording.

After the coal was unloaded and the decks scrubbed clean, we waited a few days for a shift of wind. Headwinds, southwest to northwest prevailed. We needed an easterly breeze, a fair wind back to Vineyard Haven. One morning Capt. Zeb decided not to wait any longer. A cold nor'wester was blowing. We lowered the yawl boat and cast off the dock lines.

We rounded Brant Point with Tom Tilton operating the yawl boat as bow fendered pusher against the *WENTWORTH'S* stern. The yawl boat was a miniature tug boat that was used to push the schooner out of the harbor into open waters where the sails could be safely raised. The long channel between the granite jetties was too narrow to tack the schooner, so we would have to get outside before hoisting the sails. While Tom was adjusting the engine, the yawl boat rudder, with the tiller attached, jumped out of its pintals and was soon floating far astern. Tom shouted, "Let's go back and get it!"

Capt. Zeb yelled to us on deck, "Hoist the jib!"

There was a long oar in the yawl boat for just such an emergency. Tom used it skillfully to steer in a tight circle to starboard. With a boat hook, we grabbed the drifting rudder and made another fast circle back to windward, after which we continued in the channel to the open expanse of Nantucket Sound.

We had to "lay to" in the sloppy sea conditions long enough to hoist the yawl boat and get it secured under the stern davits. Then, up with the sails, jibs, foresail and mainsail. Fortunately, the *ALICE S. WENTWORTH* was equipped with a gasoline-powered donkey engine with double winch heads that did the heavy hoisting for us. Snatch blocks, conveniently located, guided the hoisting lines properly.

We made long zigzag tacks, bucking a choppy sea and a six-hour head tide. We deliberately sailed across shoals that would have grounded a deeper draft vessel. Salty ice formed on the rails and lower rigging. Steering at the unsheltered wheel was a very cold occupation. One hour at the wheel was enough, even wearing woolen clothes and oilskins. A series of short watches were rewarded by a big mug of hot tea. A gallon-sized metal teapot brewed on the hot stove all the while.

It was a long, cold day unless we were in the cozy main cabin. We dropped anchor in Vineyard Haven in the dark of a winter night after thirteen hours of uphill sailing since departing the Nantucket wharf.

Not long after that Nantucket adventure, sometime after midnight, there were signs of a northeast storm. The "glass" had dropped two-tenths, and there were reports of easterly snow squalls. Such a 24-hour period of calm conditions, especially in mid-winter, is usually known as a "Weather Breeder." We should have paid attention to this one. However, Tom Tilton was on the phone saying, "We need to set the big anchor. If you will give us a hand, we'll see you at the coal yard in twenty minutes."

"Okay," I answered.

We launched the *WENTWORTH*'s big dory, with wind and surf increasing. Two pairs of ash oars were held in place by their respective thole pins, as Zeb and Tom rowed to windward. We soon boarded the vessel. The Tiltons ran forward and Zeb shouted, "Tie the dory astern and grab the wheel!" They quickly hoisted the inner jib and hauled the boom to starboard. Then came a yell: "Hard-a-port!" At the end of a short tack, the Tiltons dropped the six hundred pound storm anchor, attached to suitable fathoms of barlink chain. The *WENTWORTH* was "bridled." Now she could ride out a hurricane!

After furling the big jib and trying the cast iron deck pumps for bilge water (the *WENTWORTH* hull was tight except for the deck, which leaked during rainy weather), we scrambled into the dory and rowed ashore, where we dragged the dory well up into the coal yard beyond the flood tide reach of the surf. The storm, a northeaster, blew in full force for three days, as usual. A number of small craft wound up high and dry on the beach, having parted from their moorings. The only sizable craft in such a spot was a 75-foot Coast Guard patrol boat that had snapped her docklines on the southside of Steamboat Wharf and gone aground in front of Benny Crowell's coal yard. Capt. Zeb was one of many volunteers who wielded a scoop shovel for hours to remove enough sand to allow a salvage tug to float the vessel and tow her to a shipyard for repairs.

Eventually the *ALICE S. WENTWORTH* came to the end of her active era. She was sold to a Boston waterfront restaurant owner, whom she served for a number of years as a nautical attraction. The wild northeast gale and snowstorm of March, 1978 completely destroyed the grand old schooner.

After Capt. Zeb had retired, he was invited to appear on a radio broadcast program in New York City in a grand finale to his famous career.

Chapter 10

On the Briny... and Below

Tom Tilton had turned to commercial fishing before the *WENTWORTH* was sold. After operating a boat on shares for a while, he acquired the 40 foot gasoline-powered dragger *QUEST*. His younger brother Alton operated the dragger "*3 AND 1*", similar in type and size. They were both two-man boats, both fishing for flounder: Nantucket Sound blackbacks in the springtime, five-day trips for fluke (similar to halibut) south of Nantucket during the summer. Most of the fluke were caught during the night, so it was customary to go off looking for swordfish during the day. The winter season, about six months of the year, was the rough and tough yellowtail flounder season.

At that time yellowtails were most plentiful on sandy bottom in depths of water ranging from 18 to 30 fathoms. I made an occasional trip with either Tom or Alton as a "transient", or reserve deckhand. We generally worked in areas that were twenty miles or more southeast to south of Noman's Land Island. The work was mostly a matter of weather, trying to get out and back between winter gales. Weather forecasts didn't mean much.

On one occasion we waited an hour or so for a weather report. Soon enough the radio voice suggested "fair" for a day or two and, as a parting gesture, said, "Whether it's cold or whether it's hot, we will have weather, whether or not!" We cast off and went fishing in windy weather that we hoped would moderate. It didn't. That particular trip was worse than usual because with each tow, we'd scoop a netful of sculpin along with the yellowtail flounders. This meant a deckload of bony critters with sharp prongs on their heads that penetrated boots and clothing and made slow, painful work of trying to shovel them overboard while separating the mix of flounders and codfish. In the middle of all that rough work, Alton shouted, "This is a hard way to make an easy dollar!"

When the deck was cleared and the market fish stored safely below in the hold, there would be time for a "mug-up" — coffee and a sandwich. Down forward, in the cabin, it was unbearably hot and smoky. The engine, a huge chunk of clattering, overheated iron, labored beneath the wheelhouse floor. The coal-burning Shipmate stove exhaled coal gas that blended with the carbon monoxide from leaky engine exhaust pipes. Ten minutes in that hellhole was too much! Coming up on deck, groggy and sweaty, was a real test of a crewman's durability, especially to stand leaning on the winch control levers while winding in the towing cables with splashes of freezing spray dousing the operator's face. Pure misery!

The average fishing trip was a 36-hour endurance contest, since sea conditions seemed to be at least moderately rough most of the time during the winter. Usually we fished in company with other craft, schooners from Edgartown and vessels hailing from New Bedford, though we kept out of their way. Bamboo pole flag-buoys marked areas of good fishing. Bright deck lights indicated that a dragger was stopped and that the net was being "hauled back".

Fishing in a small dragger was extremely dangerous in those days. The boats were overworked and often overloaded with fish. Sometimes a trawl door would punch a hole in the boat's bottom during a "haul back". Gasoline engines presented a constant fire hazard. Fire extinguishers and soggy life jackets were the only safety equipment. No radio or electronic devices. No skiff or dory. We didn't seem to be concerned about it until after two Vineyard boats were lost. The *ADDIE MAY*, with Earl Wade and Manuel Canha, the first casualty south of Noman's, vanished in the night. Sometime later on, the *WATER WITCH* disappeared off Nantucket with Leslie Tilton and Billy Thomas. A lifeboat would have saved their lives.

After those tragedies every fishing boat carried a lifeboat — either a big skiff or a dory on the forward deck, or on a framework over the main deck. The luxury of electronics became available after World War II: Radar, Loran, VHF radiophones, sounders that produced underwater pictures in color, the whole works.

In the old days, a boatload of yellowtails sold to the Woods Hole dealer, Sam Cahoon, would be in the one to three cent per pound range. After the gas tanks were filled at eighteen cents a gallon, and we bought our ice and fishing gear supplies, our net share for the trip was about twenty dollars! However, in the course of a year we used thousands of gallons of gasoline, from which we eventually received a "road tax" refund of four cents per gallon, a better income annually than all our fishing shares!

Now for a few adventures in commercial fishing that may be worth recording.

One of the Vineyard boats, the 50-foot *SOUTHERN CROSS*, was drifting in a brisk nor'wester south of Noman's. Having just hauled back, the crew was about to dump the contents of the cod end on deck, when a huge cresting wave came out of the night and rolled the boat over on her beam ends. All three of the crew were washed overboard: Roy Campbell, Pete Grant and Jimmy Francis. Fortunately, the net hung suspended over the rail, enabling them to scramble quickly back on board. That was enough; they were soon underway and jogging for their homeport!

On another occasion Capt. George Fisher, in his new 85 foot Eastern-rigged vessel *STANLEY M. FISHER* (largest of the Island fleet), was towing his net in deep water near the hundred fathom curve. A sudden lurch not only stopped the dragger but caused immediate sternway at an increasingly dangerous speed. The winch brakes were released, allowing the one inch wire towing cables (300 fathoms of cable on each drum) to unwind quickly. The *FISHER* was an Eastern rig with "gallows frames" fore and aft on both sides and duplicate sets of nets and trawl doors. Thus the winchman was directed by Capt. Fisher to slack the aft wire, but to hold a tension on the forward cable. While that was being done, for a brief period, the stern and then the starboard rail were under water with the tremendous towing velocity strain.

With all the strain concentrated through the swiveling hanging block in the forward gallows, the vessel took off on a wild Nantucket sleighride toward deeper water, boiling along at perhaps twelve knots or more, in imminent danger of being submerged. The crew soon

85' Eastern Dragger STANLEY M. FISHER (encountered atomic submarine NAUTILUS) years later was sold and renamed ANGELA & KRISTINE.

had to use boltcutters to sever both towing cables. The frazzled end of the forward wire jammed briefly in the deck bollard before it snapped with a loud twang and disappeared overboard. A near catastrophe suddenly averted!

Capt. Fisher promptly confirmed by radiophone that the cause of their dramatic experience was a New London-based submarine on diving maneuvers, which had encountered the voluminous trawl net of the *FISHER*. The identity of the sub was quite secret, but later there came a rumor, from Navy sources that the undersea entanglement had actually been caused by the newly-commissioned atomic-powered submarine *NAUTILUS*, at sea on its original trial operations. It was reported that the sub crew had heard some loud thumps on the forward hull of the sub (probably the half-ton trawl doors) and that the sub had suffered a temporary steering problem. Evidently during maneuvers, before the sub surfaced hours later, the *FISHER*'s equipment had disappeared. We heard about scratches on the hull but, fortunately, no cable or gear was caught in the sub's propeller. The *NAUTILUS* went on to make history by navigating under the ice at the North Pole. Eventually, Capt. Fisher was reimbursed by the Navy for the loss of his fishing equipment.

Chapter 11

Danger on Dogfish Bar

My early days at Menemsha Creek are a source of stories and adventures. Boats and fishing became an obsession, especially after a series of unpleasant shore jobs. (More in a forthcoming chapter.)

Menemsha Basin was a busy place with shanties, piers and lobster boats all around the shoreline and stacks of wooden lobster traps too. The "salthouse", George Butler, proprietor, was located where the gas station store is now, near the breakwater beach. George made frequent trips over to New Bedford in his big catboat *LOUISE* to bring back bags of coarse salt and all sorts of lobstering supplies. Al, a paunchy character, was the storekeeper.

At the inner end of the Basin, the general store and post office was an active business run by Carl Reed. His front porch was a gathering place for fishermen on windy days. Nearby was a shanty with a sign over the door inscribed with the legend, "Mystic Knights Of The Sea." Poker and other card games were the principal pastimes there.

Outside, near the clubhouse door, was a convenient pay-station telephone. That was before the development of "Dial-Your-Own-Number." The caller would simply lift the receiver off the hook, drop a nickel in the slot, and a pleasant feminine voice would say, "Number, please." As it was the only public phone in the immediate area, it was a real money-maker. It also provided a few of us with a steady supply of nickels, dimes and quarters, as a locked cover on the front of the money chamber could be readily pried open, allowing a flow of silver coins to pour into the hands of the culprit. A supply of pocket money!Adjacent to the nearby town landing were a row of shanties, piers and the "creek" lobster boats. The owners were the familiar names of the era: Ernest "Horsepower" Mayhew, Carleton Mayhew, Jerry Look, David Butler, Herbert Flanders, Steve Gardner and Percy Tilton. Reginald Norton, with his boat *MADELINE*, was located at the far end of the peninsula. Tourists came from down island to enjoy the scenery and the powerful aroma of the ample supply of lobster bait. Of course, the 1938 hurricane wiped out the entire scene, but, fortunately, most of the boats survived to be repaired and refloated. Although Menemsha was eventually restored, the original atmosphere and character of the place were lost forever.Another of my early adventures occurred in the Gay Head suburb known as Lobsterville. Gale Huntington of Chilmark happened to be down island one day when we met on the Vineyard Haven waterfront. He said to me, "I have a big dory and fifty lobster pots on the beach at Lobsterville. How about if the two of us give it a try? You could live right there in my beach shanty."

I said, "It sounds okay, but I don't have a car right now."

Gale replied, "You don't need one. I have a skiff that you could use to row to Menemsha for supplies."

It was springtime, herring season (good lobster bait) so the idea had an appeal to it. The shanty contained two bunks, a wood-burning stove, a two-burner kerosene cook stove and several kerosene lamps. Otis Jeffers and his family lived in the only year-round house on the beach.

The isolation caught up with me after a few days. Finally, on a calm sunny morning, I launched the rowboat, grabbed the oars and about an hour later, entered Menemsha Basin and landed on the beach close to Carl Reed's store. After a few hours of social activity, I bought several boxes of groceries and a five-gallon can full of kerosene. Rowing out toward the Creek jetties, I heard a shout. There I saw Roger Trump, a pal from Vineyard Haven who had shipped aboard the *MADELINE*.

Roger shouted, "Come alongside and wait for the tide to turn." Rowing against a boiling head tide was not good sense, so I tied up for a visit with Roger, an ex-Merchant Marine sailor who had been a patient at the Vineyard Haven Marine Hospital. After being discharged when his injuries healed, he found he liked the island and stayed to become a fisherman. As I climbed over the rail, Roger said, "Come on below, it's suppertime." He fired up the coal-burning Shipmate stove and greased a big, black, iron frying pan with bacon fat. He cooked flounder fillets, sliced potatoes and onions quickly in one complete batch.

We had a good feed with plenty of coffee to drink, while we sat and talked about adventures of the past. It was near dark by the time we went up on deck. It was Roger's idea to forget about leaving so late in the day. "Stay aboard here tonight, then get an early start in the morning," he said. Reginald was due on board at six A.M. to go on a fishing trip. After more talk, we lowered the pipe bunks and turned in for the night. But the weather changed during the night. Soon after daylight I went up into the wheelhouse to have a look around.

The surface of the basin was ruffled by a fresh breeze from the northeast. Waves breaking against the boulders of the east jetty created showers of spray. The flow of the outgoing tide kicked up quite a rough water scene beyond the channel entrance. Definitely unfavorable conditions for rowing a low-sided skiff. Roger appeared and commented, "We ain't going nowhere today! I'll fry some bacon and eggs for breakfast."

By mid-morning the tide slacked, making for more moderate wave conditions. Northeast weather generally lasted for two or three days, while that day only a moderate breeze of probably fifteen to twenty-five miles an hour was blowing, a fair wind toward Lobsterville. Common sense told me to find a volunteer who would provide a ride overland with my supplies and the skiff in the back of a truck. But that was too easy! The challenge to row back across Menemsha Bight became an obsession, some sort of a mental quirk. Roger lent me a pair of rubber boots and an oilskin jacket. As I rowed away in the chilly mid-April weather, he yelled, "You gotta be nuts!" It was quite sloppy when I cleared the breakwater, but the old skiff waltzed along to leeward with my oar action maintaining direction.

However, upon approaching Dogfish Bar, danger loomed. Boiling white breakers ran the entire length of the bar, but a calm lagoon lay within the semi-circular barricade. At the west end of the bar was an opening, a gully about ten feet wide and about five feet deep, which I had intended to use as a safe entrance.

In normally calm weather, the gap was easily visible. But the surf was pouring over the place. Three big waves breaking across the entire bar followed by a brief lull seemed to be the pattern. After a period of jogging bow to windward but close to the breakers, there appeared to be a chance to get across the bar. I rowed like mad and almost made it. However, a sharp wave suddenly built up and tumbled in over the stern, submerging the skiff and washing me overboard!

Inside the bar relatively calm conditions prevailed. Wooden boxes full of supplies drifted toward the beach. Likewise the kerosene can. When I grabbed the gunwale of the skiff, the cranky thing promptly rolled over — bottom up! I managed to kick off my heavy boots while yelling for help. Nobody home at the Jeffers' house. Only the swooping seagulls answered my call.

Finally the wind and sea pushed the boat and me into shallow water near the beach. When my feet touched bottom, I walked ashore pulling the bowline of the skiff. With the boat grounded, I salvaged the five gallon can of kerosene and ran up the beach and into the shanty.

Shivering like a wet dog, I quickly lit the stove and all the lamps to create heat. After peeling off my wet clothing, I found enough dry clothes to replace them, including a warm woolen jacket. After awhile I was able to go back to the beach, roll the boat right side up and haul it above the high-water mark.

Some of the groceries proved to be useable. I ate an early supper of baked beans and hot dogs and drank a mug of hot coffee. In the midst of a good night's sleep under warm woolen blankets I had some strange dreams about being shipwrecked on Noman's Land, which was only a few miles away.

As usual, experience is a great teacher. Any future attempt to go surfing in rough weather would be done with two of us rowing a big seagoing dory. A logical reaction!

Chapter 12

My NEMESIS

It was back in the late twenties when I acquired my first fishing boat. Joe Tilton sold me his tired old double-ender *NEMESIS* for 100 dollars. The engine was from a Model T Ford. My pal, David Dorn, a summer resident of Menemsha, became a pardner in the venture.

After a day of repair work, including installing new steering cables, we were anxious to take the boat out for a trial run. The Model T engine came to life at full throttle and in high gear. We started at the upper end of the basin where lobster boats lined both sides of the narrow channel. Almost immediately, the *NEMESIS* proved to be just that for me, as steering a straight course in her proved impossible. My efforts to control the boat must have been comical, except that we sideswiped several boats before Dave could stop the engine. Earlier that day we had renewed the steering ropes from the hub of the wheel at the cabin bulkhead to the tiller under the deck in the stern. Somehow we must have crossed the cables, much to my surprise and embarrassment. Our steering mishap was soon corrected as we drifted along.

We finally got our act together and set a string of patched-up lobster traps off the old brickyard east of Menemsha. We also hand-lined for scup and sea bass. However, the engine was troublesome and needed repair work, like new rings and bearings, an expensive problem that required money. Dave Butler was sympathetic. He owned a big high-sided skiff which contained a mile-long string of trawl gear rigged with small hooks for catching fluke (summer flounder). Butler said, "Get some squid from the fishtrap boat when they come in so that you can bait the trawl. Give it a try anyway."

Baiting hundreds of hooks was a tedious job. Then the entire trawl had to be coiled smoothly into a large tub. The boat was heavy and impossible to row against an incoming tide. The alternative was to push-pole the boat along the jetty boulders where a favorable counter-current provided the necessary propulsion. Once clear of the jetties, I had to row a few hundred yards to the westward before dropping the trawl anchor. (All this early in the morning.) Getting the trawl set out required about three hours of steady rowing while trying to flip the trawl line over the side with a stick, in the direction of Dogfish Bar off Lobsterville. When the entire trawl was set out and anchored, it was a matter of rowing back to the origin, hauling up the anchor and trawl line and proceeding to "under-run" the gear.

By that time there was a "land breeze" blowing from the southwest that necessitated a long hard pull to windward, a job that required plenty of time and energy. There was something on nearly every hook, mostly skates and sea robin, but a good supply of fluke, too, in a wide range of sizes. Gradually I learned that the smaller fish migrated toward the beach during the afternoon. They were feeding on schools of still smaller fish like pogies and silversides. Seining for fluke along the beach had been common in an earlier era.

It was late in the day when the long trawl line was all coiled back in the tub. By that time Menemsha lobster boats were rounding Gay Head headed for home. The skiff was loaded with five or six barrels of trash fish, which I sold to the lobstermen for a dollar a barrel plus a free tow all the way back to Menemsha Creek.

My day's catch of large, medium and small fluke in a separate pen at the stern of the skiff usually weighed from 300 to 500 pounds. It sold quickly to down island fish dealers for a price that ranged between 10 and 35 cents per pound, a week's pay in one long busy day. This occupation was really a two-man routine, but I could not seem to find anyone who was willing to serve as "dorymate." However, when the wind came from the northeast, it provided a vacation day in port, a good chance to repair the trawl line and replace many bent hooks with help (sometimes I managed to re-bait the hundreds of trawl hooks with pieces of squid by mid-day, ready for fishing on the following day. At the end of each week Dave Butler received his share: one-third of the gross earnings for the use of his boat and trawl gear, a satisfactory deal.

Steamboat wharf and Seaman's Bethel—100 years ago. Credit - Duke's County Historical Society.

Vineyard Haven village and Town wharf. Credit - Duke's County Historical Society.

Navy Salvage Tug in for supplies and to refill tanks with Tashmoo Springs water. Bethel boat Madison Edwards at berth. 1930's. Credit - Duke's County Historical Society.

Draggers - "Southern Cross" Capt. Alton Tilton, Dragger ROAN - Capt. Roy Campbell.

Fleet of steam-powered tugboats at the Vineyard Haven wharf during Northeaster.

Vineyard Haven Harbor—before breakwater. Early paddle wheelsteamer leaving wharf. Credit - Duke's County Historical Society.

Inner Menemsha Basin—early 1900's. Menemsha Creek in backgraound.

Before dredging and widening—Menemsha Basin looking north, early 1900's. Distant building the Salthouse, owner George Butler. Elizabeth Islands across sound in distance.

Owens Park from Bandstand—late 1930's. East Chop in distance. Credit - Dukes County Historical Society

The time came to revive the old *NEMESIS*. The worn-out Model T engine was replaced with a secondhand Redwing four-cylinder direct-drive engine. It was a pleasure to set and haul lobster pots and handline for scup, sea bass and fluke once again and enjoy the wonderful independence of self-employment!

Chapter 13

A Treasure Comes and Goes

After I found a buyer for the ancient double-ender *NEMESIS*, a better boat became available, the 35-foot dragger, *VEGA*, owned by Weston Chase of Oak Bluffs. A ruggedly-built boat powered by a three-cylinder Palmer gasoline engine, her fishing equipment included one worn-out net, a pair of trawl doors and a big coil of rope towline. It was one of those simple deals — a down payment and the balance over an undetermined length of time. Bill Little came aboard to help rebuild the net and decided to stay for the summer fluke season. We went fishing nearly every day at dawn, usually around the Lucas Shoal area. The first tow of the day was generally the best, especially with a westerly tide. Twenty-five or thirty jumbo fluke gave us a good start for the day. By mid-afternoon we pursued the fish in along the shallower depths of the Menemsha shoreline, the same locale where I had kept busy with the hook and line trawl in the big skiff during the previous summer. By five P.M. every day we arrived at the creek town landing where we sold our day's catch to Colley Church, an Oak Bluffs fish dealer.

The *VEGA* was too small and underpowered for winter fishing. However, we managed to pursue the fluke when they began to move toward deeper water, first in an area southwest of Gay Head during September, then south of Noman's in October. Once in calm weather, we made a tow after dark. Within a short time the boat acted as if she were hung up, so we promptly hauled back. There was more than a normal amount of weight in the net. When we managed to get the cod end alongside, we were amazed to find it was solid-full of sea scallops! We made two more 20-minute tows that filled the fish hold and a surplus that made a deckload. We had discovered a mother lode!

Daylight fishing had produced a few scallops with each tow, but we were suddenly made aware of their nocturnal habits. It was evident that sea scallops sat still in hollow spots on the sandy bottom during daylight hours. After dark they became active, swimming freely in pursuit of whatever marine organisms they preferred for food.

Early next morning we unloaded the *VEGA* with shovels and bushel baskets after renting a shanty near the bulkhead and building the necessary shucking benches. The *VEGA* was moved to a winter berth at the upper end of the basin. We hired some local people to help with the shucking process. Women were the most adept at it.Then we activated the 40-foot dragger *WATER WITCH*, a boat with plenty of towing power and carrying capacity. We worked with the shuckers until mid-afternoon, then cast off and headed for the 21-fathom scallop grounds in order to be there by sunset. We went three-handed, each one getting an hour of sleep in the wheelhouse bunk while the other two took turns steering and keeping each other awake. The six weeks of steady production became an arduous repetition, with only an occasional break during windy weather. Then, one night in mid-November we made a half-hour tow after setting out our lighted buoy (dry cell batteries) and hauled it back on board with only a few bushels of yellowtail flounders in the cod end. Not a single scallop!We spent the night prospecting in all directions. On the theory that the scallops had moved out into deeper water, we made a series of short tows off to a depth of 30 fathoms. No luck. The previous night we had, as usual, loaded the boat during the nighttime hours. It was unbelievable that a seemingly unlimited supply of sea scallops could have vanished completely in a matter of a few hours, but they did. Other boats that worked the area with us had the same experience, a typical feast-or-famine occurrence common in the fishing industry.

The scallops never did return to that particular area.

Rather than fish for cheap yellowtails, we decided to tie up the boat for the winter months and try to find jobs ashore. Cold weather had arrived on schedule and the Christmas season was approaching. Opportunities to earn money were scarce. The only project in sight was a form of fresh-air exercise, a state-financed contract to move gravel to be used in highway repair from the high-water mark at West Chop up beach to a nearby paved parking area. It was a cooperative deal with a horse and tip-cart wagon, owned by Albert Fisher, with Dolph Manning, a powerful Gay Head Indian, as driver. It was a two-man job, eight hours a day, 50 cents an hour, that helpers quickly quit. It seemed to be worth a try when Dolph requested my participation.

Chapter 14

Hard Labor

Next morning at seven, I was sitting with Dolph on the lofty wagon seat as we clippity-clopped our way along the Franklin Street extension to the beach at West Chop, the same beach where the four-masted schooner *AUGUSTA G. HILTON* had grounded earlier. A freezing northwest breeze was busy washing more gravel ashore to supplement the existing supply. We lashed a heavy woolen blanket around the horse as he stood on the ridge of gravel. Dolph handed me one of the super-sized scoop shovels and demonstrated how to transfer a full load of gravel directly up into the wagon with a single swing of the scoop. With me, it was dig, swing back, then swing forward with a grunt, doing twice the work with limited accomplishment.

We had to be careful not to overload the wagon. The horse had to struggle to pull the load along the beach. Dolph coaxed him until he was on the pavement and backed him into the heap of gravel where we dumped the load. Our daily goal was to dump at least ten wagonloads before we headed for home at about four P.M. In the process we worked up a considerable sweat. (The "wind chill" was then an unknown factor.) At noon we rode up the hill and parked in the lee of a big vacant house for a half-hour lunch of sandwiches and Thermos bottle-coffee. Then we'd hit the beach again before the shivers set in. We completed the job over a period of ten working days. Fortunately for us, a northeast storm provided a few days of relaxation.

With that endurance contest completed, I began to think about easier ways to make a day's pay. A newspaper ad appeared with the slogan: "Become a `Speedo' can opener salesman and you will be a winner!" A post office money order soon brought a package of a dozen newfangled can openers. A vee-shaped wall bracket held the removable unit in place on the kitchen woodwork. With a can held in place, it was a simple matter of turning a crank handle to remove the top smoothly by rotating the can one complete turn. No ragged edges. A great door-to-door product. Every demonstration resulted in a sale! Price: $2.50. Profit: 75 cents a unit. Demand began to exceed supply and I had visions of becoming wealthy. Until the day a similar product suddenly became available at a lower price in the local hardware store. However, it was a good experience, a chapter in the process of my education.

Soon after the can opener business ended, I happened to meet Mrs. Wilfred O. White on Main Street one day. She said, "I have just hired Fred Fisher for a beach plum project. His brothers Ozzie and Arnie are busy with farm work, but I need another helper." She explained her plan to transfer beach plum bushes from her land near West Chop to an acre of land owned by her family in the hills of Chilmark near Middle Road. The plan was to establish a crop of cultivated beach plums. My new job began the following day. We carefully dug the plum bushes out of the sandy ground, wrapped the root ball in burlap and placed each bush on a platform truck. In the course of several springtime days, we had successfully planted more than a hundred bushes. We filled each planting hole with a mixture of sand and in-land earth. There was plenty of shoveling involved, but it was a pleasure compared to scooping gravel on the beach.

When the beach plum project was completed, Mrs. White suggested that someone should harvest bayberries for use as candle wax. Acres of bayberry bushes — all of them loaded with small gray berries were clustered everywhere on that former pasture land. Fred returned to the family farm, but I gathered a bucketful of bayberries to take home for experimenting. We had a kerosene cook stove in a storeroom near the kitchen. I poured the bayberries into a large cook pot of boiling water with the result that in a short time I managed to skim off a worthwhile sample of bayberry wax. A pleasant aroma was allowed to flow into the kitchen and throughout the house.

After processing several bushels of bayberries, I had sufficient wax to make a start on the production of bayberry candles. The first batch was done the hard way — the dipping

The record established during three years of fishing operations was the recommendation for the *MONTE CARLO* being chartered, by the scientific group, to take into the rough and hazardous North. A 10,000-mile search was made for a boat that would meet the requirements. The most fitting benediction to her abilities was voiced by Fr. Linehan when he said that through hurricanes, thunder and lightning, rough seas, and bad ice conditions, the engine continued to purr.

The *MONTE CARLO* is a 73-foot boat, built as a dual-purpose trawler and dragger by Harvey Gammage from the design of M. Rosenblatt & Son, of New York, in collaboration with Francis Minot, Maritime Consultant. She is owned by Captain Edwin B. Athearn of Falmouth, Mass. The Burmeister & Wain ALPHA Diesel which powers her is 180 bhp., 3-cylinder, two-stroke cycle, valveless design of 9" bore and 15 3/4" stroke, designed and built by Burmeister & Wain in Denmark, to meet the requirements of rugged simplicity and reliability.

The cost of spare parts needed for the Burmeister & Wain ALPHA Diesel engine and controllable pitch propeller unit due to normal wear and tear has amounted to approximately $5.00 per month during its first three years of operation. Cylinder wear rate to date indicates a cylin-

process. Fortunately, a neighbor came along with a candle mold that provided the answer to candle production.

For several reasons, the candle business proved to have its limitations. My folks decided against a household candle factory. The profits were limited compared to the time and effort involved. Probably I became bored with the candle making routine. Anyhow, the urge to do something more adventurous was the principle factor.

Eventually, I learned that Mrs. White's beach plum orchard was a success and that the surviving bushes provided an ample crop of plums.

Early that summer, I was hired by Harry Peakes along with Sam Newcomb for a season of trapfishing. Sam was a native of Provincetown who, during his younger years, had sailed in fishing schooners and dory trawlers, working on Georges Bank in the winter and away out on the Grand Banks during the summer months. He had survived many wild gales while his vessel was laid to under a "three-reefed foresail." His stories were essentially a series of seagoing adventures.

The fish weirs were located off the north side of Naushon Island near Kettle Cove. The traps, long hickory poles set in a place by a scow and pile driver supporting small-mesh, tarred netting, was heavy and difficult to handle. Peakes' base of operation at Vineyard Haven harbor was at the location now occupied by the Gannon & Benjamin Boatyard facility. The shop and net-storage loft was the building that burned to the ground in 1990. (Special tools and some fine boats were gone forever.) A new building was quickly built in a great example of community volunteer effort providing labor and materials.

The two Buzzards Bay weirs required frequent changes of netting. Grass and sea moss soon clogged the netting. Spare sections of trap nets had to be tumbled out of a door that opened toward the beach, where they landed on an ancient platform truck (chain-drive) to be moved out on the nearby pier in order to dump them into the two big flat-bottomed boats. These were towed behind the powerboat *SQUID* all the way to the traps, usually with a boiling head-tide through Woods Hole Channel. Handling that dry netting in the loft was an extremely dusty job. Sweat and pulverized dirt lent me the appearance of an emerging coal miner. The wet, grassy nets would be removed and brought home to be hauled by truck to a distant vacant field, there to be spread out to dry. Tears and broken meshes would be mended as well. It was a busy routine: haul and reset the traps in the morning, sell the fish at Sam Cahoon's Woods Hole market, then return to the Vineyard where we worked at net repairs in glaring heat until late afternoon. The pay? Eighteen dollars a week and plenty of fish to take home.

Harry Peakes' other enterprise, was the ice business. He owned and operated a freezer plant on Beach Road between the Vineyard Boatyard and Mobil Oil storage tanks. Retail ice came from the Lambert's Cove ice house and was rehandled from a small cold-storage building behind the trapfishing headquarters. A two-man team, Pete and Burgess, delivered ice by truck to any residence that displayed a big card with the word "ICE" prominently displayed in the front window.

Chapter 15

Some Thoughts on Boats and Boatmen

This chapter will ponder the subject of boats, specifically the genuine breed nowadays known as wooden boats. (Those of us who have a special enthusiasm for boats and ships of wooden construction are blessed with the wonderful magazine, *Wooden Boat* — six annual issues of entertainment and education.) From my point of view, a wooden craft is like a living creature. Each one seems to have individual characteristics. Some of them are known to be good "seaboats," comfortable and well-behaved in rough sea conditions. Of course, there are many variations of performance in powerboats and sailboats that often depended on the ability of the skipper and his crew.

Island people are naturally involved with boats. But to those who are "landlubbers" — islanders or inlanders — all vessels are referred to as boats. On the other hand, true seafaring people will tell you that if a so-called boat is too big and heavy to be hoisted and carried on the deck of a ship in the manner of a lifeboat, it is classified as a vessel of some sort. Sailing craft had various rigs (and still do) such as sloop, yawl, ketch or schooner.

Commercial fishermen are an exception. Their vessels, regardless of size or tonnage, are known as boats. Most of us, seafaring or otherwise, when commuting to or from the mainland by Steamship Authority ferry, speak of "catching the boat." The name "steamship" is impressive, although the fine old steamers are gone and about the only steam on the modern, diesel-powered ferries is in the snack-bar hot dog cooker.

Larger vessels of wood construction became known as ships, including sailing ships, especially the magnificent square-riggers that carried their cargoes across the oceans and around the world. The zenith of wind-powered ships was, of course, reached during the past century, the era of the clipper ship. The famous ship *FLYING CLOUD* was a perfect example of the clipper's beauty and efficiency. Marvelous figureheads, generally of female form, provided a guiding spirit for those 'round the world sailing ships. The philosopher's words — "A thing of beauty is a joy forever" — must have been inspired by the sight of a clipper ship under full sail in a raging gale! German grain ships especially!

Many of my experiences with boats consisted of sailing on fishing draggers. The 38-foot *RELIANCE* was an excellent seaboat, similar in size and capability to the *ELMARDO*. Both were wonderful wooden boats with great qualities of character and substantial construction, almost like living creatures in their behavior. Another interesting boat was the 40-foot *JUNIOR*, a bulky double-hulled craft built to carry bottled booze in special compartments. As usual, I managed to buy the *JUNIOR* with the blessing of Mr. S. C. Luce and his Martha's Vineyard National Bank. Insurance for the boat (including "War Risk") was handled by Lloyds of London, the only underwriter willing to insure fishing boats at that time. By coincidence, I took ownership of the *JUNIOR* soon after I had become an employee of the Woods Hole Oceanographic Institution.

Fortunately for me, Captain Ben Mayhew, Jr. and Eric Cottle volunteered to operate the boat out of Menemsha. They rigged the boat as a dragger and made a success of catching boat loads of yellowtail flounders in areas south of the Vineyard. The boat was powered with a Superior diesel engine that proved to be reliable and economical, special advantages in those days.

When World War II ended in 1945, many of us had the notion that the U.S.A. would plunge into another economic depression. We didn't immediately realize that the demand for goods and services would be greater than ever before. A good example of the post-war prosperity we would soon enjoy was in the boat market. Pleasure craft that had been stored for years in boatyards suddenly became available for use or for sale to new owners. Designers and builders became busy with new craft of all types and sizes.

Shipyards, particularly in Maine, made the changeover from producing military vessels to their normal business of signing contracts for commercial fishing draggers. A combination of favorable circumstances presented me with the opportunity to proceed with having a new vessel built.

The recent newspaper accounts of the exploits of the *F/V MONTE CARLO* in the ice near Meecham Island inside the as yet uncharted Bering Channel, have as much significance to boat owners and operators and marine power users as to those interested in the scientific aspects of the voyage.

The *MONTE CARLO* was chartered from her owner to make a scientific expedition to the Arctic and the Magnetic North Pole. She left Portland, Maine, skippered by Captain Wilbur E. Dow, Jr., of Short Hills, New Jersey carrying a team of eleven members, headed by Father Daniel Linehan, famed Jesuit Seismologist from Weston Observatory.

The details of how she became frozen in the ice of the Northwest Passage and would still be there except for a dramatic rescue are already well known. However, there are many other important and interesting phases of this story that have not yet been underlined. The rugged dependability of the vessel's Burmeister & Wain ALPHA Diesel engine, and the flexibility and reliability of the controllable pitch, three-bladed propeller which becomes an integral part of the engine through a hydraulically-operated friction clutch and reverse mechanism, played a most important part in the successful 8,000-mile trip of the dragger. Of special interest is the fact that when the fishing boat was freed from the ice by the Canadian Navy's Arctic Patrol vessel, *LABRADOR,* the *MONTE CARLO* proceeded under her own power through the freed passage.

On several occasions, the vessel was squeezed out of the water by the ice and when the ice would weaken the dragger would slip back in. Often, when squeezed up, the vessel would list to 45 degrees before settling back. The rounded design and strongly built hull is all that prevented her from being crushed by the ice.

der life of between twelve and fifteen years.

The trouble-free operation of the power unit is best expressed by Captain Wilbur E. Dow, Jr.: "The Burmeister & Wain ALPHA Diesel engine and controllable pitch propeller demonstrated its ruggedness and dependability to my complete satisfaction throughout our successful 8,000-mile trip."

MONTE CARLO upon return to Boston from Hudson Bay expedition in 1954.

One of the many boats that I was privileged to operate out of Vineyard Haven was the *MYRTIE B. CROWLEY*, owned by Benjamin C. Cromwell. The *MYRTIE* was a converted yawl boat salvaged from a six-masted schooner, the *MYRTIE B. CROWLEY,* built in Rockland, Maine which had been wrecked during a winter gale on the shoals outside of Muskeget Channel. Sam Jackson and his crew in the fishing boat *PRISCILLA* of Edgartown defied the raging weather and sea to reach the big schooner in time to rescue the captain and his wife along with the entire crew. Their safe return to port was celebrated as a great event. Captain Sam and his crew eventually received medals in honor of their great courage and marvelous accomplishment.

In that same era: — the six master — *WYOMING* — became a disasterous wreck off Nantucket. The Vineyard Gazette librarian and historian, Mrs. Eagan, provided further information in her recent letter.

"About two months after the *RUTH E. MERRILL* sank in Vineyard Sound, the world's largest six masted schooner: — *WYOMING* — measuring 100 feet longer than our Island Ferry, *EAGLE*, and a draft (depth) of 30 feet, was lost with her 15 crewmen in a roaring Northeast blizzard off the Pollock Rip lightship somewhere East of Chatham, on March 11, 1924.

It was hoped that she had managed to find refuge until her stern and other wreckage washed ashore on Nantucket.

This was the last great marine disaster involving loss of life on the waters immediately surrounding Nantucket Island.

The magnificent WYOMING was the 10th and the last of the era of six masted schooners. She was also the largest six master and was built in Bath, Maine, during the year of 1909. In fact the WYOMING was known to be the largest wooden ship in the world. In contrast, her handling qualities were considered to be the best of any vessel in the fleet.

Anyone interested in the history of sailing ships should acquire the marvelous book entitled *"Yankees Under Sail"*, edited by Richard Heckman and wonderfully illustrated with pictures including the *WYOMING* and the ultimate steel hulled seven master:—*THOMAS W. LAWSON.*

The 23-foot yawl boat, originally an open hull, had become a decked-over workboat with a raised cabin forward. She was rigged for swordfishing, with a fairly tall mast and suitable bow pulpit. She was probably about the smallest swordfishing boat in existence, requiring flat, calm weather to go seaward beyond Gay Head. My use of the boat consisted mostly of tending lobster traps off the north shore of the Vineyard during one summer. The Model A Ford engine

MONTE CARLO plowing through drift ice in Hudson Bay, 1953.

proved to be temperamental and somewhat unreliable.

Ben Cromwell maintained a hardware store in the corner building adjacent to the Martha's Vineyard National Bank. Captain Hartson Bodfish, a retired Arctic whaleman, was the store manager. He was a big man with a jolly disposition who sported a goatee and puffed on a curved pipe. He entertained his customers with wonderful whaling stories in the Barnacle Club above the hardware store. Regular members like Rod Cleaveland (whose weather predictions were always wrong, according to author Joe Allen) sat near the front windows and watched all of the Main Street activities.

Another small craft was the double-ender *FILLY*, a utility boat handled by Erford Burt when he was manager and boat builder during the era when Bill Colby owned the Vineyard Haven boatyard. Erford was a man of exceptional energy and a real talent for designing and building fast, able sail and powerboats. He and the *Filly* were fun to watch as they dashed around the busy harbor.

Captain Bob Douglas of Vineyard Haven has safely sailed his 108-foot Topsail Schooner *SHENANDOAH* on weekly passenger cruises for 30 consecutive seasons. He also owns the 90-foot former pilot schooner *ALABAMA*, plus an assortment of wooden craft, of all shapes and sizes, many of them in storage. He seems to have become the guru of the wooden boat fraternity, at least along the Eastern Seaboard. Back in the sixties, he sold me a small catboat; I paid him with a bank check that I forgot to sign.

✶

Years ago, on my coastwise travels, I would come upon a vessel, usually a schooner, that I knew would appeal to Capt. Douglas. Another example of our mutual "wooden boat fever."

The former schooner yacht *JANE DORE* was secured on the north side of Longo's Wharf at Stonington, CT. The graceful 75' vessel had served on submarine patrol duty during World War II, after which she was auctioned as surplus property and sold to a commercial fisherman. She proved to be unsuitable for use as a dragger and was offered for sale by the young owner.

It was during a cold January evening when I returned to my headquarters and promptly called Capt. Bob at Vineyard Haven. In a matter of minutes after listening to my description of the *JANE DORE*, he said, "I will be on the first (ferry) trip in the morning and will meet you in Woods Hole!"

Next morning, with our pal Eddie Crosby of Osterville along for the ride, we were on our way to Stonington. A strong Northwest breeze had caused the air temperature to register 10 degrees above zero! We parked on the pier with the engine heater going full blast in the car while Douglas wandered around aboard the schooner in a state of preoccupation and oblivious to the 'wind chill factor!' for an hour or more.

Finally, he returned to the car, all excited about the vessel. We went to a nearby waterfront restaurant where we had hot coffee and a bowl of fish chowder.

A few days later, in warmer weather, we returned to inspect the vessel where she was dry-docked on the steam powered marine railway in the Thames Shipyard at New London. A survey inspection produced a favorable report, resulting in Capt. Bob becoming the new owner whereby he and his crew delivered the *JANE DORE* to Kelly's Shipyard in Fairhaven, MA to be made ready for the passenger cruising trade.

Chapter 16

Swordfish and Somersaults

Captain Steve Gardner at Menemsha needed a crewman for swordfishing on his big seagoing catboat *HELEN*. It was an easy job for the summer as Gardner was in the party fishing business and advertised swordfishing trips south of the island as his specialty. For the comfort of the passengers, we tried to foresee good weather on a daily basis.

Captain Steve, who was noted for consuming from 12 to 20 cigars a day, studied the weather signs at sunset and made plans for the following day accordingly. He would phone the prospective party with instructions to be at his pier at an early hour on the following morning. He would also notify our other crew member, Linus Jeffers, a Gay Head Indian, to be available. It was my job to make a sunrise trip to get Linus at his Gay Head house and transport him to Menemsha in the Model T before the party arrived from down island.

The Ford Roadster featured a special oversized steering wheel with a hub that could be locked with a key, a device intended to prevent the car from being used "without permission." Roger Trump, a waterfront pal, came along on what proved to be my last trip to Gay Head in the Model T car..

It was a fine sunny morning as we rolled along at full cruising speed (about 40 M.P.H.) through Chilmark center and up over Great House Hill on the road to Gay Head. Just as we passed the top and began to gain speed downhill, the steering wheel suddenly ceased to function. I twirled the wheel madly in hope that it would re-engage and become steerable quickly. Compounding the problem was the fact that the brake system was mostly ineffective. Ahead of us a man and a woman were strolling along the edge of the road, backs to us, a few hundred yards away. I tooted the squeaky horn but they paid no attention to the impending calamity. Fortunately, the old Ford gradually eased off the hardtop onto the sandy shoulder, causing the car to plunge down a steep embankment, plowing a tunnel in the bushes until we struck a stone wall that stopped us quite abruptly. Roger was catapulted over the partly folded-down windshield and made several "loop the loops" before landing in a squatting position in the thick underbrush, stunned but basically unhurt.

For a few moments we tried to get our wits together. The Model T was a total wreck. Colliding with that wall of boulders had smashed the front end; the wheels and the entire steering mechanism were pushed back to a position directly under the seat, nearly touching the rear wheels. A most abrupt, "end of the road" situation.

The two of us, bruised and suffering nervous reaction, managed to crawl through the bushes and emerge onto the highway we had recently exited. Within minutes, Amos Smalley came along in his fish truck going in the direction of Gay Head. He stopped quickly and said, "It looks like you two clowns need a ride somewhere!" Three of us made a tight squeeze in the driver's seat, but we rumbled along and after a brief stop to pick up Linus, Amos said, "I'll give you guys a ride to the Creek and while I'm there, maybe Campbell and Flanders will be in from their fish traps with enough seafood to keep me in business today". Linus and I sat on fish boxes in the back of the truck where we could enjoy the scenery en route to Menemsha. (By the way, I should mention that Amos Smalley was a whaleship crew member in his younger days and was somewhat famous for having harpooned the huge white whale that provided reality for the original classic sea story and the name Moby Dick by author Herman Melville.)

Captain Gardner and his party of six passengers were getting impatient by the time Linus and I jumped on board the big beamy *HELEN*. Captain Steve had chewed through two cigars and was lighting a third as we cast off and became outward bound on a flowing ebb tide. We had an exciting day southeast of Noman's Land, sighting numerous sharks and four wild swordfish. About mid-afternoon, Linus, the striker, managed to "iron" an underwater swordfish. It was my job to jump into the big skiff and get towed over to the keg buoy that was boiling along toward deeper water by the pulling power of the powerful swordfish. With the keg in the skiff, it was a matter of hauling in the buoy line as the skiff surged over the ocean swells. It was an hour's work to get the fish secured with the "fluke rope."

For anyone who has not experienced the procedure of "tending" a harpooned swordfish, here is how it is done. When the keg-buoy is picked up, the buoy line is quickly placed in a chock or roller near the stem of the skiff or dory. The crewman, sitting in the middle of the boat with a pair of new gloves on his hands, pulls on the rope hand over hand and tries to coil the slack line in a neat pile, clear of his feet, on the floor of the boat. Meanwhile, the boat is being towed at a lively pace toward deeper water. Usually, within an hour, the fish tires from pain and exhaustion and is hauled up alongside the boat to where his tail can be gaffed and the fluke rope secured. An upended oar is the signal that the battle is over. But there are exceptions. A crazed fish will often turn quickly and follow the rope up and drive his sword directly through the bottom of the boat in an attempt to destroy his tormenter. On other occasions, a wild fish will "breech" out of water, then dive at high velocity straight down into the ocean bottom, an example of suicide as a last resort. Generally it is impossible to remove the fish as the harpoon dart usually pulls out and the fish is completely lost.

It did not occur to us as fisherman, that the harpooning of sea creatures such as swordfish and tuna, or in an earlier era, whales, was a cruel and barbaric procedure. Of course, the necessity for food is an incentive but, as ever, the overpowering urge for money is the primary motive. Our caveman instincts are basic, and the desire for money seems generally incurable.

At that time, we had no idea that eventually all marketable creatures of the sea would become so scarce that the possibility of extinction was a reality. International rules now control the whale population. Federal and state regulations likewise control the production of nearly all forms of marketable seafood. The new laws apply to sport fishermen, too. As ever, when it is nearly too late, drastic action is of immediate necessity. Now there is a good chance that all species will regenerate as the result of controlled production.

Chapter 17

To Florida and Back

The effects of the 1929 economic crash reached the island of Martha's Vineyard about a year later. Everywhere it was a matter of survival as the Depression lingered year after year.

There were reports that Florida was in better financial condition. Jobs there appeared to be more available, boatyard work in particular. The promise of steady work in a warm climate was quite appealing. I needed a car, however. A neighbor offered me her 1928 four-cylinder Chevrolet open-touring car for 75 dollars. The folding top was worn out. It had disc wheels with fairly new tires. Aunt Millie loaned me 50 dollars to go with my 25. She had financed my first car, a 1925 Model T Ford sedan, for 25 dollars and having paid her back, my credit was very good. A boyhood pal, Paul Fletcher, decided to join the expedition. Somehow we managed to get started in mid-October with about a hundred dollars each for travel expenses.

We soon landed in Woods Hole with our duffel bags in the back seat. At that time the main highway south was Route 1. We stayed on it for several days and nights at an average speed of probably forty miles an hour. We were headed for Coconut Grove, a village south of Miami because someone had given us the address of a boarding house there. The magnificent Pan-American seaplane base was located on Dinner Key, irectly across the highway from our new home.

Huge Sikorsky four-engine Flying Boats, known as "Clippers," made regular flights from Dinner Key to Rio and other South American cities. They needed an additional boatman to operate the launch that was used to patrol the Biscayne Bay seaplane take-off and landing areas, clearing floating debris out of their way. He would also tow the big seaplanes to the landing ramp, where a group of swimmers installed the landing gear so that tractors could tow the colossal aircraft up to a concrete servicing area. The job paid 25 dollars a week, with clean, white Pan Am coveralls provided. It was an inspiring occupation.

The Pan American Administration Building was an attractive three-story white structure with an immense lofty foyer. In the center of all the tiled floor space was a magnificent globe of the world, protected all around by a shiny brass guard rail. It must have been at least ten feet in diameter. Continents and other land areas were shown in gold with oceans a contrasting dark blue. Solid lines indicated existing South American flying routes established by Pan Am, while dotted lines encircling the world to all major countries predicted ambitious plans for their future.

The aircraft were generally serviced during the night in the glare of floodlights. The four big Wright Whirlwind radial engines were tuned and run at all speeds, sometimes all at the same time. The volume of that combined roar was nearly intolerable! The prevailing easterly wind carried the din for miles inland. Real estate devalued except for our rooming house, the neighborhood had been vacated. In order to sleep at night, we finally had to resort to earmuffs such as the mechanics wore during their engine work. We managed to adapt.

The Coast Guard Air Station was adjacent to Pan American. Their patrol planes were Flying Boats powered by two water-cooled V-12 engines. Fortunately, engine testing was usually done during daylight hours, but night time take-offs did happen on occasion.

The Coconut Grove Boatworks was separated from the Coast Guard base by a high, chain-link fence. The boatyard specialized in yacht repairs and refinishing. Whenever my Pan Am boss gave me a day off, he actually presented me an opportunity to make an extra day's pay by doing sanding and painting on one of the many fancy yachts there that required continual cosmetic work. In the meantime, Paul had become night manager in a super-sized Miami automotive service station, so that he could sleep peacefully during daylight hours, mostly free of the customary nighttime aircraft engine noise.

The tropical scenery was a pleasant change of atmosphere. The stately Royal Palm trees rustled their fronds in the steady east wind in contrast to other coconut trees and common Florida vegetation.

The water supply for drinking was a problem for newcomers. The water had a very strong odor and taste of sulphur. For a thirsty Northerner, it had the added disadvantage of acting as a laxative. As ever, it was a matter of gradual adaptation. Milk and soda pop served as alternatives.

When a mid-winter cold front reached southern Florida, dropping air temperatures down into the 30-degree range, the discomfort was far greater than a winter day in the North. With only one or two thin blankets on the rooming house beds, there were occasions when it was necessary to put on all available clothing and walk over to an all-night diner to enjoy the warmth and the jukebox ragtime music until sunrise, when it was time to go to work. It was also a good place for an early breakfast.

During normally warm weather, the best source of amusement came from watching the nightly roller skating derby which consisted of a series of exciting races on an oval, steeply banked track, at a huge stadium over in the village of Coral Gables.

By the first of May it was time to think of heading north. The climate was getting altogether too hot and sultry. A shipyard pal had suggested going to Port Washington, Long Island. Such an active yachting center needed painters and especially riggers for boatyard work. Paul decided to go along on the return trip north. This time we traveled close to the coast on Route 13 from Brunswick, Georgia all the way to Norfolk, Virginia. Narrow bumpy roads, but a nice change of scenery. We explored the cities of Charleston, Beaufort and Moorhead.

We parted company in New York City at Grand Central Station. Paul said he would buy a train ticket to Woods Hole via Boston. After leaving the Brooklyn Bridge traffic, I had a fairly easy ride to Port Washington. It was late in the day but, by luck, a policeman directed me to a first-class rooming house. The lady proprietor was pleasantly talkative while we looked into available rooms. Today such an establishment would qualify as a "bed and breakfast" enterprise.

Pan American "Clipper" Sikorsky flying boat, powered by four Wright Whirlwind radial air cooled engines. Dinner Key at Coconut Grove - 1933

Chapter 18

Shipping Out on the SANJANA

The Port Washington Yacht Yard was only a block from the rooming house. Main Street paralleled the waterfront. A man by the name of Monty was the boatyard manager. He hired me immediately when he learned that my talents included rigging work. Stainless steel wire-slicing became my specialty, much of it done high up on a tall mast in a bosun's chair.

After a month or so of rigging work, a new tenant appeared at the rooming house. He introduced himself as Walter Carter, a yacht captain from Bluehill, Maine, a seagoing Master Mariner with an unlimited ocean license. A yachting job was his version of a sabbatical. The Palmer family of Cleveland, Ohio were summer residents in their granite castle on a high hill overlooking Bluehill Bay. Captain Carter was a distant neighbor who had taught the Palmer children the art of sailing boats.

The Palmers had recently bought a 52-foot Dawn cruiser that had been stored for several years in Monty's nautical warehouse. Captain Carter was hired to do an inspection survey on the boat. The report proved to be favorable. The Palmers bought the boat, subject to its being in commission within ten days. Sanding, varnishing and painting the topsides and bottom — a month of yard work, ordinarily. The work went on, daylight to dark, including weekends. In the midst of the frantic pace of getting the yacht *SANJANA* ready for launching, someone mentioned that the movie *"CAPTAIN'S COURAGEOUS"* was the new attraction in a New York City theater.

It was Saturday and time for a night of recreation. Capt. Carter and I boarded a Long Island Railroad train in the late P.M. for a fast ride into the City. We had supper in an Automat restaurant — (a choice of foods in glass doored wall boxes similar to a Post Office.) A novelty for us.

After viewing that wonderful sea story film and several extra features, we strolled leisurely back to Penn Station where we discovered that we had missed the last train for the night by a matter of ten minutes. We could not afford a hotel room - probably about ten dollars, so we had to spend the night stretched out on the hard wooden station benches. The train service resumed

Roomate Jim Blakely with 1928 Chevolet touring car. Winter in Florida at Coconut Grove, near Pan American Airways.

at eight A.M. that Sunday morning. We were a bleary eyed pair by the time we returned to our boatyard work on the *SANJANA*. But we had seen a marvelous film story that provided a memorable interlude.

The boat, originally *SEABIRD*, was renamed *SANJANA* and launched on schedule. The Palmer family was due to arrive at five P.M. that day. We had just finished putting the last of the furnishings on board when the owners arrived by taxi. We had been too busy to stop for lunch, but there was a fresh stock of groceries in the galley. While the taxi driver unloaded the baggage, Captain Carter introduced me to the Palmer family: Mr. Bruce Palmer, his wife Emily, brother-in-law Duncan MacLeod and his sister, Betsy. We were soon underway toward Long Island Sound. It was late in the day for the trial run that we had anticipated. A decision was made to begin the cruise toward Maine right away.

The twin Hall-Scot engines, under the carpeted deckhouse floor, were turning at a leisurely 1200 R.P.M. Up on the flying bridge, engine and exhaust noise was at a minimum. We were on our way into a series of new adventures.

By the time we reached the Long Island shipping channel, the darkness of night enveloped us. The sky was overcast; the conditions flat and calm. With me at the wheel, Captain Carter studied the chart-laid courses and checked each flashing navigation buoy by searchlight for its correct number as we passed by. Mr. Palmer joined us on the bridge and asked, "Where is the nearest harbor where we can anchor for the night?" After a glance at the chart and a look at the Connecticut shoreline, the skipper answered, "Bridgeport would be the best choice, about an hour's run from here."

A 90-degree turn to port put us on a northerly course toward the myriad of bright lights, some steady, some flashing, all in strong contrast to the dense blackness of the night. With one eye on the compass, the trick was for me to try to keep on the lookout ahead. A huge shadow that blanked out a section of shorelights ahead quickly loomed much larger. The skipper and Mr. Palmer were leaning on the chart table casually talking. In a hair-raising instant, I made a sharp turn to starboard that swerved us past the stern of a huge four-masted schooner! We passed directly under the schooner's yawl boat suspended from davits above the vessel's transom. It was a shocking moment!

We slowed and circled back around the huge vessel, which was drifting slowly with the tide and all sails set while waiting for a breeze. The dim sidelights, starboard and port, green and red, were barely visible. In those days, sailing vessels were not required to have the additional white lights of powered ships. A beam of light trained on the sails would have prevented many disastrous collisions. We turned on our searchlight, which we should have done when the blackout first appeared, and swept the vessel fore and aft.

On board the high-sided schooner we could see two men on watch. One man was forward, peering over the rail. The other man was sitting on the wheelbox aft. We stopped nearby, turned off the engines and had a "gam." "What vessel are you?" shouted Captain Carter.

"We are the *LAURIE ANNIE BARNES*, out of Parsborough, Nova Scotia," was the reply.

"We watched you coming at us and yelled as loud as we could." Captain Carter replied, "We didn't hear you, we didn't see you, so we damn near had a disaster! Why don't you use a flashlight on the sails?"

"We had one but dropped it on deck and now it don't work. Maybe you could lend us one."

We eased in alongside where the crewman dangled a fishline, which we tied to one of our new lantern-type flashlights. He thanked us and went on to say that they had recently discharged a full cargo (including a deckload) of Canadian Spruce lumber at Providence, Rhode Island. Now they were in ballast (cobblestones) bound for City Island, New York where they would load hard coal for the return voyage to Yarmouth, Nova Scotia. (*LAURA ANNIE BARNES* was in collision with a loaded inbound tanker sometime later enroute to Nova Scotia. It was a nighttime disaster that happened too quickly for any of the schooner crew to survive).

We wished them well and parted company. We proceeded into Bridgeport, where we dropped anchor away from the main channel and gave the anchorline plenty of scope. The sounding leadline indicated that we had about two fathoms of water, plenty for our five-foot draft. Time to relax.

Passengers and crew gathered in the aft cockpit for a "happy hour." A bottle of Haig & Haig Scotch appeared along with soda water and ice cubes. We were all starving hungry. That first big drink knocked us for a loop! By the second or third, we couldn't talk sense. Mr. Palmer volunteered to produce a steak dinner. It was after midnight by the time we turned in, drunk and exhausted after eighteen hours of intense activity. The crew's quarters were in the bow: we called it the "chain locker," two folding pipe berths and a barely accessible "hopper."

Sometime before daylight, I realized I was having difficulty staying in the portside bunk. The boat seemed to have a considerable starboard list. A quick climb up the bulkhead ladder revealed a strange sight. The boat was aground on mudflats. In the early light of dawn, all sorts of hazardous clutter were visible. Most embarrassing! I called the skipper. After a bleary-eyed look around, he uttered an unquotable line. The anchor was in deep water at the edge of the channel. Fortunately, there was an incoming tide. We cautiously worked the anchor winch to tighten the anchor line. We were in a nervous dither that the owner, or one of the family, would arrive on deck. Wavelets lapped in over the flats until the bare ground was covered. During the next hour or so, we must have smoked two packs of cigarettes. Gradually, the tide rose enough to lift the boat to an even keel. We wondered about hull damage. We could have been sitting on an old rusty engine block, for all we knew!

Then we noticed that a big towboat had entered the harbor and would pass by us in the near-by main channel at full speed. The bow created a sizeable swell that became real waves as they tumbled over the flats toward us. We cranked the winch handles until the manila anchor line was stretched like a fiddle string. The swells rolled in around us, the boat lifted and moved ahead. We cranked like mad to keep a strain on the anchor rope. In a matter of minutes, we floated free and had retrieved the anchor. We got underway and proceeded slowly down the channel while listening for any possible noises that could originate from damaged propellers or bent shafts. Everything proved to be okay as we gradually reached our standard cruising speed. No indications of hull damage. No leaks visible.

About an hour later, our passengers came out on deck. Betsy provided us with mugs of hot coffee and Danish muffins, delivered on a tray, a real treat that was crucial to counteract our hungover conditions.

No mention was ever made of our grounding dilemma! Perhaps our companions knew about it and were discreet enough not to mention it. For the crew, the whole thing was considered just a bad dream.

Somewhere east of Fisher's Island we came upon a swordfish, a big critter that was sculling along leisurely on the calm swells with dorsal fin and tailfin flashing in the sunlight. The beautiful creature must have known that we didn't have any harpoon equipment on board, as there was no sign of its being disturbed by our commotion.

South of Point Judith, we saw an occasional shark and several schools of mackerel. By that time a breeze from the southwest ruffled the placid ocean surface. At the entrance to Buzzards Bay, we slowed down and stopped close alongside the Vineyard lightship. The Palmers had rolled up and tied a bunch of magazines, which we passed to a crew member who stood in an open doorway in the starboard side of the lightship where they normally received their supplies. Such a delivery was a common practice before the advent of television. The crew on deck gave us a cheer as we safely made our departure. Fenders were not necessary. The other lightship, "Hen and Chickens" was located to our northwest near a bunch of boulders by that name. But we had no more magazines or newspapers. Eastward, toward Cuttyhunk Island, a clanging bell buoy with a flashing light on top marked the outer end of a rocky ledge known as "Sow and Pigs" ledge, the scene of many horrendous shipwrecks, of sailing ships in particular. It was and continues to be an area often blanketed by dense fog.

We followed the buoyed channel northerly, passing close to Cleveland Ledge Lighthouse toward Wings Neck Lighthouse and the winding entrance to the Cape Cod Canal. When the canal was later widened, the dredging included a deeper, straight-line channel approach. Fortunately we had a favorable tide through the canal with only moderate traffic in both directions. Near the east end, a Corps of Engineers patrol boat came alongside to check our dimensions and destination. By mid-afternoon we had entered Cape Cod Bay and departed from the sea buoy on a compass course toward Gloucester, 60 miles away, with a fresh southwest breeze as a fair wind. Typical summer weather. We could see the scattered fleet of Provincetown fishing draggers on the horizon to the northeast.

We saw a variety of shipping in the Boston "Steamer Track," from trawlers to a Cunard ocean liner. There were freighters and oil tankers, inbound and outbound, towboats and barges and several "coasters" — two and three-masted schooners. The Port of Boston was a busy place in that era. Long before electronic navigational systems, inshore vessels depended entirely on their compass, sounding lead line and the skipper's judgment. In thick weather, foghorns sounded from all directions. At dusk, we entered Gloucester harbor and tied up alongside the fishing schooner *ALVIN T. FULLER*, a dory trawler.

In the morning we went ashore and had breakfast in a nearby diner. Captain Ben Pine, famous racing skipper, sat nearby. We heard him say that his new schooner, *GERTRUDE L. THEBEAUD*, would win the next race against the Canadian fishing schooner *BLUENOSE*. The Nova Scotia skipper Captain Angus Walters was equally famous and usually outsailed his competition. Captain Ben also remarked that he now had a lively "mastheader" by the name of Sterling Hayden. Sometime later, Sterling served as mate with Captain Irving Johnson on his first *YANKEE*, a former North Sea wooden pilot schooner, sailing around the world. Of course, he eventually became a successful Hollywood movie actor and best-selling author of *Voyage*, a novel about the age of sailing ships.

We moved the *SANJANA* to a fuel dock where we refilled the gasoline tanks. Our passengers went on a walk along the waterfront, sightseeing and returned with food supplies for the galley. After lunch, we got underway and after a look around the harbor to admire all the picturesque vessels that were in port, cruised leisurely through the Anasquam Canal, thereby avoiding the long run around Cape Ann. Outside, we had a moderate southwest breeze, a hazy atmosphere and a long swell from the southeast. By the time we saw the Portland Lightship, dense fog had rolled in and closed our view ahead. The deep boom of the foghorn grew louder as we arrived for a close view of the lightship before turning to compass course that would take us directly and safely into Portland Harbor, a good place to be during a night of dense fog.

Visibility quickly improved when we reached the inner harbor. Late afternoon sunlight illuminated the waterfront and the hillside city of Portland. We tied up alongside the sardine carrier *CONQUEROR*, a comfortable spot for the night. The ten-foot rise and fall of the tide was simplified by securing to another vessel where we could use short docklines and fenders, smooth-sided floating conveniences, over the side.

A drinking party with dinner on board occupied the evening. Distant and nearby foghorns were doing their part to add to the mystery of the unusually thick fog. Such conditions, according to local mariners, were known as a "dungeon of fog," conditions which made for difficult navigation during that era before radar became available. Experience and instinct had to be the basic elements applied during periods of thick weather.

The weather had changed overnight. A breeze from the northeast had blown the fog away. We hailed a small harbor supply tanker, the *PENOBSCOT GULF*, which came alongside to refill our gasoline and water tanks and deliver a case of engine oil.

By mid-morning, we were underway out of the harbor on the way toward our destination at Bluehill Bay. Captain Carter knew all the short cuts between islands and ledges and a channel shown on the chart as Deer Island Thoroughfare. Outside, the northeast wind kicked up a choppy sea but we were in the lee of islands most of the time. We even went out of our way to make a side trip into the far end of Sommes Sound, a deep water fiord between the mountains.

We picked up our mooring buoy in Bluehill Bay in the late afternoon, just in time for the cocktail hour. The Palmer family mentioned that they were pleased that their two-man crew had the capability of matching them drink for drink whenever the boat was safely moored. They didn't want anyone who was sober to watch their silly antics!

It was time to celebrate our safe arrival at the homeport after an adventurous three-day cruise from Port Washington. A sailboat came out toward us. The three Palmer children and their governess, an attractive blonde, greeted us with yells of "Welcome home!" They came alongside, where we helped them to climb aboard. They were naturally curious to see the layout and interior of the "new" boat. The lively crew clamored down into the sailboat and headed back ashore when reminded that it was time for their supper.

The 12-foot lapstrake varnished dinghy sitting in chocks on the aft cabin was swung out on her davits and lowered until afloat alongside. It was my pleasure to row our passengers ashore. Five people was a boatload. They disembarked on a floating pier. Another round trip was necessary to ferry all the baggage ashore. Fred Simmons, the year-round caretaker of the Palmer estate, arrived in his truck to deliver the baggage up the hill to the "castle," an imposing three-story granite structure. As an employee, I was privileged to join the household servants at mealtime in the kitchen. Captain Carter commuted daily from his house in Bluehill Village.

There was about a month of routine activity, beginning with cosmetic maintenance every morning. Usually in nice weather there would be a cruise with the entire family out around the local islands during the afternoon. We made several stops so that the kids could try handlining for codfish. It was my job to clean the fish when we had returned to the mooring. After those trips, it was cocktails or highballs for the grownups, soda pop for the kids. When the party was over, my final chore for the day was to scrub the fish gurry that would stain the aft cockpit's teak deck.

Sometime in mid-July, having completed another codfishing cruise, Mr. Palmer announced that they were making plans for a tuna fishing expedition to Nova Scotia. Giant bluefin tuna was the objective. At first, we thought he was anything but serious. The SANJANA, a fragile yacht, was rather impractical for that type of activity!

Chapter 19

Stormtossed

It soon became evident that Mr. Palmer was intent on proceeding with plans for a Nova Scotia tuna-fishing expedition. Captain Carter and I tried to convince him to forget it. A custom-Dawn power yacht was known to be of outstanding quality when it came to material and workmanship. However, these yachts were intended to be "good weather" boats of rather light construction that would generally be limited to day-cruising between yacht clubs. A Dawn had a spacious deckhouse with too many large windows. It was a typical "cocktail boat" and not suitable for a voyage across the Bay of Fundy. A William H. Hand-designed Motor-Sailer would be the ideal craft for such an ambitious cruise.

But our advice was to no avail. An armful of Canadian charts were brought aboard followed by a dinghy-load of tuna-fishing equipment, including a pair of super-duty Penn reels, another pair of VonHoff reels of similar capacity and a bunch of big husky rods and spools of maximum test fishline. The reels were big and very heavy with drum-type brakes and asbestos brake bands normally used in the operation of trucks. A leather harness was snaphooked to the reel, and with the butt-end of the rod placed in a swiveled rod socket, provided the means of keeping the fisherman in his elaborate fighting chair whenever a big fish was hooked. A "star drag" on the side of the huge reels was used to control the fishline tension. However, as Mr. Palmer further explained, upon our arrival at a chosen "Novy" fishing port, he would hire two Canadian skippers and their lobster boats that were equipped and specialized in the sport of bluefin tuna fishing.

We departed our Bluehill Bay mooring in mid-afternoon of July 31, which happened to be Bruce Palmer's birthday. The children and others waved farewell from the shore. We cruised over to Bar Harbor where we received official customs clearance for the Canadian trip for the four family members and the two of us, the crew. After refueling and loading a truckload of food supplies, we moved to an anchorage in the outer harbor.

A birthday party for Mr. Palmer was to be the evening program. There was an ample supply of liquor stored on board. We celebrated nearly all night. Snacks and more drinks. A portable phonograph produced loud music from a table in the aft cockpit. Shouting and singing disturbed the peaceful serenity of the entire harbor. We should have been boarded by police, but we had no interference. Finally Mr. Palmer fell overboard! The two women quickly jumped into the icy-cold water to make a dramatic rescue. We used the boarding ladder to haul the shivering revelers back on board. That sobering experience ended the noisy affair.

We huddled in the galley for a while, drinking hot coffee and eating sugary Danish pastry. We began to recover from our indiscretions. Dawn was lighting the eastern sky. It was time to get underway. We cast off from the mooring, started the twin Hall-Scot engines and steered eastward toward the red ball of the rising sun.

It was a shame to suffer a hangover on such a beautiful morning. We all felt better after a large drink of tomato juice. The calm, clear weather made us feel better too. We steered a compass course toward the Lurcher lightship, the navigational guardian near Lurcher Shoals in the mouth of the Bay of Fundy. From there we would go into the Port of Yarmouth, Nova Scotia for official clearance into Canadian jurisdiction. We hoped to reach the lightship in about eight hours at our cruising speed of twelve knots. However, by mid-morning, we encountered a moderate southwest breeze, the forerunner of an extremely dense version of North Atlantic fog. Visibility near zero. A saturating wetness that dripped from everything, including one's eyebrows and nose. At the same time, the notorious Bay of Fundy tide was turning from ebb to flood, a six-knot northerly current that would necessitate a 15-degree change in the steering direction toward the lightship, still nearly an hour's run ahead of us.

The coast pilot book was a valuable source of information, especially in regard to tidal conditions. Arrows indicated the direction and velocity of currents at various stages of each six-hour duration. We had to keep in mind that we would be subject to a rise and fall between high and low tide of 20 to 30 feet, depending on the stage of the moon.

We groped along listening for foghorns until we had reached the vicinity of the lightship. The chart indicated a combination bell-and-whistle buoy in the area. We stopped the engines and listened. South of us we could hear the periodic moan and occasional bong of a big bell-buoy. In the distance to the southeast, we could also here the deep, rumbling two-tone roar of the lightship's foghorn. We had a compass bearing on the buoy but we had to stop and start several times before we could see it, and no wonder: the huge buoy was heeled over at an angle by the force of the boiling current! Fortunately, from there, we were able to locate the bellbuoy off the entrance to our goal, Yarmouth Harbor. As we approached the channel, the fog thinned until suddenly we arrived in clear air and bright sunshine! The contrast in atmosphere was simply wonderful! A great waterfront landscape. It was high tide when we docked at the City Wharf. The skipper hailed a taxi for a quick trip to get cleared through Canadian customs.

In the morning the ladies went on a shopping tour around town. When they returned the tide was low, but we had tied to a float at the pier stairway, making it easy for them to return aboard with their bundles. The harbor was a strange scene. Mudflats everywhere except between the buoys in the main channel. Extremes of high and low tide.

We emerged from Yarmouth Harbor in bright, sunny weather. A dry breeze from the northwest provided ideal conditions. The tide was in our favor, too. We soon rounded Cape Sable, keeping a sharp lookout for lobster-pot buoys, hundreds of them, all shapes and colors, many of them partly submerged in the flowing current.

The famous fishing village of Wedgeport was abeam and we talked about going in there to inquire about tuna fishing. However, a Yarmouth fisherman had advised us to go on up the east coast to Shelburne where we would find plenty of big tuna and a minimum of competition. By late afternoon we had entered Shelburne harbor and found a suitable anchorage that was within easy rowing distance of a granite block pier. We noticed that a crude chain-propelled hoisting device was located at the outer end of the pier. It was evidently a place for unloading big bluefin tuna.

Before the day ended, we had hired two local fisherman as guides, along with their 38-foot standard "Novy" lobster boats. Both boats were equipped with special fishing chairs that were located in the center of a circular slope-sided tub, which served as a foot brace at any angle during the process of trying to conquer an extremely powerful tuna.

Every day during the month of August we had a busy sort of around-the-clock routine. The two guide boats arrived alongside at 2 A.M. It was my pleasure to go along with the Palmers in one boat while Captain Carter went with the MacLeods in the other boat. Near the harbor entrance we stopped at a fish weir in order to scoop out several bushels of sea herring with dip nets, to use as bait. From there we proceeded to moorings at the mouth of the harbor. The two boats were positioned about 500 yards apart, each one equipped with a quick-release device on the mooring buoy for a fast getaway the moment a tuna was hooked. Each boat had a hand-cranked meat grinder clamped to the rail. The herring that went thru the grinder became "chum" that was carried away by the tide and became an immediate attraction for tuna that picked up the scent and quickly followed it back to the source. We looked for swirls on the water around the boat. One of us would be in the fishing chair "pit" secured to the rod and reel, with a fresh herring dangling on a hook over the side about two fathoms deep. Whole herring were tossed over the side to excite the monstrous fish. We had about two hours of fishing time, from early dawn until sunrise and full daylight. Then the fish would disappear completely.

Usually we would hook a fish in the semi-darkness. Frequently both boats had a fish hooked at the same time. Then the trick was to keep out of each other's way and not get the lines crossed. If we didn't lose the fish or part the line, the battle to bring the huge tuna alongside lasted about two hours. An exhausting sport!

An Oklahoma oilman soon appeared on the scene, adding a third boat to the early morning excitement. He always wore a cowboy hat, and when he hooked a fish, he would whoop and holler and wave it as though he were riding on a wild horse! We called him "The Cowboy."

Back on board the yacht, we decided that one of the reels was due for a renewal of fishing line. One of us cranked the new line on the beveled reel while someone else volunteered to hold a strong tension on the line by standing a few feet away and allowing the line to squeeze thru a piece of rubber inner tube. It was a slow, but usually effective, process. However, the following morning, Mrs. Palmer invited me to take her turn in the fishing chair. Moments later, a fish grabbed the bait and took off like a torpedo. Suddenly the line jammed on the reel, causing me to be instantly yanked out of the chair, and flung to the deck with my knees jammed under the rail! The enormous strain was pulling the boat backwards while I was trying to squirm out of the leather harness. Our boatman, Murdock, came to the rescue and cut the line with his sharp knife. What a relief! That ended the morning fishing. We returned to the *SANJANA* in order to work on the faulty reel. The jammed line was cut away and replaced with new line, which was carefully wound into place on the big reel.

Next morning, before daylight, Mrs. MacLeod, on the other boat, hooked a fish and away they went! Her portable phonograph was spinning her favorite theme song, "Begin the Beguine" — entertainment that could be heard for a mile in the flat calm conditions. She had the fish alongside within an hour, quite remarkable until we learned that the big bluefin had snagged a soggy lobster pot, which slowed the fish considerably. We had caught an average-sized (500 pounds) tuna that morning, so by nine AM we had hoisted both fish up into a truck on the stone pier where they traveled to the coalyard scales in town. However, the big tuna caught by Mrs. MacLeod was picked up by the coalyard crane to be weighed separately. At 865 pounds the monster tuna would set a new world's record for a bluefin caught by a woman!

After the usual errands in the village of Shelburne, we returned to the yacht for a special celebration. The drinking program was by now a routine thing day and night anyway. On this occasion, it was discovered that the supply of liquor was low. It was my spare-time job to drive the rented station wagon to Liverpool, seventy miles up the coat, to the nearest commissary, the government-controlled liquor store. It was a long bumpy trip over rough pavement. The cargo of bottles in boxes had to be ferried out by dinghy to the Dawn "mothership." The procedure took several trips!

My shipmates had achieved a great state of inebriation by the time I returned with a fresh supply of booze. They were of no real help in unloading the dinghy and getting it all stored in compartments below.

Somehow we survived with a minimum of food and sleep until one day near the end of August, when Bruce Palmer received a telegram requesting his return to his office in Cleveland, Ohio right away. His company, American Steel and Wire, had a problem to resolve.

Next morning, on our final fishing trip, we caught one tuna, the smallest one of all, a 300-pounder. We decided to keep the fish and take it back to Bluehill for the kids to see. We spent an hour securing the fish on the forward deck, using pot-warp to lash it to slender stanchions and other light-weight hardware, including the chrome-plated anchor winch. (We had first retrieved the anchor.)

At the fuel dock we filled the gasoline tanks and two 55-gallon steel barrels that we secured on planking on the aft cockpit deck as a reserve supply for the return voyage to the U.S.A. After farewells to our Novy guides, who marveled at our endurance, we departed Shelburne by mid-afternoon and pursued a course to the south whereby we cleared Cape Sable in the early evening. The weather was calm with a dark, overcast sky. A small barometer mounted on the cabin bulkhead was more ornamental than useful. Changes in atmospheric pressure had very little effect on its indications. The battery-powered portable radio provided news and music, but we heard no weather forecast from any of the available broadcast stations.

We decided to siphon gasoline out of both barrels on the aft deck, which we did by using a section of rubber hose to refill the fuel tanks, thus lowering their center of gravity in the event of rough weather ahead. It proved to be a good idea. A few minutes later we noticed a puff of wind from the east. It proved a forerunner of what came next: rumbling thunder and brilliant

Mrs. MacLeod with cup of coffee. Capt. Carter with rod and reel.

flashes of lightning, with spatters of rain. Possibly just a passing squall. We promptly put on our boots and oilskins. Two crew members stood on the flying bridge, while the owner's party was below in the deckhouse.

The wind velocity quickly increased from the southwest. The ebb tide was flowing full force to windward, a dreaded condition in the notorious Bay of Fundy. Captain Carter went below to secure the furniture and anything else that could get loose and fly around. The four passengers, scared and seasick, were advised to stay in their bunks for safety's sake. My job, steering, was a real challenge. The storm quickly became a rip-roaring southeaster with huge waves, the size and contour of cone-shaped mountains, topped by boiling whitecaps. The *SANJANA* bounced around like a ping-pong ball, pounded from all directions. She became nearly useless.

In the midst of all that chaos, we worried about the tuna on the forward deck. The searchlight revealed that the lashings had become slack, allowing the fish to roll around! The heavy fish could crash through the fragile deck. There seemed to be no practical way to try to cut the fish loose. It would take a suicide mission.

Then the port engine slowed down and came to a stop, creating a real state of emergency. With the starboard engine in neutral, the boat drifted out of control as we removed the deckhouse rug and opened the hatch over the port engine. Dirt and water had to be removed from the fuel filters. Captain Carter had to do a tough job in the worst of conditions with me back on the bridge trying to maintain headway and control in the wildest of seas.

It was a great relief to get the port engine restarted and in operating condition. Now it was my turn to check the filters for the starboard engine, which was done by slowly draining the contents of the container with the engine at idle speed. Plenty of dirt and water appeared before clear gasoline refilled the two filter tanks. It was a hot, dirty job, but it was our best insurance for survival. With both engines working we could outrun breaking waves that threatened to swamp us.

Capt. Carter and our tuna fish of a successful morning.

The *SANJANA's* oversized plate-glass deckhouse windows presented another dangerous feature. We suffered a few beam-end knockdowns whereby tons of water could have wiped out the windows completely. But we had the good fortune to rebound and we tried to keep the buoyant playboat pointed in the general direction of Bar Harbor.

The storm was a nightmare that lasted for several hours! Gradually conditions improved. The wind moderated and the tide slackened as if by mutual consent. We had somehow survived the battle. As daylight replaced the darkness of a fearsome night, we rode easily over the long swells at a leisurely six or seven knots. The tuna on the bow had stayed with us but showed considerable wear and tear because of the rope lashings. The interior of the boat was wet from the pressure of wind-driven spray forced through every available seam. After pumping out several inches of bilge water, we were pleased to learn that the hull was intact, with no lcaks of any importancc.

Crew on flying bridge with Duncan MacLeod as we rounded Cape Sable en route to Bar Harbor. An hour before the bay of Fundy Storm.

We had a ceremony, all six of us, up on the flying bridge, where we each downed a full-sized drink of Scotch and soda in a toast to King Neptune. Then we had hot coffee and sandwiches for breakfast, our first food in something like fifteen hours. We felt that we had a new lease on life!

Eventually the U.S. shoreline began to appear on the horizon. Cadillac Mountain, a welcome sight, was a blue hump in the distance. By mid-afternoon we had entered Bar Harbor bay and dropped anchor to wait for the customs inspector to appear. We hailed a lobsterman who obliged us by taking our well-worn tuna ashore to be put into cold storage. By that time it could only be classified as lobster bait. In those days, a freshly-caught tuna had a market value of between seven and ten cents per pound. The Japanese market was in the distant future.

While at anchor, we launched the dinghy so that I could tackle the ambitious job of scrubbing dirt streaks from the white topsides. A startling surprise was in evidence. All along the mid-sections of the topsides, loops of cotton caulking and

Capt. Carter in pit fishing chair with VonHoff tuna reel and special rod.

Ed Athearn in fighting chair with Mrs. Palmer and boat skipper in backgroud.

pieces of compound protruded from the planking seams, especially in the engine room area. The sheer planks had split and the toe rails were cracked. Several of the deckhouse panel sections showed damage. The boat had taken a terrific beating with all sorts of twisting action while being pounded from every angle during the sudden southeast storm and the crazy sea conditions of the Bay of Fundy.

A few days later, the "seagoin'" yacht *SANJANA* was delivered to a Boothbay shipyard to be surveyed and completely repaired. The Palmer family was so proud of the *SANJANA* and her life-saving performance that they commissioned an expert model-maker to create a three-foot detailed duplicate to be put on display in their Bluehill castle.

Chapter 20

Pierce-Arrow to Indian Scout

The subject of automobiles revives all sorts of memories. The annual town meeting provided a special temptation, as the nearby streets were lined with parked cars, all with their ignition keys in the switch position. Two or three of us young scamps would each "borrow" a car for a ride around the block. The fun developed into a contest to find out how many cars we could use and return to their original parking spaces within an hour. The town meeting was usually a two-hour affair, but we knew better than to stretch our luck too far.

Our activities gradually extended to the assortment of automobiles that were stored in the

Mr. Palmer between two super blue fin tuna (shelborn, Nova Scotia)

Big bluefin tuna hoisted on crude chain and axel device.

The 300 pound tuna lashed on the bow, ready for the trip to Bar Harbor.

Dukes County Garage. (Now Douglas Boat Storage at the "Five Corners.") The big front door was always open and all the cars had their ignition keys in place. According to the law of averages, at least one of us should have been caught, but we were lucky and evidently had sense enough to quit while we were ahead. We three culprits completed our car-stealing activities by "borrowing" one of Bart Mayhew's cars, a big Buick taxicab. We drove all the way to Gay Head and back successfully. However, it was a nerve-wracking journey which cured us completely of the habit.

Soon after those illegal adventures, I came upon another exceptional vehicle, a monstrous dark gray Pierce-Arrow four-door sedan which the Cochrane family of Vineyard Haven had traded to Manuel Campbell for a standard Chevrolet. The Pierce-Arrow was built like a truck, with a huge six-cylinder engine featuring a twin-ignition system. The headlights were molded into the front fenders, an outstanding characteristic. The headlights, being far apart, had the appearance of two approaching motorcycles in the dark of night.

It soon became evident that I had purchased an expensive form of transportation. At an average rate of ten miles per gallon of gasoline (eighteen and nine tenths cents per gallon at that time) at Percy McDonough's Texaco service station on Beach Street. The big P-A was a frequent and welcome visitor there.

When I finally realized that my conspicuous Pierce-Arrow was not suitable for routine transportation, I parked it in my backyard near Daggett Avenue. The spacious leather-covered rear section became my private den, a place to do my high school homework. The eight-passenger car had plenty of floor space to accommodate "jump seats" that folded into the back of the front seat. Furnishings, when completed, included a small table for use as a desk and a portable Victrola with some records to provide musical entertainment. With the arrival of winter, I managed to find floor space for the installation of a small stove mounted on an asbestos pad, a cute cast-iron model that could burn either coal or chunks of wood. The stovepipe required a three-inch space at the top of an open window; a vertical extension about five feet high created a stronger draft. Bunches of tinfoil filled the open space on each side of the pipe to retain the heat and prevent cold air from entering. Usually though, the little stove radiated so much heat that it was necessary to remove the tinfoil and eliminate the excess warmth.

A neighbor, Esther White, lent me her portable Royal typewriter. Gradually, I learned to use all my fingers on the keys. A boxful of interesting books and a variety of delectable snacks completed the picture.

That state of contentment continued for several weeks, until the arrival one day of the local fire chief and the building inspector, both of whom were personal acquaintances. After inspecting my abode, they concluded that the hot stove was the only real violation of town rules. As it was located directly above the gasoline tank, vented gas fumes could create a sudden explosion. Somebody nearby had complained. I was told to remove the stove and I would not be disturbed otherwise.

It was time to find a new owner for the Pierce-Arrow. I should have given some thought to its future antique value. At that time, no one on the Vineyard seemed to know what to do with such a big automobile.

I was employed then on weekends by Paul Bangs, storekeeper and member of the Vineyard Haven Board of Selectmen. It was my job on Saturdays to load a full cargo of supplies aboard the 40-foot former fishing boat *MILDRED* for delivery on Sunday to his store on Cuttyhunk Island. Paul knew about my Pierce-Arrow problem and he came on board to check my cargo inventory. While there, he said, "I have a prospect for you. While you are at Cuttyhunk, be sure and stop at the Allen House (a well-known hotel and seafood restaurant) and talk with Clarence Allen. His mother and his wife want him to get a combination taxi and truck and I'll bet you a buck that they will buy your big car!" Before leaving, I found some snapshot pictures of the Pierce-Arrow and took them along.

When the Allens saw the pictures, it was a unanimous deal."

We will buy the car," they said," but how will we get it over here?"

"No problem," I said. "Captain Pinto has deckroom on the freight boat *EBEN A. THACHER* and Captain Tilton has plenty of deck space on his schooner *ALICE S. WENTWORTH*."

They decided that they would prefer Captain Zeb to transport the car. They knew him from previous experience in the transport of bulky objects. Also, several Tilton families had become natives of Cuttyhunk. Island families usually are good neighbors.

The Pierce-Arrow was promptly sold to the Allen House for 350 dollars in cash, 50 dollars more than it cost me to own it. Captain Zeb delivered the car safely to Cuttyhunk for an even hundred dollars. Of course, he worked the tides — high tide to load and unload and a fair tide all the way via Quicks Hole. The Cuttyhunk ferry ALERT arrived just as the P-A landed on the wharf. Clarence Allen had an immediate payload of people and supplies and soon learned the knack of shifting gears on the way uphill to his headquarters.

Brother Tad Athearn on 1931, 4 cyclinder Indian motorcycle. Tad's 1925 Buick sedan in background.

The marvelous Pierce-Arrow served the Allens faithfully for many years. Finally, a sudden period of freezing winter weather cracked the engine block (Clarence forgot about anti-freeze!) Repairs were too costly. For another decade, the big car was used as a fenced-in chicken house. A humble ending for a magnificent vehicle.

Soon after I sold the Pierce-Arrow, our island state trooper, Officer Cleary, appeared on Main Street one day astride his bright red Indian Scout Motorcycle. He and I were acquainted, as I had talked with him about ways and means of becoming the owner of a motorcycle like his. Cars seemed to be too commonplace. A motorcycle — ah, real adventure!

My introduction to Officer Cleary had taken place during the previous year, soon after the Chilmark General store burned to the ground one night. Paul Mayhew, a Chilmark resident and one of my pals, had suggested that maybe we could salvage some of the stock from under the burnt debris of the destroyed store. Legality never was considered, so we boldly drove my open Model T to the location during daylight hours and loaded the back seat with burlap bags filled with scorched cans of food. The lack of labels created an air of mystery about the contents.

When we had gathered a full load, we drove toward Gay Head until we came to the entrance of a wagon road that led us to Squibnocket, where the Mayhews had a summer camp. We unloaded the car and stored our loot in the kitchen closets. We opened one can that we hoped would be baked beans; it proved to be sliced peaches! Still, we drove out of there with the notion that we had a cache of food supplies for future use. It had been a profitable weekend, we thought.

During a Monday morning class (in the old school) our principal, Henry Ritter, appeared suddenly in company with Officer Cleary. I was invited to join them and depart the room. A most embarrassing situation, especially because I was not yet aware of what it was all about. In Mr. Ritter's office, Officer Cleary brought up the subject of my part in the raid on the burnt store. He went on to say that, because neither Paul Mayhew nor I had any court record that it was simply a matter of returning the stolen goods to the store owner — Carl Whitcop, I believe — and our indiscretion would be forgiven.

That expedition was a necessary part of my education. We learned that salvage work of any sort required legal permission. It was obvious that any activity related to stealing was to be entirely avoided. Only an occasional slip, like picking apples from a neighbor's orchard, would be allowed.

Back to Officer Cleary. He parked his Scout and waved to me. "The Indian motorcycle dealer, Crandall & Hicks in Boston has taken several Metropolitan Police `bikes' in trade for new ones. Now is your chance to get a good deal," he advised.

Somehow, I managed to gather some money, about 300 dollars, and promptly traveled by steamer to Woods Hole and steam train to Boston.

By mid-day, I owned my first motorcycle and was learning to ride it, first on Commonwealth Avenue, then on Route 28 toward Woods Hole. In the late afternoon of that bright October day, I rolled down the gangplank at the signal of the mate in charge of unloading the ferry steamer.

My parents were not aware of this latest escapade, so I parked the Scout in the bushes behind the house for the night with the hope that I could think of some logical reason for being involved with such a hazardous form of conveyance. The status of the motorcycle was gradually tolerated when it was proven to my folks that its gasoline economy was a real advantage. Of course, I hadn't mentioned the related expense necessitated by the approaching cold weather: the cost of special windproof clothing, high boots, a leather jacket and aviator-style helmet and goggles.

I took two memorable off-island trips with that Indian motorcycle. The first one was in mid-December when Osborn Tower suggested that we ride to Boston for a visit to the big Sears-Roebuck store for Christmas shopping. The bike had a rear "tandem" passenger seat. We made an early landing in Woods Hole and quickly reached Falmouth, where we foolishly made a wrong turn on the highway. Instead of arriving at the Canal Bridge, we roared along through a series of villages until we came upon an old guy with a horse and wagon. We stopped to ask how to get to the Cape Cod Canal Bridge and how many miles would it be.

"Waal, boys," he drawled, after a few puffs on his corncob pipe. "You ain't goin' in the right direction. Better turn around and go back about 50 miles on this North Shore road until you get to the Canal Bridge. Right now, you are in the town of Truro!

Too embarrassed to admit where we had come from, we thanked him and roared away in the "right direction." The ride to Boston was uneventful, but we enjoyed the warmth as we explored the merchandise displayed on several floors of Sears-Roebuck's. We bought what items we could pay for and arranged to have mailed to our Vineyard address. We had a smooth ride back to Woods Hole and arrived home by suppertime. That was an adventurous journey.

The next off-island expedition happened in January. It involved the 50-foot dragger *STELLA* that was for sale in Provincetown. The boat was nearly new; it had been built over in South Dartmouth (Padanaram) five years earlier and had operated out of Vineyard Haven for about three years. A husky vessel powered by an Atlas diesel engine, the *STELLA* was an ideal vessel for year-round commercial fishing.

While on a fishing trip with Captain Tom Tilton in his 40-foot gasoline-powered dragger *ARTEMISIA*, I preached to him about buying the *STELLA*. We needed a larger boat that was equipped with a wire cable winch for setting and hauling back the heavy trawl net. Our double coil of rope towlines caused us plenty of misery in freezing weather. The *STELLA*, I thought, would require a three-man crew, and I was dreaming about the job of engineer. The comfort of visits to the warm engine room was quite appealing.

Finally convinced, Captain Tom decided that it would be my responsibility to journey to Provincetown to inspect the *STELLA* and negotiate the selling price. At the first chance, while we were in port during a cold nor'wester, I landed the Indian Scout in Woods Hole and was soon on the road to Provincetown (a familiar route) and readily located the owner of the *STELLA*.

4 Cylinder Indian motorcycle at Bert Cahoon's shop in West Tisbury. Chevrolet school bus and Agricultural Building (Fairgrounds) in the background. (see sheepskin pads on both seats of motorcycle

The owner, whose name I have forgotten, was not a fisherman. We met at the Town Wharf, launched a nearby dory and rowed out to the *STELLA*, swinging impatiently at her mooring. The boat needed plenty of cleaning and painting, but otherwise appeared to be in good condition. The big diesel engine started readily and behaved properly. The spacious pilot house, located forward, had access to the living quarters below. The engine room was under and somewhat aft of the wheelhouse with watertight bulkheads and a separate entrance hatch in a roomy deckhouse.

The boat was completely equipped with a Hathaway two-drum winch and wire towing cables shackled to the trawl doors. In addition, a new-looking net was flaked out on deck. Full headroom in the fish hold, too!

We rowed ashore and entered a coffee shop to talk about the situation. The owner explained that he was disillusioned with the fishing business. He came to the subject of price: "Right now," he exclaimed, "I will sell the *STELLA* for $2,500! And that includes the dory!" I couldn't believe it! A fraction of the original building cost! An unheard-of bargain price! We parted company with my promise to report to him by phone very soon.

The two-hour ride back to Woods Hole was made in below freezing temperatures. My Indian bike had no protective windshield. Only the inspiring thoughts of Tom Tilton's buying the *STELLA* eased my discomfort.

By the time I reached the ferry dock I was practically numb all over. I zoomed up the loading ramp and parked the Scout in an out-of-the-way corner. The ferry steamer was soon underway while I was allowed to make the homeward trip_stretched out on the boiler room grating in 100-degree dry heat. When it was time to disembark, I had just about become comfortably warm again.

After a visit with Tom at his house to tell him the good news, I rode the motorcycle home where I arranged to store it in a neighbor's garage for the duration of the winter.

Early the following morning, Captain Tom phoned to say, "Let's go fishing, the weather has moderated."

"But, Tom," I said, "what do we do about the *STELLA*?"

His answer was, "I want to think about it for a couple of days." It was a disappointing response.

We stocked up with groceries and coal and took a favorable west tide toward the fishing areas south of Noman's Land for another 48-hour endurance contest for a boatload of cheap yellow tail flounders. We made the trip, sold our catch at Sam Cahoon's market in Woods Hole at the usual price of two or three cents per pound, and returned to the Vineyard to recuperate.

Perhaps I was too insistent about acquiring the *STELLA*. Captain Tom seemed reluctant to take advantage of that great opportunity. He told me, "I would have to `hire' the money from the bank and try to make the payments." Insurance for the boat with borrowed money was another of his concerns. Reluctantly, I notified the owner of the *STELLA* about the decision and thanked him for the opportunity while trying to conceal my disappointment.

Soon afterward, he sold that marvelous boat to a Provincetown fisherman, Fred Salvadore, who operated the *STELLA* successfully for many decades. Eventually Captain Tom Tilton realized his mistake and was required to move into a larger and more practical fishing dragger. It became his lifetime occupation.

With the arrival of spring's warmer weather, the Indian Scout was reactivated. I rode it during the Tashmoo road oil project (previously described) and while commuting to the Bigelow (Mink Meadows) golf course construction occupation, where I'd ride that jouncing tractor all day

It was an era of temporary prosperity. The Boston motorcycle dealer mailed a notice advising that among their recent trades was a four-cylinder Indian. The following day, I made a quick trip to Boston on my Scout and promptly traded for the much larger former State Police Highway Patrol machine. Compared to my old Scout it was like riding a race horse. Its ample power and speed, along with flywheel torque, made turns toward the right somewhat challenging. I learned about that torque trait one day when I was in a hurry to get to Menemsha for a swordfishing trip with Norman West in his new Post boat, *HERSHEL B.*

At the intersection of State Road and North Road, Officer Cleary was sitting on his Scout in a grassy triangle, apparently enjoying the scenery, which included a huge oak tree in a nearby field, an island landmark. When I suddenly appeared on my zooming four-cylinder Indian, he cranked up his Scout in hot pursuit.

At such high speed, it was very difficult to negotiate turns to the right — due to that flywheel torque. Left turns, of course were easy. On straightaways, I could look back and see Officer Cleary in the distance. The race ended at the Town Landing, where I parked on the jiffy stand and awaited results. When my competitor Cleary came to a stop nearby, he glanced at my speedometer. My red needle set-hand was right on the 90 MPH mark. I had neglected to turn it back to zero. Cleary remarked, "That's all the evidence I need, but we had a good race, so it's okay." Because he was such a good sport, I invited him to ride my machine, which he did on several occasions. By the way, that 4 cylinder Indian motorcycle provided an exciting ride in wet weather. The four spark plugs were located on the left side of the air-cooled cylinders. Splash from the front wheel soon soaked the rider's pants below the knee. A careless moment with the left leg moving within two or three inches of the spark plugs resulted in high voltage blue sparks shooting outward from two or more of the plugs that produced powerful stings on the rider's left leg—a perfect electrical grounding action that nearly made the rider leap off the machine!

That incident took place on many inattentive occasions—a reminder of the hazards of a magneto generated ignition system.

Before dawn next day, the *HERSHEL B.* was underway on her first swordfishing trip with her owner Norman West, David Dorn and me. We reached the fishing area by mid-morning on a glassy, flat calm day in hot weather. Then we discovered that the four one-gallon jugs stored in the cabin were empty. Each of us had forgotten to fill the jugs with water before the voyage began. Fortunately, we hailed a Block Island boat, the *STANLEY*, which supplied us with a gallon of clean, cold water that tasted simply wonderful and saved the day for us. The day was made more memorable by our catch: two medium-sized swordfish.

Now for one more motorcycle incident. Toward the end of the summer, I was doing some maintenance work on my super-highway motorcycle. I had removed the wheels to check the bearings and was surprised to find that both tires were badly worn. Wilson Thomas, an Edgartown friend, had recently bought a new pair of Dunlop tires for his Indian Chief motorcycle. Somehow, they did not fit his wheels but they happened to be exactly the right size for my machine.

The only other motorcycle in town was an ancient model 74 Harley-Davidson owned by John Downs Jr, a clerk in Paul Bangs' store — "The little store with the big business." John happened to roll into my yard on his Harley for a visit. When I told him about the new tires in Edgartown, he volunteered to let me use his Harley to bring the tires home while he was at work in the store the following day. He explained that I would need to get familiar with the controls, which I soon discovered were completely opposite to my Indian's. The clutch, the shift lever and the throttle had the distinction of functioning on different sides and opposing directions.

By the time I had traveled to Edgartown the next day I had become adept with the mixed-up controls. I bought the new tires and discovered that they would fit snugly around the rear seat. In fact, they formed sort of a backrest for the driver of the machine.

On the return trip, things went smoothly until the throttle suddenly became disconnected. The big Harley immediately became nearly airborne. In a flash, I reached down and grabbed the carburetor choke lever, which brought the beast under control. With several miles to go, I managed to maintain a comfortable speed. The drivers of the few cars that I roared past must have wondered about my single-handed riding mode.

The Charter Oak, West Tisbury. *Photo by Alfred Eisenstaedt*

In a matter of minutes, I was at the Mount Aldworth section of the Edgartown-Vineyard Haven road where the downhill highway intersected with the up-island state road. I was ready to switch off the ignition and coast in neutral all the way to the Bangs' store on Main Street. At that moment, I came upon a large spread of loose gravel that must have spilled out of a dump truck earlier. The ensuing action was crazier than any Hollywood movie stunt. The motorcycle, probably speeding along at 40 MPH, whirled into a sideways skid until reaching bare pavement, where the machine and I parted company. I can vividly remember flying through the air in a sitting position as the big bike passed overhead doing a couple of barrel-rolls!

Is there anyone who would believe that I made a perfect one-point landing on the pavement, the contact point being the left side of my rear end? A leather wallet in the pocket of my dungarees took the full impact. The wear and tear included a hole in the single dollar bill that the wallet contained. An improbable story, but, oh, so true! It really happened!

While I was sliding to a stop, arms and legs upward, the Harley crash-landed a few feet downhill and spun madly in a circle with the engine at full throttle. Somehow, I was able to stand up, leap upon the machine and yank loose the spark plug wires. Peace was restored.

The one witness to that performance was Carl Magnussen of West Tisbury, who stopped his truck at the intersection to watch the whole unbelievable circus. He jumped out of the truck and helped me to lift the battered bike into an upright position. Looking at my tattered posterior, he commented, "You must be numb all over — and you have a raw bruise on your butt as big as your head!" I could hardly walk and was obviously unable to sit, but the two of us managed to push the Harley over to the roadside curb before any traffic appeared. The bike was a mess of spattered oil and bent handlebars; the twin bullet-shaped headlights were twisted out of shape. The new tires, by luck, had dislodged and rolled out of the way. They were scuffed but generally okay.

When I phoned John Downs from a nearby house and described to him the events that had transpired and the condition of his motorcycle, he was, of course fit to be tied. My condition was entirely incidental.

It seemed to be my responsibility to get his Harley-Davidson repaired and returned in satisfactory condition. The work could not be done on the island. The nearest dealer and repair shop was in New Bedford. When we learned that Captain Zeb Tilton was going there to load coal for Nantucket, he obliged by taking the Harley on deck and hoisting it onto a truck upon arriving in New Bedford. After a while, the repair work was done and the dealer found a new owner for it. Gradually, over a period of several months, I was able to pay the whole cost of the restoration.

My recovery from that rough landing was slow and rather painful: it took time and dozens of aspirin tablets. But, after a while, I managed to get my four-cylinder Indian back on the road for its daily quota of mileage. The worn-out wallet that had served so well as a chafing pad was kept in a bureau drawer at home for several years as evidence of my extraordinary experience.

The next motorcycle adventure was a journey to New York City to explore the waterfront. Milton Silvia, a Vineyard Haven boy, was a volunteer passenger on the rear seat. Route 1, a bumpy, two-lane, concrete highway, the expressway at that time, was the main highway from Maine to Florida. During the night, somewhere in Connecticut, I realized that we had taken a wrong turn, away from Route 1; I promptly slowed and made a quick-180 degree U-turn. Milton, dozing on the tandem seat, flew off at the edge of the road and tumbled down an embankment. I turned around when I heard his shout and went back to where he was sitting in a pile of leaves, uninjured.

Farm buildings nearby suggested a place to stay for the night. We walked in and found a barn with an open door and an inviting haymow overhead. We climbed a built-in ladder and tumbled into that sweet-smelling hay, a great place to sleep. Soon after daylight, we were awakened by voices on the ground floor. Several men seemed to be busy sorting a truckload of tomatoes while jabbering in a foreign language. Occasionally, one of them would look in our direction, so we realized that they knew that we were trying to hide in the hay. Of course, the motorcycle parked near the barn must have surprised them when they came to work.

When we made our appearance, we were greeted pleasantly by the work crew. After thanking them for the comfort of the haymow, we said goodbye and resumed our journey. A roadside diner provided us with breakfast.

Soon after crossing into New York State, we saw an exit sign that read, "City Island." This was a well-known anchorage for coastwise vessels waiting for a change of wind and tide, or in need of a berth to load or unload cargo. Located at the western end of Long Island Sound, at the entrance of that busy waterway known as the East River, it seemed a good destination to begin a tour of the waterfront.

City Island proved to be a yachting area with boatyards and piers all around the shoreline. Only one commercial vessel was in the anchorage, a three-masted schooner that appeared to be deeply laden with cargo. A boatyard owner gave us permission to park the motorcycle and to borrow his clumsy workskiff for a closer inspection of the schooner.

Milton sat in the stern while I rowed. As we circled the vessel, we discovered the name — *GYPSUM QUEEN* — and the hailing port in faded lettering — Parsboro, Nova Scotia. She was loaded with a powdery product known as gypsum, a wall-plaster ingredient. A shaggy old character sitting on the wheelbox invited us to come aboard and introduced himself as Captain MacDonald. He resembled Lionel Barrymore, the movie star of *Captains Courageous.*

He told us that he was shorthanded and offered us a job as crew members until his company could provide Canadian seamen. The motorcycle was no problem, he said: "The harbor supply boat will bring it out in the morning and we'll hoist it aboard!" They were awaiting a tugboat that was expected to tow the vessel to Hoboken, New Jersey, where the cargo would be unloaded. Then they would load the cargo of hard coal for the return voyage. Captain Mac did warn us that the dust raised while unloading the white gypsum and loading the black coal caused numerous complaints from the crew.

Milton and I decided to join the crew as an adventure, and because of a shortage of money for travel expenses. We hoped to work our way back to Vineyard Haven and earn crew wages of $3.25 per day.

The Captain and Mate, with their living quarters in the main cabin aft, had their meals delivered in a covered basket by one of the crew. The crew sat on benches at the galley table. The crew's galley and bunk space was located in a deckhouse forward of the main hatch, as on all coasting schooners.

By now it was suppertime, and — as crew members — we were hungry. However, when the cook placed dishes of food on the table, a regiment of huge cockroaches suddenly appeared, a rather revolting sight. The cook simply removed his apron and swished them away from the table.

One of the regular crew advised us not to worry: "They're tame and won't bite you." So we ate our beef stew and biscuits and tried to forget the ship's pets. We seemed to be having what would soon be known as a "learning experience.

"When it was time to turn in, we discovered that the two empty bunks, an upper and a lower, radiated a strong aroma of "B.O." The soiled bedding was long overdue for replacement. I climbed into the upper bunk and stretched out on the dirty blanket. Before I could get to sleep, I began to feel some sharp bites, which I soon recognized as the work of bedbugs! Hundreds of the little red devils! Milton, sound asleep, was unaware of my dilemma.

Out on deck, I removed my clothes to shake the bugs loose. My next move was to climb up into the furled foresail and wiggle under the folds of heavy canvas. Luckily the night was calm and fairly warm. Soon I heard a loud orchestra broadcasting from a dance pavilion on the outer end of City Island. The volume of the shouting and singing indicated that a large crowd of weekenders were in a mood for entertainment. The combination of noises seemed to amplify as it rolled across the calm bay.

Sometime after midnight, after a short snooze, I came to a decision. I crawled out of the folds of sail, returned to the deck and awakened Milton in the deckhouse bunk. I whispered, "Let's get out of here!" He rubbed his eyes and came out on deck scratching his bedbug bites.

We brought the boatyard skiff, tied astern of the schooner, alongside quietly in order to escape. We used the oars as paddles to avoid the noisy oarlocks. A night watchman greeted us at the boatyard, unlocked the front gate and allowed us to take off on the motorcycle.

By dawn, we had reached New London, Connecticut, and after touring the New Bedford waterfront, arrived in Woods Hole just in time to board the ferry steamer *NOBSKA* for the trip to Vineyard Haven. Our parents greeted us like homecoming heroes! We had made a safe return from a rather hazardous journey.

About a month later the three-master *GYPSUM QUEEN* dropped anchor in Vineyard Haven Harbor. Austin Tower, in the Seaman's Bethel boat *MADISON EDWARDS*, went out alongside and learned that the schooner was making her last voyage. The company had acquired a modern steam-powered freighter that was to take over the name *GYPSUM QUEEN*. The old schooner was sold to Newfoundland, where she would end her career in the codfishing trade. Captain Mac told Austin that he didn't really blame us for leaving as we did. He was still shorthanded when he sailed on the following day with a favorable wind and tide.

We eventually learned that he unloaded the cargo of coal in Halifax, Nova Scotia and safely delivered the schooner to the new owners at St. John's, Newfoundland.

My final fling on that four-cylinder Indian motorcycle came during the Labor Day weekend in that summer of 1931. Ed Roth had organized a group of young people (primarily girls) for a beach party at South Beach. He invited Emory Flanders and me to follow him in his mother's tan Buick touring car. It was a great party on a nice moonlit night: plenty of food and things to drink, including some bottled booze, which was scarce during Prohibition. Sometime after midnight, we cruised over to Menemsha and parked in front of Carl Reed's store. One of the girls demanded a ride on the rear seat of my motorcycle. We roared up to the top of the hill in front of the Joe Tilton house where we turned around and zoomed back down the road and around a particularly dark curve (the moon had set by that time). To make matters worse, the headlights were dim and we were traveling at a high speed. I actually had to glance upward at the open, starlit sky, which made a path of light between the tree branches, in order to stay in the middle of the road. I prayed that we wouldn't skid on a patch of sand or gravel and crash into the roadside trees.

The other four girls in the car each insisted on an equally thrilling ride. Somehow, by good fortune and heavenly guidance, we completed each trip safely. On the return trip to Vineyard Haven with Emory on the rider's seat, we raced the Roth Buick, sometimes showing off by going alongside so that I could put my foot on his running board. Then he would swerve and nearly force us off the road. Somehow, we survived and arrived home successfully.

It was the dawn of a new day when I coasted into my backyard and parked the Indian after a night of wild adventure. With further good fortune, I tip toed upstairs in my stockinged feet and rolled into bed.

When I awakened at midday, I lay there for a while and thought about the activities of the previous night, some of which had the qualities of a nightmare. I realized that it was time to avoid that sort of foolishness. My decision was to sell that four-cylinder Indian motorcycle right away.

While having an easy brunch, I decided to ride up to West Tisbury for a visit with Bert Cahoon. Bert was a well-known, up-island automotive mechanic who also liked to tinker with motorcycles. His shop was located behind the Socony (later Mobil) service station that was managed by his grumpy father-in-law, Captain George Donaldson, a retired whaling captain. The station, located at a bend in the highway near the fairgrounds, is still there yet today.

After a leisurely ride, I wheeled into Bert's driveway and came to a stop in front of the shop doorway. "Make me an offer for this motorcycle," was my greeting to Bert.

Bert stomped out his cigarette and replied, "Let me take a ride." He was gone about 20 minutes. When he returned, he switched off the four-cylinder motor and promptly offered to buy the Indian for 150 dollars.

I said, "It's a deal, but you'll have to give me a ride in your car." He paid me cash and drove me home in his blue Pontiac coupe. His dog, Bill, rode with us. That transaction completed my motorcycling experiences. The end of the trail brought a feeling of relief and satisfaction.

As a replacement, I bought a 1929 Model-A Ford roadster, a red car with a tan cloth top. It had been owned by the caretaker of senator Butler's Lamberts Cove estate known as "Mohu". I've forgotten his name. But the car was a bargain at 400 dollars, the most sensible deal I had ever made. And the rumble seat was a fun feature!

Chapter 21

High School Graduation Trip

The Tisbury High School senior class celebrated their graduation from the "new school" in the spring of 1931. Somewhere in my storage files, there is a copy of the "Bomb", the school magazine for that year. The individual graduates, about a dozen of us, had our pictures represented along a descriptive commentary relating to our particular characteristics that required three pages of print.

The grand finale of graduation was the off-Island expedition. The destination was a choice of Washington, D.C. or New York City. We voted in favor of New York. From Woods Hole we traveled by train and bus to Fall River where we boarded the palatial steamer *COMMONWEALTH* for the overnight cruise to New York.

We had clear weather beyond Newport until we reached Brenton Reef Lightship, where the ship turned westward into an atmosphere of dense fog. Being the only mariner in our group, I became curious about the problems of navigation in near zero visibility while the ship continued at the customary speed of twenty knots. Frequent blasts from the ship's fog horn blended with the horns and whistles of other craft in the vicinity. At that time, the miracle of Radar was in the distant future. With luck, I was introduced to Chief Mate McKinnon when he appeared on deck after completing his four p.m. to 8 p.m. watch. He explained the whole routine. First, the quartermaster had to steer an accurate compass course while the other A.B. seaman was at the bow on lookout duty. The direction and velocity of the tide in Long Island Sound was carefully considered because of daily variations. In addition, the distance between navigation buoys was reported from the engine room by the number of RPM's of the steam powered propeller. (The same procedure was used on the earlier paddle wheel steamships).

It is no wonder that the Captain generally felt obliged to stay awake and be on watch all night to try and insure the safety of the voyage.

By dawn, the steamer *COMMONWEALTH* had rounded Throg's Neck and entered the East River entrance to New York City in clear weather. Breakfast was served in the main deck dining room while we bucked a head tide in the hazardous and narrow passage known as Hell Gate. Marine traffic all around us.

After docking at 79th street, we disembarked and were delivered by bus to a midtown hotel for our five day stay. Our Tisbury school Principal, Mr. Henry Ritter was in command of our expedition. His normally stern and disciplinary disposition was greatly modified as we proceeded on our tour of New York City.

Our first objective was the new Empire State Building completed that year of 1931. The elevator zoomed us up to the observation tower some eighty four floors high where we viewed the amazing features of the city including the magnificent Chrysler landmark that had previously been the world's tallest building. With it's handsome tower distinguished by graceful curves, the Chrysler building continues to be the most identifiable building in all of the Manhattan skyline.

We all had a great time exploring the big city, riding the roaring subways for many miles with a turnstile fare of one nickel.

Some of us rode around on buses while others walked the streets and went window shopping. A ferry trip over to visit the Statue of Liberty was the real climax of all our travels. In the evening, after a fancy dinner, we usually attended one of the Broadway stage shows. As I recall, Radio City Music Hall was being completed at that time.

By the end of that seven day excursion we had experienced more memorable adventures than we ever thought would be possible

Chapter 22

Mildred and the Bon Voyage

So, here was the boat I had orders to deliver. I walked along the New Bedford wharf, looking at the *MILDRED* from different angles. A forty-foot, sloop-rigged, fishing dragger... her weathered appearance indicated she had been neglected for months.

An Island merchant had recently bought the boat and hired me to bring her home. The tide was down, so I had to leap into the slack rigging to get aboard. One of the hatch covers lay bottom up on the deck. Not an encouraging start, I thought, mindful of one of the old superstitions of the sea. However, I righted the matter and turned my attention elsewhere.

With the help of the pump handle, I pried open the cabin door. The atmosphere below was heavy with many stale odors. A large rusty gasoline engine occupied much of the cabin space. It took an hour of intense effort to get the old hand-cranking mill started. A few adjustments, as it warmed up, made it run smoothly.

Being young and impatient, I didn't stop to look for safety equipment or to get any supplies for the trip. The fuel tanks measured nearly full, so I decided to get started. A bystander threw the lines aboard and we were underway. By coincidence, the noon whistles blew as if saluting a lone voyager. It was the latter part of January with a freezing Northwest gale blowing. Though it was a fair wind, it wasn't the right time to start out alone in an unfamiliar boat.

There was not much activity in the harbor. Even the gulls seemed to have gone for shelter. At the mouth of the harbor the bell buoy clanged a noisy warning as we squared away on the twelve mile run toward Woods Hole.

Wild foaming seas boosted us along. With the wind on the quarter, I decided to hoist the riding sail. It was a tussle to get it sheeted aft, but it was worth the effort as a new driving force was quickly evident. *MILDRED,* having a sailboat-shaped hull, behaved well as we drew away from the land and the sea grew rougher. She plunged along in lively swoops, steering easily. Stinging wind-whipped spray came hissing aboard, freezing instantly. Hull and rigging were soon coated with ice.

It was quite comfortable in the wheelhouse. I opened a forward window to clear up the bluish haze of leaking exhaust smoke. At this rate I figured I would get home in a couple of hours. This pleasant state of mind soon changed when the engine suddenly began to cough and slow down. It wheezed to a stop before I could get below. I discovered the gasoline strainers to be full of dirty water. With the boat drifting and tumbling around, it was difficult to get at the trouble. In a short while, however, I had the engine running again. Coming out on deck, I was surprised to see the Cuttyhunk mail boat *ALERT* approaching. Circling around, the skipper hailed, asking if we were in need of a tow. I assured him that everything was all right. The *ALERT* went plowing to windward in a smother of spray.

Shortly the engine failed again. The *ALERT* was far out of reach and I began to regret having turned down the offer of a tow. The engine would run only briefly. There seemed to be an endless amount of rusty water in the fuel tanks. Cleaning out the fuel system soon became an exhausting routine. It was hot dirty work in very cramped quarters. The crazy motion of the boat didn't help any.

During a breather on deck I worked out a balancing combination of sail and rudder, which kept the boat surging along in the right general direction. A deep-laden, ice-covered oil tanker, headed for the Cape Cod Canal, crossed my bow too close for comfort. There was no other shipping in sight.

In my spare time I rigged an anchor and overhauled a coil of rope in readiness for the lee shore ahead. The daylight was going and I was anxious to get into Woods Hole channel before dark. The engine began to cough and backfire again. I was busy coiling rope on deck when suddenly there was a jarring explosion! Smoke and flame burst out of the open cabin door. The gasoline soaked cabin floor was a roaring mass of flames. My first desperate reaction was to escape the burning boat, but *MILDRED* carried no dory or skiff. It would have been difficult to launch a small boat in any case. The fire extinguisher which I pulled from a bracket in the wheelhouse proved to be nearly empty. I grabbed the deck bucket and started bailing sea water into the blazing cabin. I bailed in a blind frenzy until I simply had to give up, completely exhausted.

Meanwhile *MILDRED* drifted side to the wind, rolling like an abandoned wreck. The sheet rope had parted and the thrashing sail was threatening to dismast the boat. The deck was covered with several inches of slushy ice. Smoke and steam were billowing up out of the cabin. Realizing I must try to smother the fire, I jumped into the hold and came up with a couple of wet burlap bags. One of these I cut into strips and used for caulking around the cabin door. The other I crawled forward with intending to stuff it into the cabin stove pipe. At the moment I reached up to do this a great rushing comber struck the boat, almost burying her as she rolled down on her beam ends. For an instant I hung suspended with arms clamped around the pipe. The rusty bailing wire stays quickly parted, one by one, then the pipe snapped off at the base. Overboard I went, grabbing in all directions for a handhold! The frigid water felt like an electric shock. Reaching up I caught a rigging turnbuckle, hooked a knee over the rail and tumbled back aboard, as the boat righted herself. For a few minutes I lay there shivering huddled between the rail and the hatch.

Rather than freeze on deck, I gathered myself together, crawled forward and yanked open the cabin door. After a dense cloud of smoke had cleared I was greatly relieved to see no sign of fire. The cabin floor was covered two feet deep with water rushing from side to side with the wild rolling of the boat.

By now it was nearly dark. I took a renewed interest in living by getting the boat off before the howling wind once more. The long job of pumping began. By working the crude deck pump I soon became reasonably warm again.

Sometime after dark, at the mouth of Woods Hole channel, I sailed *MILDRED* through a boiling tide rip where the confused pointed seas made steering very difficult. The ebb tide, flowing to windward, created a chaos of breaking seas. Gradually I worked the boat into the lee of Uncatena Island. It was a real pleasure to be in smooth water again. Close-hauling the sail, I eased *MILDRED* in along the shore, at last bumping into the wharf I had been looking for.

The sail was quickly lowered and the boat secured. Cheerful warmth was glowing from the windows of the caretaker's house up on the windswept hill. A path led me to the kitchen door. After repeated knocking, a barking dog brought an elderly man, who let me in. My shipwrecked appearance was explained to the caretaker and his kindly wife. They hustled me up some dry clothes and served a batch of delightfully hot quahog chowder. Although I was invited to stay for the night I felt obliged to try and get started again. The old man insisted ongoing down aboard with me to help get the engine ready to run. The thermometer outside registered 18 degrees! The roaring wind had much more of a bite to it after the cozy comfort of the house.

The icy cabin presented a hard place to work, especially with only a flashlight to see by, but after a while we had drained and reassembled the entire gasoline system. With the ignition system dried off, the engine came to life again. It was nearly midnight by the time we had test run the engine at full load for a while. Before I cast off the old fellow gave me his flashlight with the suggestion that it might come in handy.

I hoisted the sail and headed for the tricky Woods Hole passage. A huge full moon had just come up in the southeast. Millions of bright stars were blinking overhead. The wind continued to blow a full gale. Buoys in the channel were bobbing under in the boiling flood tide as *MILDRED* swept past the flashing green beacon.

A moment later, with no warning whatever, the engine stopped! It was hard to believe it could happen again. This presented another kind of problem, a six-knot current with rocks all over the place. I leaped out on deck and hove the anchor over the rail. With the line coiled on the hatch, there was no time to go forward, so I ran aft and barely caught a turn around the towing bitt. The anchor held as I snubbed the boat to a halt with little rope to spare. The racing current slammed the rudder over, forcing the boat across the channel. The strain was terrific. I hurried to get the engine started again. Before I could do much the anchorline parted, the stern lifting with the released pressure.

Away we went, *MILDRED* and me, spinning slowly in the tidal whirlpools toward dangerous hidden ledges. About that time I lost interest in the whole thing! I leaned against the wheelhouse door and listened to the wind in the rigging and the gurgling sound of the racing current in the nearby rocks. I waited as the minutes went by, expecting to fetch up with a crash. Strangely, nothing happened. I looked around and was amazed to see that the boat had gone clear of all the channel ledges and was drifting serenely out of Woods Hole Harbor towards Vineyard Sound.

At this point a new danger presented itself. Great Ledge lay directly in my path; a cluster of sharp black rocks at the mouth of the harbor were visible between breaking seas. There was a very real danger of drifting into deep water after punching holes in the bottom. I tried blinking the flashlight to attract attention ashore, realizing it was probably futile. I then thought of the sail and maneuvering around the rocks. Casting off the sheet, I scrambled up on the bow and by hauling the sail forward, made it serve as a jib. Slowly the bow swung off until the wind came nearly astern. Then I hustled to sheet the sail aft again. The boat promptly picked up enough steerage way to sail out around the threatening danger.

Reaching the comparative safety of Vineyard Sound I decided to continue sailing and not bother with trying to gt the engine started. With a strong fair wind and full moon flood tide, I expected to work the boat into Vineyard Haven Harbor, my destination. I shivered a little in my borrowed clothes at the thought of not making the harbor before the tide started to ebb to the westward. The steady white glow of West Chop lighthouse was the goal.

A sizeable vessel was approaching from the eastward. Lofty navigation lights indicated, possibly, a coastal freighter, or tanker. As the lights drew nearer it looked more like one of the offshore Coast Guard vessels. This seemed to be a chance to get towed in somewhere. I pulled out the flashlight and blinked a series of "S O S". The vessel responded with a string of flashes which was only confusion to me. I blinked back at a slower rate and waited to see what would happen. The big craft drew cautiously closer until I could hear the sound of engine room bells. A loud megaphoned voice came from up on the bridge, "What are you?" was the question. I yelled back, "A fisherman with engine trouble!" The booming voice replied with an accent that sounded British, "Stand by. We will throw you a line." "What vessel are you?" I called. "Tug *BON VOYAGE* of Liverpool, England," was the answer.

This, I thought, is the most colossal tug I have ever seen. Heavy rope fenders were lowered along the tug's guard rails. A heaving line landed on deck. With that huge bulk to windward *MILDRED* lay almost becalmed. In a few minutes, with the help of crew members on the tug, the bobbing ice-coated dragger was secured alongside. Invited to come aboard I climbed up to the bridge and entered the warm spacious wheelhouse. The Captain, a stocky red-complexioned Englishman, introduced himself, the Mate, and the young Quartermaster on watch. By coincidence, they had thought I was the Coast Guard as I thought they were. When they saw the blinking light they had thought it was a warning to keep out of danger.

"Now, son," the Captain said, "I will have to tyke you in somewhere. I can't leave you drifting here, it wouldn't be human." Then he went on to inquire about my knowledge of local waters. "The *BON VOYAGE*," he said, "has a draft of 18 feet." I pointed toward my homeport and convinced him that Vineyard Haven Harbor was a regular port-of-call for deep-draft ocean tugs. It took some more convincing to satisfy him that I was capable of piloting his command in there. Finally he said, "All right, take over." Turning to the Mate he ordered, "Slow ahead, both engines." This was a new and very interesting experience. When I said to the Quartermaster, "Starboard a little," I was surprised to see him roll the wheel to port. "She steers opposite," the Mate explained.

We steamed slowly into the harbor, the big tug's two 1500 H.P. steam engines turning smoothly. The Captain took over as we approached the town wharf. He eased the *BON VOYAGE* in across the end of the dock where we tied up for a while. Hot coffee and sandwiches were brought up from the galley. While we sat around on the cushioned benches, the skipper unfolded an interesting tale of his recent adventures.

Sometime previously the *BON VOYAGE* had been sent out to tow a disabled freighter from mid-ocean to Montreal, Canada. The next orders were to proceed to Vancouver, British Columbia, by way of the Panama Canal. Coming down from Nova Scotia they ran into a Northeaster which reached hurricane force. At the height of the storm, the tug was carried across a shallow area on the northern part of Georges Bank. Mountainous seas crashed aboard carrying away most everything movable, including one of the lifeboats. I had noticed the heavy wooden paneling around the bridge was splintered and missing in sections.

Soon after the storm moderated, they hailed a Boston trawler to get a bearing and a course for Nantucket Lightship. Following the course given them, they somehow had arrived at Pollock Rip Lightship late the next day.

Rather than go out around Nantucket Shoals, the Northwest gales forecast, he decided to navigate through Nantucket and Vineyard Sounds. He showed me the chart he was using, an offshore number covering an area between Nova Scotia and New York. A magnifying glass was needed to see the spot where our signals brought us together. His caution in approaching was understandable.

With a final swig of coffee, the skipper announced that they must get moving to make up for lost time. I drew out a rough sketch and marked off a series of courses which would take him westward through Vineyard Sound and safely out to sea. As we shook hands, I thanked him for the rescue and expressed the hope that the big vessel would continue to live up to her name.

The crew helped move *MILDRED* around the corner of the wharf. I stood there fascinated as the *BON VOYAGE*, monarch of all tugs, lighted like a village, swung around and cleared the breakwater, outward bound!

Turning to the *MILDRED*, I looked and rubbed my eyes. The boat had gone adrift and was halfway across the harbor! I raced the length of the wharf and along the beach where, luckily, there was a skiff with a pair of oars in it. By rowing like mad, I caught the boat, grabbed the trailing bowline, and after a long hard pull, managed to work her in to the nearest wharf.

The dawn of a new day was showing in the East by the time I had reached home after a two mile uphill walk.

This all actually happened many years ago, but the details are well remembered. Of numerous boating adventures, before and since, this one takes the prize for variety.

As I wearily climbed the stairs to my room that morning, I thought of the words of a philosopher: "Of all the teachers holding classes here on earth, experience is the dearest one, but you always get your money's worth."

Chapter 23

A supplementary chapter to commemorate the following experience with shipmate Emory Flanders, recently deceased, August 1994

Marvelous 40' Seaboat MILDRED

Over a period of several months, I had a regular weekend project of delivering a boatload of general supplies to the island of Cuttyhunk.

After unloading the Cuttyhunk cargo, it was usually necessary to make a round trip to New Bedford for a deckload of twenty-five steel barrels filled with Shell gasoline. Leaky fill caps caused a puddle of gasoline to slosh around on the top of nearly every barrel. A Cuttyhunker, Louie Ramos, stood in the pilot house with me and watched sparks of hot carbon shower to leeward from the overhead dry exhaust pipe. We also flicked our burning cigarette butts across the barrels and hopefully overboard! Ignorance and plenty of fresh air were our favorable circumstances.

It was usually late in the day when the heavy, 400 pound barrels were unloaded, and nearly always at low tide. The hoisting procedure consisted of barrel hooks, a four-fold block and tackle from the swinging hoisting boom with four or five turns of manilla rope wrapped around the brass winch head which was chain driven from the slow turning six cylinder Lathrop engine running leisurely in the warmth of the cabin-engine compartment.

Louie always tried to convince me to wait for high tide, but I was too impatient and anxious to be on the way to Vineyard Haven and home for the night.

The deckload of twenty-five full barrels of gasoline had a total weight of about five tons. With no cargo in the hold, the *MILDRED* had a tendency to roll in an uncomfortable way. Of course, the "center of gravity" was dangerously high, a factor not yet a matter of concern to us boatmen. Evidently the Anderson Shipyard in Wareham, builders of the boat *MILDRED* (also the 50' *SOUTHERN CROSS*) had proven their reputation for seagoing boats of exceptionally strong construction and stability.

The ultimate freight project with the *MILDRED* was presented unexpectedly. That was the summer of 1939, when the Dutcher Dock and bulkhead was being built at Menemsha. The original wharf had been destroyed during the 1938 Hurricane. Captain Pinto and his crew with the Vineyard freighter *EBEN A. THACHER* had the contract to carry all the building materials from

Woods Hole to Menemsha. The piling and timberwork had been completed and was ready for the deck planking. At that stage, the *THACHER* had been called upon for an emergency towing job and would be gone a week or more.

A partially unloaded railroad flatcar sat on the tracks at the Woods Hole pier. The dock-builder, Taylor Marine of Fairhaven needed a boat and crew to transport the final load of dock planking immediately. Paul Bangs arranged the deal and hired Emory Flanders to work with me. We didn't realize the nature of what we had to do — not until we had arrived in Woods Hole and tied up close to the flatcar. We examined the stack of planking which consisted of 2" x 10" hard pine creosoted planks in 10' and 20' lengths. The 20' planks each weighed 300 pounds! Heavy as lead — sticky to handle. Instead of trying to hoist each plank, a tricky job, we lifted and lugged one plank after another until we had built up a sizeable deckload. Common sense indicated the need for two round trips to Menemsha. But foolishness prevailed until the flatcar was empty and *MILDRED* overloaded.

Fortunately, the weather was fine with a light southwest breeze and the tide was in our favor. Some of the plank cargo extended out over the bow and the stern. We two crew members had barely enough open space to steer and control the boat as we proceeded into Vineyard Sound and in the direction of Menemsha.

The deeply laden *MILDRED* with too much weight piled high on deck was in an ideal condition to quickly capsize. The first roll from the wake of a passing boat indicated our dilemma. A balancing act was our only chance. Full throttle engine power plus responsive steering seemed to be the best way to prevent the top-heavy boat from going into a sudden roll-over. Emory, a husky lad, tried to counteract the rolling tendency. By the time we arrived at the Menemsha entrance, we were in a lather of anxiety. Slack tide between the jetties was the final factor in our favor. The turn into the calm waters of the Basin went smoothly with instant relief from our intense anxiety. Slow momentum carried us to the new bulkhead construction. Docklines were quickly secured. We had hoped to get some help with unloading, but there was nobody in sight at that late evening hour. We did manage to slide all the planking ashore and to stack it across the existing stringers before night caught up with us.

We had only one visitor, Mrs. Everett Pool (Emily) who was watching our actions from her house on a nearby hill. As a newspaper reporter, she was curious about how we happened to be involved with the *EBEN A. THACHER* transporting project.

The nighttime cruise back to Vineyard Haven with a flowing flood tide and a warm fair wind was a genuine pleasure. Starlight and a rising full moon completed the idealistic atmosphere. We had done a good day's work and defied gravity along the way. Memories of the original homeward trip, the winter time *MILDRED — BON VOYAGE* epic was in stark contrast.

That was my final cruise in that wonderful boat *MILDRED*. She was eventually sold and returned to her previous

This is a view of the old MILDRED owned and operated out of New Bedford. In recent years the boat had been known as VERJOY. This scene was at Union Wharf in Fairhaven, a few months after Hurricane "Carol" destroyed the waterfront in 1955.

homeport of New Bedford. Her new owner, Tony Ellen, re-rigged her as a fishing dragger and used her actively for many more years.

✶

Sometime during the mid-forties, the management of the Steamship Company had become inspired to acquire an ancient New York Ferryboat by the name of *HACKENSACK.* Evidently they had a glimpse of the future that indicated an ever increasing tonnage of bulk freight to be transported from Woods Hole to Martha's Vineyard.

For native Islanders, the existence of such a vessel as compared with our seagoing steamers was cause for all sorts of comments. Like it was just a playful experiment. The *HACKENSACK* appeared to be a clumsy self-propelled barge. But, of course, we came to realize that ferryboat transportation had opened up a whole new era.

Automobiles and loaded freight trucks simply rolled on board at Woods Hole and rolled ashore at Vineyard Haven. Suitable landing ramps had been built to handle the traffic to and from the mainland.

After several months of year round operation during which the *HACKENSACK* (renamed *ISLANDER* at times) was held in port waiting for weather conditions to improve.

Eventually, a full scale ferry was designed and build specifically to be capable of servicing Martha's Vineyard and when necessary, the island of Nantucket as well. The "new" ferry *ISLANDER* proved to be a complete success and now after decades of continuous operation it is going strong today as the forerunner of all the island ferries including the *NANTUCKET,* the *EAGLE* and the most recent luxurious *MARTHA'S VINEYARD.*

✶

The Menemsha Coast Guard Station, a big two story building, was originally located on a strip of beach at the eastern end of Cuttyhunk Island. A hurricane washed out the beach and isolated the Station building. Consequently, the Government decided to relocate the building and to thereby establish a Coast Guard Station at Menemsha where boats and boathouses were anyway — miles from the original Gay Head Station

With the engineering skills of Gordon Linberg and the experience of the Falmouth marine contracting firm of Turner and Brievogel, the huge building was jacked up and rolled on board a big barge. The combination was towed out through Canipitset channel, a narrow gap between Cuttyhunk and Nasawena Island in calm, foggy weather and by good fortune arrived safely in Menemsha Creek. It was a slow cruise on a gentle swell that threatened to capsize the house at any moment, particularly during the first mile or more of the nerve wracking miracle of marine engineering that took place on a summer day in 1952.

The immense structure was jacked up and carefully moved ashore at high tide and with the pulling power of every available tractor and truck, it was very slowly moved on timbers and rollers to the top of a nearby knoll that overlooked Menemsha Creek and the Homeport Restaurant. A location previously occupied by Reginald Norton's house that had to be moved away from the C.G. site.

The impressive, all white structure had the appearance of a hotel except for the lookout tower above the peak of the roof.

Now, after many decades of practical usefulness, the Menemsha Coast Guard Station is about to be decommissioned in the process of eliminating many similar outlying stations — such as Provincetown — a Federal government economy program that is subject to plenty of complaints and opposition. The plan is to consolidate all activities at the main Base in Woods Hole. Senator Gary Studds, our most influential marine representative in Washington is working diligently to prevent such abandonment of important Coast Guard Stations. The Menemsha Station continues active with a smaller crew (10 men).

Senator Studds is also very active in protecting the requirements of the commercial fishing industry and related problems.

Chapter 24

"The Real McCoy!"

Prohibition during the 1920's and the early 1930's was a period of mysterious adventure, especially on the high seas. The U.S. Coast Guard represented the federal government in its all-out war against the "rumrunners". The original three-mile limit was extended to a twelve-mile limit. Supply ships came from faraway ports with their cargoes of alcoholic beverages and anchored outside the limit of the law like floating stores. The supply fleet eventually became known as "Rum Row". Activities extended from the coast of New Jersey to the Gulf of Maine. Areas south of Nantucket and Long Island were especially busy. Early rumrunners came out from shore in a variety of makeshift boats with plenty of cash. In a fever of greed, many of those unseaworthy boats were overloaded by inexperienced people. Too often they led to disaster in rough weather conditions.

Another phase involved commercial fishermen. A vessel and crew would be hired by a stranger to bring in a load of booze for money temptation that was irresistible. An "agent" was put aboard with a bundle of money. Arriving at the supply ship in daylight, the crew would transfer the cargo. In good weather, they would lay alongside against the big ship's spongy fenders. Rough weather made it necessary to use dorys to handle the cargo, with the two vessels at a safe distance from each other. The contraband was carefully placed in the fish hold where it was covered with heavy canvas. The next step, before entering the twelve-mile limit, was to catch some fish, either by net or tub trawl. The top of the cargo soon consisted of a deep layer of codfish and flounder above the protective canvas. If they were stopped and boarded by the Coast Guard, a glance down the opened hatch was sufficient. Arriving in port, the fish were unloaded in the morning, the real cargo at night.

However, one of those fishing schooners, the *ETTA M. BURNS,* went ashore in a thick fog on the south shore of Martha's Vineyard when the skipper fell asleep while steering. The lookout man on the bow saw the breakers too late. At dawn on a new day in smooth, calm weather, a beachcomber reported the stranded vessel to the island Coast Guard station. A big cutter soon arrived on the scene. A motor whaleboat came in at high tide with a manilla hawser in tow. The schooner was nearly afloat in unusually calm conditions. She could have easily been pulled off into deep water at that moment.

However, the skipper and his crew refused help, making the ridiculous excuse that the schooner was leaking badly and could possibly sink if she were refloated. It was not true. They could have been floated and safely towed into the port of New Bedford. No problem and with the cargo intact. Nothing unusual. Their one chance, lost to bad judgment.

The whaleboat crew, with a bos'ns mate in charge, their curiosity aroused, decided to board the stranded vessel. They noticed that the deck was dry; the auxiliary deck pumps had not been recently used. Then they removed the two hatch covers to find only solid layers of fish. They inspected the crew's quarters forward and the engine room aft. To them, everything appeared quite normal. They returned to their ship bewildered. They were soon underway and back on routine patrol. They reappeared early the next morning. The Coast Guard captain had become suspicious.

The boarding crew returned in the motor whaleboat. Overnight, the schooner had swung around parallel to the beach and was listing to starboard, toward the shore. The *ETTA M. BURNS* was by this time officially a wreck. The crew had gone ashore in their dory and were nowhere to be seen. Once again the hatch covers were removed. The C.G. boys had a hunch. With a pitchfork and a pump handle, they worked down through the fish until they struck the canvas cover. After pitching enough fish out on deck, they were able to cut out a section of the canvas to reveal the true cargo. There was excitement! Several V-shaped sacks labeled "Old Mac" — Scotch whiskey — were hauled out of the fish hold and put aboard the whaleboat as evidence. The poor old schooner was declared under arrest and two armed guards remained on board. As the news quickly spread around the island, people swarmed to the wrecked rumrunner. State and town police appeared on the scene to help control the liquor cargo.

An increasing swell brought in a pounding surf. There was an onshore breeze from the southwest. Typical summer weather. The Coast Guard crew pitched the fish overboard to be strewn along the beach highwater mark. The booze, or most of it, was relayed ashore and stacked on the beach. The stuff was hauled away by a team of horses pulling a low-slung wagon, known as a dray. Some of it managed to reach a warehouse for protective custody. There were broken bottles in the vessel's hold. A strong aroma of alcohol wafted inland for several weeks after the schooner was abandoned.

Those who were privileged to taste "Old Mac" and other bottled products from the wreck expressed disappointment. An Indian would have called it "firewater"! It was later reported that the cargo came from a rusty steamer at anchor 30 miles south of Montauk, New York, a floating distillery, complete with bottles, labels and packaging materials. Belgian alcohol was said to be the basic ingredient of scotch whiskey production. The Gloucester fishing schooner *CONSTELLATION* became another victim of disaster on South Beach in circumstances similar to the fate of the *ETTA M. BURNS.* However, I was away somewhere at that time and missed that particular adventure.

Rumrunning experienced further changes. Enterprising boatmen began to acquire boats that were designed and built as rumrunners. Some were seagoing speed boats 40 to 50 feet long, of low profile, with a small pilothouse forward and a dory secured in chocks on the stern deck. They were powered with two or three converted aircraft engines; such craft were capable of thirty-five knots with a full load. However, rough winter weather required special qualifications. The answer became a series of husky vessels that appeared to be fishing draggers combining an easy-driving hull and a pair of big, high-powered engines. They had names like *MADAM X, HI-QUEEN, TOSSUP* and *OLD LADY.* These new seagoing boats were built by Casey Shipyard for Charlie Travers, who was an expert boatman and an all-weather operator . . . king of the inshore fleet. They would mingle with the fishing fleet during the day, then run offshore to pick up a load at night. A Vineyard fisherman, Frank Butler, was one of the boldest and most successful skipper of these boats and many of the speedboats as well. The "rummies" developed a smoke screen system that consisted of piping a supply of dirty, black drain oil into the flaming hot manifolds of their high powered engines. Dense smoke prevented Coast Guard pursuit.

It is probable that the most consistently successful type of Rumrunner was the development of the double bottom fishing vessel. The inner hull was similar to the exterior vessel except that there was a two to three-foot storage space between the two hulls. Secret sliding doors provided access to the cargo space. These specially-built boats ranged from 40 to 60 feet in size and were much wider and of deeper draft than standard fishing draggers. They were so burdensome that they carried a full load of booze plus a hold filled to capacity with fish, with no indication of being deeply laden. Prohibition was nearly ended before the Coast Guard became aware of the existence of these clever smugglers. In later years, the writer acquired and went fishing in the double-hulled former rum boat *JUNIOR* — a great seaboat!

The most common Coast Guard patrol boats during the mid-1920's were the "Seventy-Five Footers", which were often referred to as "six-biters". They were rugged seagoing boats powered with twin gasoline engines. On the forward deck a "one-pounder" gun was mounted. However, the crews were generally newly-enlisted men who spent most of their sea time in a state of seasickness (or hauling fishermen's lobsters at random). They were only a moderate annoyance to any of the professional smugglers.

By this time, the Coast Guard was improving their skills and equipment also. A captured rumrunner became their latest weapon. The former rum boat TRAMP had been captured recently by the Coast Guard and was on patrol one night off Cuttyhunk. The *NOLA*, queen of the newer speedboats and armor-plated in all crucial areas, was inbound that night with a full load of alcoholic beverages, including a deckload of alcohol in five-gallon cans. The Coast Guard had somehow been informed about the probable destination of the *NOLA* and her load of booze. There were three C.G. craft on the alert at the Vineyard Sound entrance. One was a "Four Stacker", a former Navy destroyer. The *TRAMP* intercepted the *NOLA* and fired warning shots with a 50-caliber machine gun. The fully loaded *NOLA* bored on, gradually outrunning the *TRAMP.* A burst of gunfire suddenly ignited the cans of alcohol on deck. A mass of flames quickly spread, fanned by the boat's 35-knot speed. Within minutes, the intense heat cut off the flow of oxygen to the engines. The boat came to a stop. Captain Frank Butler and crew were rescued after first transferring a wounded man who had been hit by a tracer bullet in the leg. A volunteer crewman, who after leaving the safety of the steel-plated pilothouse, had gone out on deck in an attempt to toss the cans of alcohol overboard before they caught fire. *NOLA* burned until she sank. Frank Butler was captured by the *TRAMP*, a boat he had skippered only a few months earlier! It happened one night while unloading at a pier. Frank and his crew escaped inland, but the boat and cargo were seized.

Many years later, by coincidence, Capt. Tom Tilton, a nephew of Frank Butler, while fishing off Cuttyhunk, caught the *NOLA* in his net. His dragger had enough lifting power to bring the bow up to where it was visible. But the strain was too great. Rising on a swell, the towing cables suddenly parted and the wreck disappeared, taking the net and trawl doors with it.

It was in that same vicinity that we had always avoided a sunken wreck, the steamer *JOHN DWIGHT*, scuttled by hijackers after they'd killed the crew. This tragic incident took place on a foggy summer day during the gangster era of Prohibition. Booze and money on a big scale. During that time, there were other similar violent mysteries.

Sometime toward the end of the Prohibition campaign, an incident of profound tragedy happened. The big speedboat *BLACK DUCK,* with a full cargo of liquor, while negotiating the narrow Newport, Rhode Island entrance at night in thick fog, came up to an important channel bell buoy. Captain Charlie Travers, steering the *BLACK DUCK*, discovered that a Coast Guard patrol boat was tethered to the buoy. On a tip, the C.G. boat was awaiting the arrival of the *BLACK DUCK*. There was a blast of machine gunfire. Three *BLACK DUCK* crew members were killed instantly. Captain Travers survived sustaining just a bullet wound in his right hand while holding a spoke of the steering wheel. The incident made national headlines. A series of investigations went on for months. There was a political uproar over the pros and cons of Prohibition, which soon thereafter was repealed.

Charlie Travers, a survivor of that adventurous era, is an active old man whose clear memory has provided much of the above information.

Now we will get to the ultimate object of this historic reflection — Captain Bill McCoy and his famous schooner *ARETHUSA,* a huge former Gloucester Grand Banks dory fishing trawler.

Captain McCoy made a specialty of handling strictly first-class liquor. A responsible man with a conscience, he sold his cargo carefully to customers who had proven their credibility. His cargoes came from St. Piere-Miquelon and Nassau in the Bahamas by alternate voyages. McCoy became acquainted with Vineyard fishermen who operated in the area of his activities. On occasion, he was known to have traded, for example, a sack of Haig & Haig Pinch Bottle Scotch Whiskey for a bushel of lobsters. McCoy maintained a masthead watch. Two *ARETHUSA* crewmen, on two-hour shifts, were stationed up on the foremast spreaders with rifles, ready to eliminate hijackers.

Rough winter weather caused unloading problems. McCoy rigged a rugged towing boom extending from the foremast, from which the craft being loaded was towed slowly to leeward while the packaged, bottled goods were sent down a slippery chute and quickly restowed in the hold of the rumrunner. This innovation greatly improved a dangerous operation.

With the cooperation of reliable fishermen, Bill McCoy proceeded to store an impressive quantity of his products in a cache on the island of Noman's Land. Whenever weather conditions made it impossible to operate offshore, the reserve supply took care of immediate demands. Vineyard fishermen were available to serve as Bill McCoy's storekeeper on Noman's when such special service was required!

Before Prohibition came to an end, *ARETHUSA* had been renamed. (New name unknown here.) After loading in Nassau the largest cargo of assorted products he had ever carried, McCoy sailed some time in mid-September of that year. The vessel was so deeply laden that seawater sloshed in through the midship scuppers. Since she carried no deckload during the hurricane season, all available space below decks became storage space for cargo.

The famous vessel was somewhere east of Cape Hatteras in the Gulf Stream when they were caught in a roaring hurricane. Every sail was double furled and all hatches securely battened. Bill McCoy and his crew lashed themselves to the main boom. The schooner drifted, mostly submerged in mountainous seas! Chances of survival seemed unlikely, but when the storm subsided, they were still afloat. Sea conditions improved. It became safe to move around on deck. They tried the deck hand pumps. To their amazement, there was no water in the bilge! Likewise, the foc'sle and the engine room!

A marvelous example of an extremely seaworthy schooner.

The former *ARETHUSA* again reached her scheduled destination. Another cargo of high quality liquor was distributed to thirsty connoisseurs. The product became known as the "Real McCoy"! Now, that's a familiar expression, but usually with its origin is unknown. Since Captain McCoy's time it has described any product that claims to have the hallmark of excellent quality.

Chapter 25

Shipping Out

Another series of experiences took place during the thirties. I shipped out of Philadelphia on the coastal freighter *VOLUSIA*, owned by a company known as Merchants and Miners, a non-union line. Although rated as an Ordinary Seaman, I was called upon to serve in the capacity of an Able Bodied Seaman (abbreviated to A.B.). Underway in the Delaware river, I heard Capt. Hunley say to the Chief Mate, "put the new sailor on the wheel, maybe he knows how to steer." The other sailor, a qualified A.B. was on bow watch lookout. After several compass course changes along the buoyed channel, the Captain, in his stoic way said, "He's steering okay but he's nervous! Call the other man to steer and put this new fellow on bow watch until we are out of the Bay."

By the time we had sighted Diamond Shoals lightship, off Cape Hateras, I had become familiar with the slow action of steering a heavy ship. It was a real contrast to the way small craft responded and handled.

The voyage south required the discharge and loading of other cargo in three consecutive ports: Savannah, Georgia; Jacksonville, Florida, and finally at West Palm Beach, Florida. Stopover time in each port was usually about twenty-four hours. When I learned that the *VOLUSIA* would return to Jacksonville on the voyage north in order to load additional cargo, I spoke to the Captain about leaving the ship.

The food produced in the ship's galley was both indigestible and intolerable. Probably that situation was the principle reason for the ship being shorthanded. M & M was well known as "hungry" company.

After receiving a reluctant discharge, I went directly to the Marine Hospital in Jacksonville for some needed medical attention. The next stop was the Seaman's Union headquarters on the waterfront. A sailor's boarding house was located nearby. Several other characters sat around the Union Hall waiting for a call, a variety of seamen some of whom were qualified for engine room jobs.

Finally, my name was called for an A.B.'s job on an oil tanker. Capt. Hunley had generously provided me with an A.B. rating on the discharge document from the freighter *VOLUSIA.* A special favor.

An hour later, I had signed on as an A.B. crew member of the coastwise oil tanker *CAROLIN BARKER.* The ship was empty and sat very high out of the water. We cast off and became undocked with the assistance of tugboats. Fortunately, the other A.B. on my 4 p.m. to 8 p.m.

watch was called upon to steer the high sided ship down the river while I went forward for a two hour watch on bow lookout. By the time I took over the wheel watch, the pumpman had properly ballasted the tanker with sea water thereby causing the ship to be much more manageable.

By the way, as a seafaring career, life on an oil tanker had some advantages. The wage scale, at $62.50 a month was $10.00 more than freighter pay. But the main attraction was the galley which was similar to a restaurant. A menu to choose from and a waiter to serve the desired combinations of food. Only passenger ships provided such luxury for crew members. A marvelous contrast to life on the *S.S. VOLUSIA.*

After a pleasant cruise across the Gulf of Mexico, we reached our destination, the oil port known as Texas City, near Galveston. There, we would load the cargo of 100,000 barrels of crude oil for delivery to a northern port. Loading the ship consisted of opening and closing valves that were controlled by wheels 2' in diameter. A new experience. The Norwegian Chief Mate with a cranky disposition, tried to teach me how to keep the ship in trim. Somehow, I opened the wrong valve that allowed the huge flow of oil to enter the wing tanks also known as summer tanks on the starboard side of the ship. With the ship visibly listing, the Mate ran aft, swearing and shouting "you vill capsize the ship if I don't vatch you every minute!" Later that evening, off watch, I went ashore and exploded the hazards of the seaport waterfront.

The following day, a local Pilot came on board to take charge of the tugboats that maneuvered the fully loaded tanker out of the harbor.

Things went smoothly until we entered the Straits of Florida, off Key West where we encountered strong Northeast weather with rough sea conditions. With the ship all awash, it was necessary to use the elevated bridge known as the "catwalk" to get fore and aft. The engine room and crew's quarters were in the stern of the ship. The loud whine of the steam turbines interfered with radio reception from shore stations.

The wheelhouse, bridge and officer's staterooms were in a lofty structure amidships. Also the galley and dining space.

The Gulf Stream current flowed northerly in opposition to the gale force northeast wind. Conditions off Cape Hateras necessitated slowing the ship to half the normal engine power. The heavily laden ship was pitching and plunging dangerously. An hour at the wheel was enough with the lookout watch performed on the wing of the bridge. The usual routine of the bow watch reporting "Lights are bright, sir." (Normally the bow watch had the routine of reporting to the mate "Lights are bright, sir," meaning all the ships navigation lights are illuminated.) It was surprising to observe the ship's flexibility. Deck plates buckled while sections of deck piping were bending noticeably. The Captain, a Greek, whose name I've forgotten how to spell, paced the wheelhouse, smoking Camel cigarettes and cursing the weather conditions. Occasionally, a loud ping was heard. "She's popped another rivet," was the Mate's comment.

Gradually, the weather improved. Finally we arrived at Ambrose Lightship where we changed course to enter New York Harbor. By mid-afternoon we had docked at our destination in Carteret, New Jersey. The ship was owned by Standard Oil of New Jersey and John D. Rockefeller.

We soon heard the latest news, Union members of the U.S. Merchant Marine had voted to go on strike. It all started on the Pacific Coast.

The ship was soon unloaded whereby all the crew members were paid off and discharged — pending the eventual ending of the strike.

The prospects of joining the strike and walking a picket line in cold weather was far from appealing. Instead, my watchmate, Trent Templeton, invited me for a visit to his home in Lewes, Delaware. He said, "Maybe, with luck, we could join the crew of the Pilot vessel *DELAWARE* as regular sailors with no Seaman's Union problems." Trent was often called "T.T. the A.B." He owned a model A Ford convertible that was conveniently parked in the company yard. We tossed our baggage into the open rumble seat and headed south. As we rounded a rotary, one of his suitcases flew out, hit the concrete and popped open where the contents scattered in all directions. I tried to detour the traffic while he gathered nearly all of his belongings.

Upon arriving at the Lewes waterfront, we discovered that the *DELAWARE* was offshore awaiting the arrival of a ship that was enroute to Baltimore.

However, I was in for a big surprise! In a nearby cove was a complete combination of dredging equipment! My former employers, the Bay State Dredging Company of Boston! T.T. and I found a skiff, rowed out and boarded the houseboat where the skipper, Kevin O'Neil greeted us with enthusiasm. He promptly insisted upon hiring us at unusually attractive wages. We soon learned about his insistence. All the sections of pipeline had just arrived by railroad and was stacked on flatcars on a sidetrack which was about a quarter mile away with soggy marshland between there and the crane barge that would reassemble the pipe with the pontoons floating nearby.

That project proved to be the most difficult and dangerous project I had ever tackled. Releasing the cable lashings allowed the 20' sections of 12" pipe to suddenly tumble down the railroad embankment into an uncontrolled pile. The next stage was to balance and roll each section of pipe the length of the pipeline: a two man job in mud that was several inches deep. It was a week's work to complete the desperate challenge. Eight hours of drudgery every day.

The actual dredging job was completed in a month's time. One day, the skipper had some business in Philadelphia. I went along for the ride and bid him good-bye while there. Happily, I later learned that my pal Trent had signed on as a seaman on board the *DELAWARE,* a job with a much more promising future.

Once again, I was on board a ship operated by the Merchants and Miners Line — this time as a passenger on the ship *PROVIDENCE*, as a guest of Capt. Albert Bunting, a friend providing a special privilege on a passenger ship that was required to serve good food in a real dining room. A few days later, I said farewell to Capt. Bunting in the balmy atmosphere of the port of Miami, Florida. With a pocketful of hard-earned dredging money, it was a good time to play the part of a typical visiting tourist, a new life-style.

Chapter 26

Island Steamer Strike

Sometime during the mid-thirties, the employees of the Island steamers suddenly decided to go on strike. Elmer Rogers called me that morning with the surprising news and advised me to use his 38' boat *EVENTIDE* to ferry passengers and supplies between the Vineyard and Woods Hole. With my Federal license, I was qualified to "carry passengers for hire" in vessels of limited size and tonnage.

With Richard Thompson of West Tisbury on board as mate and deckhand, we soon had the *EVENTIDE* fueled and equipped for business.

When we arrived at the Woods Hole wharf and sized up the fleet of competitors, we decided to specialize in transport service to the Island of Nantucket. Immediately, we had a full load of people along with baggage, bicycles, pets and a variety of incidental things.

For the duration of the strike, which lasted only for about a week, we operated continually around the clock by alternating naps in the wheelhouse berth. Fortunately, the weather was calm, but fog in Nantucket Sound was a nuisance. Late one night in thick fog, we had a delay in trying to locate the Nantucket breakwater entrance. The fog siren at the channel entrance was silent. The passengers became uneasy while we hunted around. Finally, I made a couple of fast turns, creating waves, in order to wake up the entrance bell buoy that was sitting quietly becalmed. Brant Point Light was a pleasant sight as a prelude to landing our deckload of people and cargo at the Island Service Company wharf. A nearby pay station telephone was busy for awhile with calls to family members or for taxi service. It was after midnight when we decided to take advantage of the peace and quiet and stay over until daylight and get a good night's sleep for a change. A welcome interlude.

Many years later, in the month of April 1960, the Island steamer personnel went on a strike that continued for weeks until mid summer.

That was when it became necessary to establish a tug and barge operation out of Falmouth Harbor. That was my project but eventually a group of Vineyarders, Ralph Packer and others, acquired an available non-union tug and barge with a Capt. Charlie Vanderhoop of Gay Head in full charge of around the clock vehicle routine.

Somehow, with our combined efforts, we managed to transport a seemingly endless traffic of cars and loaded trailer trucks to temporarily relieve the most urgent requirements for vehicles and supplies. A fleet of small craft continuously shuttled passengers between Woods Hole and the Island.

Sometime later, in a foggy early morning trip out of New Bedford on the steamer *NAUSHON* with Capt. James Sandsbury, I learned that the Island ferry steamers were navigated with the same procedure including propeller RPM's as all other coastwise scheduled passenger and freight vessels of that era. Marvelous abilities.

Other forms of car transport were the Island fishing draggers *PAPPOOSE,* Capt. Alfred Vanderhoop, the *BOZO,* Capt Walter Manning and the *SOUTHERN CROSS*, Capt. Alton Tilton. Each boat could safely carry two cars on deck between Falmouth and Oak Bluffs during normal summer weather conditions. That was a long drawn out strike, over a period of nearly three months.

Chapter 27

Island Characters - Human and Nautical

Among the many catboat fishermen who operated out of island harbors, one man in particular was noted for extraordinary behavior. His boat, the SEABIRD, was rigged with a mast and a hoisting boom, but no sail. The worn-out, two-cylinder gasoline engine was troublesome. It had a tendency to stall at slow speeds, especially when hauling lobster pots. Charlie, whose identity I'm obliged to conceal was, in normal circumstances, a man of easygoing disposition. On the other hand, his tolerance for an overdose of aggravation had its limitations.

There came a day, on the fishing grounds off Gay Head, when Charlie's exasperation with his balky old engine overcame him completely. He came out on deck, sweating and swearing, looked up into the bright sunshine and seemed to become suddenly inspired. He went forward in his short boots to the foot of the mast. His deckhand, a young boy, watched in wonderment as Charlie proceeded to shinny up the mast all the way to the top, where he began a loud conversation with God. As he shook his fist skyward, he was heard to say, "This is as high as I can go, so I would appreciate it if you would come down here and help me to make this @!#!* *#@!*@ engine behave itself!"

Charlie clung to the gyrating masthead for a few minutes with no response from above. Slowly, he slid down to the forward deck and from there, without another word, disappeared into the cabin where the lifeless engine was located. For about an hour, the boy said, he heard plenty of grunting and swearing and the clink-clunk of tools being applied to the engine.

After a while, Charlie appeared in the companionway holding the entire engine, complete with flywheel, at chest level. With a great groaning effort, he rolled it out on deck. Charlie emerged from below, breathing hard, drenched with sweat. He gathered up the greasy beast and dumped it over the side in a grand, splashing gesture of finality!

Charlie went aft and plunked himself down on the wheelbox. Gradually, he relaxed and cooled off. After a while, he said to the boy, "We will hail the first boat that comes this way and hope that they will tow us back into the harbor."

Several of the fishermen in the vicinity had noticed Charlie's strange antics — especially the masthead exhibition. Soon, one of them came alongside; the SEABIRD was attached to a towline and pulled home.

The story about Charlie and his disposable engine soon became widely known around the island. Evidently the good Lord was in sympathy with the situation: one of Charlie's neighbors collected money to help his hard-working friend buy a new engine for the *SEABIRD* and begin a new era for a fisherman and his boat.

✶

Another one of my youthful memories is about the variations in speech represented by many of the towns and villages of Martha's Vineyard. Usually, after hearing a few words spoken by a native islander, it was easy to determine the name of the town where he originated. Whether it was a mild sort of accent of just a typical form of pronunciation, it seemed quickly apparent that the person speaking came from a certain island town.

Of course, that peculiarity was much more evident in those days than in our modern era whereby the popularity of the island has caused an influx of people with a background of many nationalities.

✶

One of many outstanding boatmen in Vineyard Haven was Captain Frank Vincent. His house, adjacent to the D.A.R. building on Main Street, provided a good view of the harbor from the upstairs windows from where he watched all the harbor activities.

His 40-foot powerboat *ONTIME* was at a mooring near the outer end of the breakwater. His principal occupation was the transport of people between the Vineyard and Woods Hole. He made a speciality of catering to the residents of West Chop, affluent folk who preferred to avoid the confusion of cars, people and the infrequent ferry service of those days. Captain Frank was available at anytime and in all sorts of weather. Most of his passengers were landed at the West Chop Pier where chauffeurs handled the baggage and delivered their employers directly to the individual homes.

With the ONTIME back at her mooring, Captain Frank would land his skiff on the beach at Owens Park. From there, he always walked slowly backwards all the way to the top of the hill at Main Street. In that manner, he could observe all the harbor activities.

✶

The Albert O. Fischers of Vineyard Haven provided many of us wanderers with a place to meet for fun. Mr. and Mrs. Fischer tolerated activities such as evening poker games in their comfortable living room. Some of us smoked cigarettes, a habit none of the Fischers practiced. The three Fischer boys, Fred, the oldest, Ozzie and Arnie were our pals. Their sister Lois was the youngest, an attractive girl who had the good sense to avoid our meetings.

Their family vehicle was a Dodge touring car with no curtains. The four-cylinder flathead engine was equipped with a type of generator that also served as a silent self-starter, a fascinating feature. The car also was utilized as a truck when necessary.

The Fischers owned an old vacant farmhouse with some acreage at the downhill end of a narrow rocky sideroad on the north side of the Lambert's Cove highway. One day, several of us went there in the Dodge car to rescue the front section of a farm wagon: specifically the wheels and framework along with the two wooden shafts that normally would be attached to a horse whose job it was to pull the wagon. Somehow, we lashed the shafts to the rear bumper of the Dodge. Before we started, Ozzie suddenly decided to ride the contraption. The weatherbeaten oak frame and wheel spokes appeared ready to fall apart. I was sure that he would jump off by the time we'd rattled up the hill to the main road. But he yelled, "Keep going! This is a great ride!" We rolled along while Ozzie whooped and hollered like a cowboy, the shaky rig fishtailing wildly behind us. It was a great relief when we somehow managed to reach the Fischer yard in Vineyard Haven safely. It is probable that Ozzie realized the hazard involved but didn't show it. Arnie, who was driving the car, said, "Let's not try that stunt again." A film of that incident would have excited a Hollywood producer!

The old farmhouse was the scene of yet another adventure. For some reason, three or four of us cronies were touring around town when somebody said, "Let's go for a visit to the farmhouse." It was early in the evening. Once inside the house, which was in deep darkness, we fumbled our way to the kitchen, where we managed to light a match and activate the only kerosene lamp that was in usable condition. Wilbur Jerrod had provided us with a few bottles of his homemade beer earlier in the evening, so it is probable that we were in a playful mood. Anyhow, Arnie Fischer and I got into a wrestling match.

We tussled our way through a door which opened to a bedroom occupied by a full-sized double bed. In the process of rolling around on the bed, we encountered a shotgun near the wall, just waiting for something to happen. It did. A sudden, earth-shattering explosion rattled our eardrums. One of our crew appeared in the doorway holding a lighted lamp and trying to see what had taken place through a cloud of blue gunsmoke.

Evidently either Arnie or I had caught a thumb in the triggers of the double-barrelled 12-gauge shotgun, which then blasted a huge hole in the plastered bedroom wall. One of the bed pillows happened to be in the line of fire, and thus a million feathers came swirling down like snowflakes.

Fresh air flowed in through the hole in the outside wall. While Arnie and I were trying to return to normal, the other boys found some short boards that served to patch the hole. We never did learn who had left that loaded shotgun lying on the bed, but that big explosion sort of climaxed our evening. Our nerves were shattered and our hearing temporarily impaired. All of us arrived home earlier than usual on that particular night.

✶

Every one of the Vineyard towns seems to have one or more unusual characters, individuals whose bubble was known to be somewhat out of plumb. Sort of an island tradition. Edgartown, for instance, could claim "Giddy-yap" Kelly whose walking gait somewhat resembled that of a horse. He should have been appointed to the job of Town Crier.

In West Tisbury, Baxter, the town handyman was noted for surprising expressions such as, "Beauty is only knee deep!"

The subject of local character sometimes included boats, especially the wooden boats of "the good old days." Despite similar design and appearance, each boat had its own mode of behavior. Harry Norton of Vineyard Haven owned a handsome Crosby catboat, the VICTOR. His specialty was trolling for fish along the Middleground shoal off West Chop, where he caught mackerel, bluefish, striped bass and fluke on zig-zag tacks under sail in the prevailing southwest summer breezes. He kept them alive in his ample fish well. Those were the days of really fresh fish! But Harry claimed that his boat had some quirky traits that kept him wide awake all day. He didn't explain what they were. Probably an occasional jibe while he was pulling a fish over the rail.

Any boat that was known to misbehave during rough weather conditions was subject to criticism; one commonly-heard expression was, "She will scare you to death before she will drown you!" Capt. Chester Robinson, a nautical philosopher, described his powerboat *LULUBELLE* that way after a rough trip from Newport, Rhode Island to Menemsha.

A few of the more interesting boats that I remember clearly were the ancient *RIVERSIDE* — owner, Norman Benson; the commercial catboat, *RANGER* — owner, Patrick Roche; the Jonesport Maine 38-foot powerboat *EVENTIDE* — owner, Elmer Rogers; the 28-foot *CARRIE V* — owner, Ben Carlton Mayhew; and the husky 30-foot catboat *HELEN,* — owned by Captain Steve Gardner at Menemsha. The *HELEN* was built by Manuel Swartz Roberts in Edgartown in 1909. When the Helen was repaired and repainted, also re-rigged, she was renamed *CHANCE.* Jimmy Taylor, a Wellfleet fisherman, became the next owner. His occupation was dredging shellfish, a rough business for such an old boat.

When World War II came to an end in 1945, it was my pleasure to buy, repair and resell each one of these wonderfully durable "character boats."

There were, of course, a great many islanders who could be classified as characters. Pilot Louis Smith was a good example. Ships, especially those deeply laden with coal would avoid the original Cape Cod Canal by entering Vineyard Sound and "lay to" off Vineyard Haven harbor while waiting for Coast Pilot Smith to come on board and take charge of navigating eastward between the tricky shoals until they were past Monomoy Point and out beyond the Pollack Rip Lightship. Normally, the voyage to Boston or Portland, Maine was easy except in rough northeast weather or poor visibility in snow or fog. Then it became a matter of frequent lead-line soundings and finding the proper buoys that were officially known as "Aids to Navigation"

— huge bell-buoys accurately positioned on the charts. The big ships of those days were powered by steam, a nearly silent source of propulsion, which compensated somewhat for the lack of electronic navigational devices of our modern age.

Between voyages, Capt. Louis was known as "the earliest man in Vineyard Haven," which meant that he patrolled the harbor beach at dawn every day. He always took along a bucket into which he dropped whatever live shellfish had washed ashore during the night. Scallops, especially. He had an expression, a way of describing an incompetent boat owner or operator: "That guy doesn't know any more about a boat than a boat knows about him."

Now for one more character subject. On the south side of the Beach Road curve was a dilapidated old shed that contained the blacksmith shop owned and operated by Elmer Chadwick. (I believe that he was also the town's fire chief at that time.) His shop assistant was Ed Luce. Together they kept busy with repair jobs, specializing in ornamental ironwork. Elmer chewed tobacco and had a habit of testing a piece of red hot iron with a splatter of tobacco juice. Ed Luce, on his side of the anvil, was protected by a deeply-stained leather apron that became nearly fireproof. The two of them walked to and from work, including lunch hour rambles to their houses in town.

The old shop with its fiery forge provided a special hangout for many of us waterfront species. A genuine form of talkative entertainment.

We are now on the homestretch with this collection of memories. On the subject of character boats, I forgot to mention an 18-foot motor dory. She was a handsome design with topsides painted in dark red. The owner, Franklin Benson of Lambert's Cove, allowed me to use the boat for a winter project of towing a pair of scallop dredges in order to catch starfish in Vineyard Haven harbor. It was a state fisheries deal intended to reduce the population; starfish thrived on shellfish, especially bay scallops. A government subsidy, a new experience!

The dory had a smooth, planked hull with a forward deck and an enclosed engine compartment in the stern, with a sliding hatch cover and a varnished wash rail around the cockpit. She had obviously been intended strictly for pleasure use.

The engine, a compact "one-lunger," was reluctant to start on cold January mornings. At the first turn of the flywheel, it would backfire and set the carburetor ablaze. A couple of squirts from the handy fire extinguisher took care of the problem. After that ritual, it would start and run all day.

On the edge of a shoal near West Chop lighthouse, the dredges brought up a surprising number of nice big bay scallops, along with a bushel of starfish. By the end of the day, I had shucked nearly a bucketful of luscious scallops. As power dredging was taboo in Vineyard Haven, I needed to find a scallop market elsewhere.

By noon the following day I had enough stock to justify a trip to Woods Hole. It was a clear calm day with a fair tide. The dealer, Sam Cahoon, was pleased to get such elegant scallops. He paid a premium price and as a bonus, filled my gas tank free of charge.

The trip back to Vineyard Haven was an adventure. By then, a fresh northwest breeze had created a sharp, choppy condition that made the little dory behave in quite a lively manner. There were moments when I thought we would be swamped, but we finally made it through the tide rips into the lee of West Chop and the smooth water of Vineyard Haven harbor. It was a successful voyage but an experience that did not require repetition.

The starfish project was completed according to contract by mid-March. The red motor dory was returned to her mooring. She was a dandy boat, one of the fondest of my marine memories. It is probable that Franklin Benson used her every summer in his spare time for hauling lobster pots along the North Shore. After the ancient boat *RIVERSIDE* was sold, Franklin acquired a 32' Maine lobster boat for trapfishing and lobstering. One day, while crossing Vineyard Sound, the engine suddenly slowed to a stop. A look over the stern revealed a sizeable shark under there. The critter had tried to bite the fast turning propeller, a mistake that instantly ended his career. Franklin dropped a rope strap around the shark's tail and gradually pulled the mangled shark free. No visible damage to the boat or propeller when they were once again underway.

New swordfishing boat Driftwood - 1934 at East Bend, Nomansland. Block Island Boat STANLEY in background after 3 day trip offshore. Note lofty topmast on DRIFTWOOD—the fastest boat in the fleet.

Soon after the starfishing job was completed, I heard about a new boat sitting idle at a mooring in Pocasset, a Buzzards Bay village near the Cape Cod Canal entrance. I went there immediately to investigate after learning that the owner's name was T. Barry Kingman. A preliminary talk with him by telephone resulted in a meeting at the Woods Hole wharf for a ride over to see the boat he had recently launched. He explained as we rode along, that the boat had been built as a "Rum-Runner," but, Prohibition had suddenly ended (1933) before the boat could be completed. In fact, with the boat framed and ready to be planked, his hired boat builder had given up and went elsewhere. Kingman learned sometime later that the builder had intended to double the thickness of the ribs before planking the boat. The boat was planked and completed, however, with the original single frames.

My first glimpse of the boat was inspiring. A 50-foot Western style (pilot house and engine forward) a handsome design, ample freeboard and plenty of sheer. We rowed out to her and climbed aboard. I wondered about the name *DRIFTWOOD*. A musical fantasy, Kingman admitted. A past romance remembered.

The engine was a shiny new eight-cylinder Lycoming with a 3:1 reduction gear. The enclosed engine space was directly under the wheelhouse, with 100-gallon steel gasoline tanks on either side of the engine room.

The spacious cabin was bare except for built-in seat lockers. Pilothouse equipment consisted of a fancy mahogany steering wheel and an eight-inch, flat-top Kelvin-White compass with points and degrees. On deck, a tall mast and a husky hoisting boom were stepped on a large oak pad directly over the cargo hold bulkhead. All standing rigging was half-inch galvanized wire.

Kingman went on to say that the *DRIFTWOOD* could not be readily used as a dragger because the engine was not adaptable for a front-end power take-off. The power take-off would be required to operate the two-drum deck winch by a system of sprockets, roller chains and steel shafting, which provided the means of setting out and hauling back the trawl doors and net.

All that sort of equipment would cost a small fortune to buy and install. As we sat on the starboard rail, talking about what to do with the boat, we came to the mutual conclusion that the simplest and least expensive procedure was to rig the *DRIFTWOOD* for swordfishing. We made a deal. I would take the boat and be responsible for getting rigged and ready for a summer season of swordfishing.

Before leaving, Barry said that he was about to establish a boatyard on the site where the *DRIFTWOOD* had been built. Kingman Marine has since become one of the largest and most active marinas on the N.E. coast.

It was mid-afternoon when I started the engine and cast off the mooring line. Barry and I shook hands as he made ready to row ashore in his skiff. It was a sunny and mild springtime day with a light Southwest breeze.

Once underway, as I carefully stayed within the channel buoys, the trip proved to be a delightful single-handed cruise southward in the Bay while listening to the quiet rhythm of the marvelous Lycoming engine. In Woods Hole channel, a boiling six-knot east tide made it a fast passage into Vineyard Sound and all the way over to Vineyard Haven where I secured the new arrival on the south side of steamboat Wharf. Before sunset, a surprising number of islanders came on board for inspection and to make comments.

The next move on the following day was to get located at the boatyard wharf where marine supplies and hardware was conveniently available. A neighbor, Raymond Authier, became a crew member and volunteered to serve as cook. Two other boys, home from college, whose names I've forgotten at the moment, who had some previous swordfishing experience, came on board, ready, willing and able to tackle the work of rigging the boat for swordfishing. Sometime later, my summer boating pal, David Dorn of Rowayton, Connecticut joined us to make up a qualified five-man crew. One man steered, the striker, positioned in the bowsprit pulpit. That was my job. Three men went aloft in the hoops of the topmast, on the lookout for dorsal fins.

The topmast, by the way, was project number one. Chadwick, in his blacksmith shop, made us a pair of steel bands that secured the topmast to the masthead. He also made up a pulpit frame for the forward end of the bowsprit.

We needed a bunch of hardware: wire rigging, shackles, turnbuckles, coils of Manila rope, not to mention harpoon poles, shanks and brass darts. The gasoline tanks had to be filled and a week's supply of food put below. The scarcity of money made it necessary to acquire most of the equipment on credit, including a 16-foot dory. By that time, I was about a thousand dollars in debt. A new experience! Credit.

Finally, the day came, early in the month of June, that we would start out on our first off-shore cruise. After loading two tons of crushed ice at Woods Hole, we proceeded eastward out around Cape Poge and took advantage of a fair tide in Muskeget Channel. Skiffs Island shoal with its foamy breakers was safely astern as we headed on a due south compass course in anticipation of adventure.

Out toward the 50-fathom area, we came upon a variety of marine life. We saw whales, tuna, sharks, schools of mackerel and finally a good-sized swordfish, which we captured. Our first fish! A special occasion!

Then we had two days of brisk southwest wind with patches of fog. That was when we discovered that the handsome *DRIFTWOOD* was limber, actually flexible. Going to windward in sloppy conditions, the cabin topsides moved in and out while storage locker doors flew open to the accompaniment of strange, creaking sounds. It was a condition that we gradually decided to ignore.

After five days of cruising (we drifted at night, changing the watch on the hour) we had only six fish on ice in the hold. It was time to head home.

By late afternoon we had the island of Noman's Land in sight. We decided to anchor for the night in a cove known as East Bend. One other boat was there ahead of us — the big Friendship sloop *BLANCHE & IDA,* owned by an old Portuguese whose name sounded like Cafuga. He said to us, "My engine broka down. Maybe you tow me someplace tomorrow."

Before dawn, a terrific thunderstorm jolted us awake. I went up into the wheelhouse to have a look around. At that moment, a jagged flash of lightning illuminated the entire scene in startling brilliance. The lightning had struck the old Friendship sloop in a spectacular way. All of her rigging was aglow and there was a huge ball of fire at the top of the mast. Captain Cafuga was visible on deck vigorously crossing himself. Evidently he thought that his time had come! Apparently that was his first experience with the phenomenon known as St. Elmo's fire. A most memorable experience!

The storm soon faded away with the arrival of daylight. But the wind shifted to the northeast with increasing velocity, a lee shore problem. We hauled anchor quickly, then went over to put one of our boys on board the sloop to secure the towline and to help Cafuga bring up his anchor.

By the time we had rounded Gay Head we slowly bucked a near-gale from the northeast. We eventually arrived off Menemsha jetties, shortened the towline and made it safely into the calm water of the basin where we tied up both boats alongside one of the Provincetown swordfishing sloops.

Catboat ANNA - owner Everett Poole Provincetown swordfishing sloops with dorys astern Summer 1928.

The swordfishing season came to an end by late September. It was a real pleasure to have had a rather successful summer in the newest and fastest (10 knots cruising speed) commercial fishing boat.

We made a special one day trip out of Menemsha with Capt. Ernest Mayhew. As we steamed along off Squibnocket, steering south east, we came upon a small wild swordfish ahead of us. I had the harpoon pole rigged and ready. We were at full speed — 12 knots, but couldn't seem to catch or gain on the fish that was about 20' ahead of us. Ernest hollered from aloft — "Nail that fish before he dives!" I raised the harpoon and threw it in a long shot. By chance, striking the active fish in the tail section. Away went the buoy line and keg. We expected to lose the fish, but by careful tending, the fish was saved. We discovered that the dart was embedded in the muscles under the backbone of the tail section. A very unusual gamble. In the course of that same day we captured a much larger and lazier swordfish that really made our day.

Captain George Fisher of Oak Bluffs liked the looks of the *DRIFTWOOD;* so much so that he became the new owner. He could afford to equip the boat as a dragger. His father, Stanley Fisher, operated a small boatyard where the boat was hauled out in order to double plank the hull — the easiest way to strengthen her flexibility.

Sometime later, Captain George acquired the husky dragger *SOUTHERN* CROSS. Horace Devine of Gay Head worked the *DRIFTWOOD* until his new Eastern-rigged *GERTRUDE D* was built and in commission. After that, Captain Jerry Vincent took over the *DRIFTWOOD*, and with George's younger brother "Snookie," went into the full-scale production of yellowtail flounders. In general, the two of them consistently loaded the boat to the hatch combings (probably 20,000 lbs.) and then steamed all the way to Boston or Gloucester where the fish sold for about one cent a pound. I remember that in the course of one year, their gasoline consumption was a total of 33,000 gallons. The four cents per gallon road tax return probably was the major part of their year's income.

Back in that period of time, when most of the inshore fleet of draggers was engaged in overloading their boats with the extremely plentiful yellowtail flounders, local dealers like Sam Cahoon at Woods Hole could handle only a limited supply. One or two boatloads and he was glutted. Other incoming boats had no choice but to make the long run to either Boston or Gloucester, where fish fillet plants could process unlimited quantities of flounder at the going rate of one cent per pound or sometimes a fraction more.

Nowadays, all market fish are nearly extinct, which has resulted in very high prices. This reminds me that I once heard a fisherman say, "I don't care what they're worth, so long as there is plenty of them!"

It is about time to bring this rambling collection of casual memories to a close. The features are all true according to the function of my clear memories of "when the good old days were new." There may be some inconsistencies as I tried to relate these incidents in the general order from one year to another, that they actually happened. But, as an excuse, I had only a few diaries for reference and of course, most of my contemporaries of that era are, as the saying goes, "long gone."

In any event, I trust that there will be readers who will find that some sections have sufficient historic value to make turning the pages worthwhile.

On the chance of providing some further entertainment, I may decide to include a few of my former magazine articles here for future reference.

One of the outstanding memories of the Menemsha scene, way back then, would have to include the "Cooper boys" — Gay Head Indian brothers. They were tall and husky with similarities in characteristics. Almost like twins.

They had two boats, a small catboat for winter scalloping in Menemsha Pond and a larger craft originally build for lobstering but used by the two Coopers exclusively for swordfishing.

During the summer months, in good weather, at sunrise they commuted from Gay Head in the scallop boat, the two of them standing like a pair of totem poles traveling down the creek channel with a fair tie, and around into the basin, alongside the "offshore boat." As they had only one usable storage battery, it was necessary to shift the battery from one boat to the other. Their next step was to fill three or four, five gallon cans with gasoline at Carl Reed's roadside pump and lug them aboard for use as the day's fuel supply. when the tide was not in their favor they chose to reach Menemsha by car, an ancient Chevy. Then it was a matter of borrowing the car battery to start and run the boat engine.

The Cooper boys had had their own special system of swordfishing. Instead of an all day trip south of the Island, they cruised slowly out to an area around the Vineyard Sound hooter buoy. The plan was to arrive there during the period of slack tide. It was an active place for all sorts of marine creatures. Lobster pot buoys were numerous, and the Cooper boys, from years of experience and infinite patience, having stopped the engine, would drift along until they would see a swordfish on the surface or playfully coming from the depths as he rubbed his sword upward along a pot buoy rope to finally whack the buoy as he surfaced. Such a swordfish was usually tame and easy to harpoon. Those ideal conditions, lasting about an hour, would produce one or more swordfish with the result that the Coopers would arrive at the town landing by mid afternoon to sell their day's catch and be home in Gay Head by supper time. The two most economical fishermen in the entire fishing industry.

✶

Two annual events in Vineyard Haven Harbor during the 1930's.

In mid summer — the arrival of three "Eagle Boats" — U.S. Navy training vessels based at the Brooklyn Navy yard in New York.

I can remember two of them as #48 and #55 in large white figures painted on the bow of each vessel. They docked at the New York wharf in Eastville. Daily shore parties headed for the fun town of Oak Bluffs. In their neat sailor suits, the young cadets easily hitched rides into town via New York Avenue. Like all visitors, they rode the "Merry Go Round" in quest of the brass ring. After a stay of about ten days, the ships departed toward other New England ports.

The other event was far more spectacular. The annual cruise of the New York Yacht Club. A huge fleet of sail and power vessels arrived on a day in the month of August and by the time they were all anchored, the harbor was really crowded. The huge clipper bowed steam yachts such as the Vanderbilt's *VAGABONDIA* and the *HI-ESMERO* — the glory ship of the Tommy Manville asbestos fortunes.

The main purpose of the N.Y.Y.C. was to utilize a magnificent fleet of racing sailboats: the marvelous J-class cup defenders especially. Tide and wind conditions taxed the skill and experience of the captains.

At night, the whole fleet provided a display of lights that resembled a World's Fair of bright colorful illumination.

As a prelude to Labor Day, the New York Yacht Club fleet demonstrated the contrast in U.S. economics while serving to bring our summer season to a memorable close with a wonderful Grand Finale.

✶

Whenever I try to bring this long series of events to a close, along comes another flash of memory. This one belongs in an early chapter that refers to another Percy Tilton/*LOIS T* adventure.

It was on a fine summer morning, soon after sunrise, when we arrived at the creek for a busy day at hauling lobster traps. However, Percy suddenly changed his plans. He announced, "This is a perfect day to go swordfishing." A surprise when he went on to say, "We will go two handed this time." We hauled the skiff on deck and away we went.

Out around Gay Head we encountered a most impressive ground swell. Percy remarked, "Must have been another big breeze went by offshore." Otherwise, it was a nice calm day with clear visibility.

Percy went aloft as we departed the Nomans hooter buoy, while I stayed on deck to steer and to unreel a couple of tuna jigs. The ocean was alive with marine creatures. Schools of mackerel were being driven by big fish from below. Swarms of smaller fish rushed above the ocean surface trying to avoid their enemies.

By mid-morning, we had seen dozens of sharks, including hammerheads, which at a distance could be mistaken for swordfish due to the similarity of their dorsal and tail fins.

Suddenly Percy yelled, "There's one — straight ahead!" as he slid down the headstay into the pulpit. We maneuvered around to meet the fish "head on." Moments later, the fish was "ironed" and the buoy line whizzed out over the rail as I tossed the keg overboard.

Percy came aft and launched the skiff over the side. As we caught up with the keg buoy, Percy shouted, "Stay close by; that's a backboned fish! (the keg wasn't moving) He may come to life and give us a hard time!" In a matter of minutes, he had the fish alongside with the fluke rope secured.

Suddenly, that swordfish became violent. The action was terrific! The critter used his sword for leverage, thrashing madly in showers of spray while the skiff danced around, nearly capsizing at times. Percy, thoroughly soaked, was in danger of being tossed overboard. He yelled and swore and waved at me to come to his rescue.

It was an extremely tense moment. At the same time, for some reason, perhaps current conditions, the ocean swells had become more frequent, with deeper hollows. The *LOIS T* and the skiff were out of sight of each other for brief intervals. The idling engine nearly stalled as it went into gear. This could have caused a problem, as it had to be started with an iron bar applied to slots in the flywheel. Fortunately, I opened the throttle just in time to keep it running. Percy was yelling, "Watch out, don't run me down!"

The maneuver to close in on the endangered skiff and occupant was a thrilling experience: a swerve at the right moment, a fling of the skiff's towline by Percy, a nifty catch by me with a couple of feet to spare and a quick turn around a big cleat on the aft deck. The next move was to get the fluke rope hooked into the hoisting tackle as Percy climbed aboard. With the crazy fish stretched out on deck and quivering, Percy hacked off the sword. Things were under control at last.

40' dragger WATER WITCH 1932. Lost with crew the following year.

That adventure would have made a lively scene to record with a modern video camera. Maybe it could be reenacted sometime!

On the way inshore, we decided to haul a string of our lobster pots. Perhaps it was a form of therapy; more likely it was a good time to use some smelly, leftover lobster bait. We returned to our Menemsha Creek pier at dusk and sold our hard-earned 150 pound wild swordfish for a price of 35 cents per pound. A most memorable day.

We later discovered that the harpoon dart was locked in crossways under the backbone of the fish. No wonder he went crazy!

✶

The 40' fishing boat *GULL* was an example of a practically perfect combination of useful features. She was one of the smallest of Eastern type fishing boats (engine room and pilot house aft) designed by the famous firm of Eldredge McGinnis and built by a Maine shipyard as a commercial fishing dragger.

The original owner intended to use the boat in the production of blue shelled mussels, but with a limited market at that time, he decided to sell the boat. After a period of being operated out of New Bedford and Point Judith, RI, Capt. Bob Walsh of Vineyard Haven became the ultimate owner. Among other activities, he made some history with the boat by going swordfishing on the Southeast part of Georges Bank. One of the boldest of ventures in a boat of that size. The boat was powered with a 6-7I G.M. diesel engine.

Among many of his remarkable experiences was the full speed run from Georges Bank to Wood Hole in company with the Larsen boys vessel *CHRISTINE & DAN* during the development of a hurricane (probably Carol) and incident that really proved the extraordinary seaworthiness of the small dragger *GULL.*

Their safe return to port was newsworthy and was cause for celebration.

40' dragger WATER WITCH at Dukes County Pier - 1932. Name being painted on stern. That Vineyard Haven Pier is now owned by Coastwise Packet Co. near the Black Dog Restaurant.

Fortunately, Capt. Bob Walsh, having survived all those adventures, and now retired in the arid state of Arizona, has written and published a book with the title "Swordfish, Sculpins and Suds." It is a very informative and entertaining book that is colorfully put together in the author's version of the English language from a fisherman's point of view.

It is my pleasure to read his book at least once a year!

The *GULL* proved to be one of the best "seaboats" of her size in the commercial fishing industry. By all means, get a copy, read it and be entertained!

✶

Another outstanding Vineyard character was Herbert E. Mayhew, a Chilmark native who was the best combination of farmer and fisherman that I had ever known. My acquaintance with Herb took place at Manter's pier (now Coastwise) where he had a summer job as skipper of a shiny motor yacht owned by a Mr. Childs.

As a contrast to Herb in his yachting uniform, I was aboard the dragger *WATER WITCH* on the other side of the pier where I was trying to clean the fuel injection system of a balky Cummins diesel engine. When I appeared on deck, covered with grease and fuel oil, I heard some comical comments from Herb Mayhew in particular.

However, we became good friends and over a period of years, whenever he decided to sell his latest dairy farm, he and I traveled by car from Maine to New Jersey in order to inspect every available fishing dragger. At night, (we usually stayed at a tourist house where we shouted comments about our day's activities - Herb's hearing aid was rather inefficient.) Other tenants in nearby rooms finally put a stop to our noisy conversation. The best boat for the price was what it was all about.

Finally, at the end of World War II, my 40' dragger *JUNIOR* was at a Woods Hole pier awaiting a new owner. Ben Mayhew and Eric Cottle had taken over a similar sized boat called the *PRISCILLA*. By that time, Ben Mayhew had become Representative for the Martha's Vineyard political scene at the State House in Boston.

A New Bedford fisherman was ready to buy the *JUNIOR*, but by coincidence, Herb Mayhew decided that he needed the boat to round out his fishing career. That took place in the early summer of 1947.

Sometime during the mid-summer of that year, I made a three handed fishing trip on the *JUNIOR*. Herb Mayhew, Herb Flanders and me went dragging several days for Menemsha Bight "lemon sole" juvenile blackback flounders and fluke of all sizes. About 12,000 lbs. of fish were iced in the fish hold pens.

Finally, it was time to head for New Bedford where the entire catch was sold to a Homer's Wharf fish dealer who was the high bidder at the early morning auction. My job was in the hold with Herb Flanders guiding the hoisting basket while Herb Mayhew took charge of the culling process up on the unloading platform. (Prevention of stealing was part of the game!) By sunset, we had returned to Menemsha with a new supply of ice in the hold and fuel oil in the tanks. My memory has no record of how much money we shared — probably a good week's pay.

It was time for a change. The next venture of that year of 1947 was to get established in a marine brokerage business that became known as Athearn Marine Agency, a going enterprise up to the present time with modern management. My favorite wooden vessels are nearly extinct, but it was a romantic and pleasant form of maritime history.

✶

One of my youthful playmates during the Eastville era was a husky young fellow by the name of Craig Kingsbury. He was a summer visitor whose family owned a cottage on the shore close to the East Chop Lighthouse. Another summertime playmate, Kimball Smith, along with Craig, hunted for turtles around the shore of a small fresh water pond. Craig had a tendency toward cruelty that Kimball and I tried to prevent. But, he was too big and strong for us to try and control.

In the course of time, Craig became a year-around island resident. Eventually, he bought a small farm on the State Road near Vineyard Haven, property that was previously owned by an elderly man who was known as "Joe the barber".

Craig and his family reactivated the farm and with his pair of oxen he occupied his spare time by doing heavy work for other farmers.

He became a familiar sight with his bushy mustache — always barefooted while strolling behind his oxen at the grassy edge of the highway during his slow travels between farms.

Occasionally he would go fishing for a change. I recall that he and I were shipmates with Captain Alton Tilton on a yellowtail flounder expedition in the dragger 3 & 1.

Quite a contrast to his farming activities.

Chapter 28

The Super Catboat – HELEN – Rerigged and Renamed –CHANCE.

The seagoing catboat *HELEN* was built by master boat builder Manuel Swartz Roberts in his spacious Edgartown workshop during the year of 1909.

The 30' boat with a beam of 15' and a draft of 4' 6" was a vessel of considerable carrying capacity. The huge fish well with it's upward sloping bulkheads would keep a ton of fish or lobsters alive. Eventually, all the two inch holes in the bottom planking were plugged — converting the wet well into a flored over fish hold.

The bulky catboat was very substantially built of seasoned white oak and 1 1/2" hard pine planking with galvanized iron fastenings.

The *HELEN* may have been built with a typical catboat trunk cabin — including oval shaped portholes. But, in my youth, when Capt. Steve Gardner owned her, she had a rather homely raised bow which provided more freeboard forward and more than full headroom in the cabin. The upper stem slanted aft a few degrees, a common shape in early catboat design.

Capt. Gardner, a fussy character, spent all of his spare time maintaining the *HELEN* in a state of perfection. His workshop and wharf were likewise kept in first class condition. The property faced Menemsha Greek and was located within the town of Gay Head boundary line. Nowadays, the wharf and building is owned by Capt. Alfred Vanderhoop, and his fishing boat *REDWING* is a familiar sight at that location. He has a house and land on the beach at Lobsterville.

The *HELEN* was powered with a four cylinder 40 HP Lathrop gasoline engine which was located aft with a small deckhouse that served as an accessable engine room. The steering wheel with an Edson worm gear mechanism in the wheelbox was at a convenient location.

A modern pilot house became the ultimate and modern improvement in the stern. A knee high rail enclosed the deck area.

On many occasions, the buxom *HELEN* was employed by Campbell and Flanders to carry a deckload of mackeral — (about thirty barrels) to the Sam Cahoon market at Woods Hole.

During the winter months, Capt. Gardner and his wife lived on board the *HELEN* at Pawtuxet Cove in upper Narragansett Bay, Rhode Island. Quite a contrast to their summer cottage at Menemsha.

After World War II, Mrs. Gardner had become a widow with the result that the *HELEN* was neglected for a year or more. By that time, my wife Doris and I had moved to Woods Hole and rented a cottage near the Eel Pond town pier. After a long cold winter of being occupied with dredging quahogs singlehanded in Buzzards Bay on a borrowed dragger, I had the urge to own a boat. A cruise over to Menemsha for a visit with Mrs. Gardner resulted in my purchase of the *HELEN* for a price of $1,500.00.

Jerry McCarthy, a Woods Hole fisherman, was along for the ride, so that we promptly rigged a towline: (*HELEN's* engine was inoperable) whereby we towed the *HELEN* directly to MacDougal's boatyard in Falmouth. (A month earlier, Jerry and I had used the Woods Hole schooner rigged dragger — *R. B. STINSON* to tow the Ben Mayhew boat *CARRIE V.* over to Woods Hole to be cleaned, painted and made ready for a new owner.

At the MacDougal Yard, the *HELEN* was completely renovated. She was re-rigged as a Ketch with two new masts and all new sails. A pair of 275 gallon custom made steel household tanks with special compartments known as baffles and coated with rustproofing were located under the deck — one on each side of the fish hold — a remarkable example of available space in a 30' vessel. We went on to rig the boat for sea scalloping, with double hoisting booms and steel sheathing on both sides. Probably the smallest (in length) sea scalloper in existence.

Before leaving MacDougal's Boatyard, the *HELEN* was re-documented, by the New Bedford Custom House. She was subjected to the new name — *CHANCE* — a salute to a schooner built for Columbus Iselin for persuing an oceanographic project along the coast of Greenland as a prelude to the development of the now world famous Woods Hole Oceanographic Institution. Also, my pal, Terry Keough was the mate on that expedition.

The cost of all that shipyard labor and material must have been impressive but it was somehow eventually paid, maintaining future credit.

It was great to be underway at last. With my two man crew, Murley and Joe Barboza, we proceeded toward Woods Hole.

The boat was rigged with a pair of 5' scallop dredges — one on each side which inspired us to make an experimental tow along the smooth sandy bottom between Falmouth Harbor and Nobska Point Lighthouse.

The *CHANCE* was equipped with a small two drum Hancock winch with 3/8" wire cable that made an easy job of hauling the dredges back alongside and hoisting them over the rail where we dumped the contents on deck. Mixed in with a collection of "monkeydunk" — yellowish chunks of a soggy substance, was an amazing supply of full sized bay scallops! A few more tows produced several bushels of the shellfish. We then proceeded into Woods Hole and tied up at the town pier near the M.B.L.

By midnight, we had shucked the scallops and built benches for culling on each side of the deck area. We managed to work the area until the supply diminished about two weeks later.

After the introductory bonanza, we rigged the boat with a quahog dredge with which we operated in the sheltered bay of Tarpaulin Cove. In the process, we gathered tons of junk that had to be removed. In the course of an eight hour day of dredging those chowder quahogs, we

Steamer NEW BEDFORD leaving Woods Hole on the way to Nantucket - 1935.

Steamer NANTUCKET leaving Vineyard Haven on the way to Woods Hole - 1935.

would have thirty 90 pound bushels in burlap bags stowed away in the hold (the former fish well) which we unloaded every night into a dealer's truck at the Woods Hole town wharf. It was a monotonous occupation that provided us with a good week's pay.

Sometime during the following summer, the *CHANCE* was sold to a fisherman at Wellfleet, on the northside of the Cape. She survived for many years as a sea clam dredger, but eventually age and severe abuse caught up with her, and like other small draggers that I had previously owned, she "laid her bones" on the saltmarsh at the upper end of Wellfleet harbor. I have sentimental memories of that very exceptional vessel by the final name of *CHANCE* Genuine marine history.

Chapter 29

Tashmoo Bonanza

The following spring (1935) I had another offer to go trapfishing, this time with Norman Benson and his son, Franklin, who was about my age. It was understood that the job would be limited to the length of time that would be required to construct their two traps — one in Lambert's Cove, the other in Buzzards Bay, near Quisset Harbor. The hickory trap poles, some of them 70 feet long, were stacked on the back side of a fairly high sand dune. Also behind the sand dune was a shed where the Bensons had kept a horse until he had died a few weeks earlier. The horse had been used to pull the heavy poles down to the water's edge. Part of my job was to help replace the horse. Rope straps attached to a pole were placed on our shoulders, and we would somehow manage to rush the burdensome thing down to the water.

Fortunately the smaller and shorter poles were launched first, as they would form the "leader" or fence toward deeper water and the bowl-shaped trap. We had to adapt to increasingly difficult physical stress. With a dozen or more poles lashed together, we attached a towline and rowed out to the anchored workboat *RIVERSIDE*. The Bensons' pile-driver scow was anchored off the beach at the eastern part of Lambert's Cove. We towed the raft of poles over to the scow and proceeded to up-end them one at a time and pound each pointed pole into the hard sandy bottom. Sometimes it was necessary to use a gasoline powered jet nozzel connected to a long two inch pipe to facilitate the job of getting the holes placed in the dense bottom.

The business end of the scow was rigged from a frame about 25 feet high, which was used to guide the up-and-down movement of a 500 pound chunk of iron that was lifted by a gasoline-powered "donkey engine" and released by a lever, which Norman operated skillfully. In fairly calm weather we could drive 25 poles in the course of a long day. A good day's work, and an early-to-bed and early-to-rise activity, to be sure.

The Bensons owned a compact shanty on the upper beach that measured about ten feet square and was furnished with a small table, two chairs, a two-burner kerosene stove and a built-in upper berth. A week's supply of groceries and jugs of water were kept on shelves in a corner closet. The shanty had a front door and windows on three sides. Norman said, "Go ahead and use the camp; save time and travel." It was a great experience, rolling into the bunk at sunset, exhausted, then waking up at dawn feeling like a fully-charged battery. The stove was within easy reach of the bunk, and the coffee pot had been placed on a burner before bedtime, so it was a simple matter to light the burner and lie in bed waiting for the coffee to percolate. Scrambled eggs and bacon for breakfast before the day's work.

What a life! A great memory. Eventually, the 1938 hurricane carried away the neat little shanty.

By the end of May, the Quisset trap over in Buzzards Bay was completed and in operation. The Bensons kept me on the job for an extra week or so because of an unusually heavy run of scup and squid. Plenty of herring too. Their traps were much easier to haul and set than Harry Peakes' similar equipment.

The Benson boat *RIVERSIDE* was truly ancient. Once upon a time she had been powered by a small steam engine. Obed Daggett at Cedar Tree Neck had been one of her previous owners. Sometime after World War II, Norman retired and sold the veteran boat to me. In time, she was sold again and went to New Bedford where she survived for several more years.

Another adventure with the Bensons came about in the early spring of the following year. Somehow I had become the owner of a house and land on the western shore of Tashmoo Lake, an area known as Northern Pines. Henry Cronig engineered the deal (a sign in the window of his real estate office read, "If you are on earth — own a slice of it!") The purchase price was $2,500. Mr. S.C. Luce in his Martha's Vineyard National Bank provided most of the money. Bill Swift was a nearby neighbor. Katherine Cornell, at her beach property, was a more distant one.

Tashmoo had been opened to the sea a few months earlier. A channel was dredged from the Herring Creek across the sand flats into the much deeper water of the lake. Increased circulation of salt water greatly improved the growth of shellfish such as clams and bay scallops. Equally important was access to the entire lake for moderate-sized boats via a navigable channel. Vineyard Haven had gained a landlocked harbor.

One afternoon early in March, I happened to arrive home before dark. Glancing out across the bay toward Herring Creek, I was amazed to see what appeared to be large schools of fish churning on the calm surface of the lake. A mystery to be investigated! I launched my skiff and rowed out around the swarms of fish, but I could not be sure of their species. It was far too early in the season for herring (alewives) to appear, or scup, which these fish resembled. I hurried ashore, ran up the hill to the house, grabbed the telephone and called Norman Benson. Right away he said, "They have got to be white perch. They discovered that new channel and, like herring, can spawn in brackish or fresh water."

An hour later he and Franklin appeared with their seine piled on the back seat of a big sedan. We made a short set for a few bushels of fish to prove Norman's theory. They were indeed white perch — and all sizes of them. We decided to wait until next morning to get properly organized for the fish seining project. The Bensons provided a big dory and two oversized flat-bottomed fishtrap boats. Pickup trucks were scarce in those days and were small and underpowered, anyway. Heavy loads would usually be carried on a homemade trailer or a horse-drawn wagon.

My job was to find a powerboat that would be capable of towing the soon-to-be loaded trap boats over to Cahoon's Fish Market in Woods Hole. A 26-foot catboat, the *FLORADORA*, a typical scallop boat with no mast, was the only possibility on such short notice. The engine, a four-cylinder Redwing, salt water-cooled and noisy, seemed to be in running condition, except for the generator, which was burned out. After a few hours of running, the two six-volt batteries had to be taken ashore to be recharged.

By the time we had our fleet of fishing boats and the seine ready for business, we had to go looking for fish. After a zigzag search, we finally located them in the far end of the lake, a charming area known as Tashmoo Springs, close to the Vineyard Haven water-pumping station. The narrow cove was full of the migrant white perch. The 300-foot seine was set out quickly in a semi-circle at a depth of ten feet. It was all we could do to bring the other end of the net ashore as it was packed with our prized fish.

The dory and the two big trap boats were brought in and over the cork line, ready for loading. Each of the Bensons was in a trap boat, while I was in the huge dory. Using long-handled dip nets, we began bailing or scooping white perch over the gunwales. By mid-afternoon, the three boats were fully loaded. Before leaving, we tied both ends of the seine to nearby trees. We sculled the heavy boats out to where the anchored catboat waited.

All three loaded boats had fore and aft bulkheads that allowed open space as a place either to bail sloshed-in sea water if it became necessary or for buoyancy. Long towlines of varying lengths were tied to the bowline of each boat. As we proceeded toward the new Herring Creek channel, we became aware of a weather change. The sky had become overcast and a moderate breeze blew from the northeast. The tide had just turned to flow eastward, which we knew would cause sloppy conditions in Vineyard Sound. We stopped between the jetties and discussed the situation. On one hand, our perishable cargo was in urgent need of being delivered to the wholesale market in Woods Hole. On the other hand, it was a dangerous gamble to try to get across to Woods Hole before dark. If we waited until the following day, the fish would need to be covered with ice. Then too, the weather by next day could become a full-scale northeaster that would effectively prevent our proposed cross-sound transit.

We made a snappy decision. Norman said, "Let's you and me give it a try. We'll put Franklin ashore on the jetty and somehow he will get back home and be close to the telephone. If he don't hear from us by nine o'clock tonight, he'll know that we are in trouble and he can call the Woods Hole Coast Guard to get underway and start a search."

So out we went, heavily-laden boats in tow. The trip to Middleground Shoal went smoothly. However, after crossing the shoal, we had a long stretch of rough water ahead.

Chapter 30

A Hazardous Gamble

By the time that we had slowly gone partway across Vineyard Sound, the smaller of the two trap boats was in need of bailing. Fish washed over the gunwales with each roll. We had to stop the catboat so that we could haul in the overloaded "flattie" alongside. We took turns scooping fish with a dip net while trying to fend off the two boats. After a while we had removed nearly half of the cargo onto the deck of the catboat and bucket-bailed the trap boat. Just as we became ready to get underway again, the idling engine stalled, putting us in a most awkward position. If the engine did not start immediately, the batteries would be dead. It was an uncomfortable state of affairs.

There was only one vessel in sight, a big dragger coming from the eastward and headed for the main channel of Woods Hole. I recognized the schooner-rigged craft as the

STANLEY M. BUTLER, a hi-liner owned by Capt. Olaf Anderson of New Bedford. The *BUTLER* was not more than a mile away when I frantically waved my oilskin jacket from atop the cabin. Daylight was on the wane but I was sure that we would be seen — four boats and a waving coat in the daylight to the west. No such luck. They continued on their way as if we didn't exist.

Norman said, "Let's try something. Let's take the spark plugs out, clean the points and heat 'em in a can." We grabbed a spare can of gasoline and poured a cupful into a coffee can where we had placed the plugs. We put the can in a deck bucket, lit a wooden match and fired up the gasoline for a couple of minutes before snuffing out the fire with a cover. Using pliers, we returned the hot plugs to the cylinder head after priming each cylinder with a squirt of gasoline. We quickly tightened the plugs with an adjustable wrench and replaced the wires. It was a now, if ever, situation. One or both of us must have said a little prayer. A push of the starter button, and wow! The engine came to life! Music to our ears. The thrill of a lifetime!

We checked the towlines of the three boats that had fortunately stayed astern of us, then carefully got underway in a northwesterly direction toward Nobska Lighthouse. We had drifted to windward with the flood tide. Gradually we crept into the east channel, past Little Harbor and Juniper Point, greatly relieved to be in calm water. By about 8:30 PM we had the boats tied up at Sam Cahoon's unloading platform. Norman went to locate a telephone while I bailed out our three boats and secured them alongside the catboat for the night.

The Edgartown dragger *LIBERTY*, schooner-rigged, arrived from offshore and tied up close by. Capt. Claude Wagner invited us to go aboard. The cook served us a big bowl of fish chowder. They found it hard to believe that we had crossed the Sound towing three overloaded boats. There were spare bunks available, providing us with a comfortable place to stay overnight. A big breakfast was also included.

Our triple cargo of fish had kept well overnight, what with the air temperature at about 38 degrees. The unloading occupied us all morning. We scooped the perch into big wire baskets that the dock crew hoisted and dumped on the culling bench. Wish I could remember or had a record of how many thousands of pounds of white perch we sold that day. I do remember the prices per pound — three sizes, small, medium and large, at five, ten and fifteen cents a pound: a small fortune in those days that was divided on a 50-50 basis between the Bensons and me. We bought two new fully-charged six-volt batteries before heading back to the Vineyard. The northeast wind was moderate, the trip back to Tashmoo uneventful.

Franklin was waiting for us when we arrived back at the seine, but so did disappointment. A bunch of kids had grabbed the corklines and hauled the seine ashore; the tons of fish had all escaped. Mark Smith at the pumping station nearby told us that it had happened right after we left the day before. He couldn't get there in time to stop the disaster.

The quantity of perch that we had lost out of the aborted seine was probably more than double the tonnage we'd delivered to Woods Hole. Beyond that loss, the kids had also amused themselves by throwing stones at the schooling fish in the cove. On the chance that we would find the perch elsewhere, we explored the entire lake. Not a sign of white perch anywhere. They were gone completely. We never saw that phenomenon again.

An island philosopher, Capt. Chester Robinson, had heard about our adventure at Tashmoo. He said to me one day, "If you took time to read the Bible, you would learn that whenever there is a reference to a fisherman, it will be as 'the poor fisherman'!" Another common expression of his was, "You can starve to death slower on the Vineyard than any place I've ever known." That was during the Depression, of course, long before tourism became the principal island industry, along with real estate and its unbelievable values.

Chapter 31

An Expedition For Herring

After recovering from the momentary wealth of the white perch expedition, the spring run of herring (alewives) was the next attraction.

Roland Authier, a neighbor, wanted to ship a load of fresh herring to Fulton Market in New York. He had a Model T touring car that would serve as a truck. We removed the back seat cushions and folded the cloth top down so that it extended out over the rear of the car. Early in the evening, we rumbled along a rutted road through the woods to the Tashmoo Herring Creek. The channel was alive with incoming alewives. We found space to back the car to the water's edge. Quite a gang of fish catchers was positioned along the shoreline. We grabbed our dip nets and bailed fish directly into the back seat until it was level full. Then we poured more herring into the folds of the overhanging top. Five or six nearby men were comandeered to help us push the straining car up onto solid ground.

We soon learned, while rolling along in low gear, that we had a problem. The weight of the fish was so far back that the front wheels had a tendency to leave the bumpy ground, causing a steering difficulty. At the same time, the throttle linkage became disconnected. We had to stop while Roland volunteered to locate himself on the right front fender to serve as ballast to hold down the front end while simultaneously performing the engineering feat of controlling the engine speed by holding the broken throttle rod. It was like a Laurel and Hardy movie, with me in the driver's seat steering, and my left foot pressed down on the low-gear pedal (on a downhill stretch we could get into high gear).

When we occasionally met an oncoming car, we would insist that they back up until we could get to a level area where we could crawl out of the ruts and let the other car pass by. By the time we emerged from the wagon road and reached a paved highway, the low gear speedband burned out in a cloud of smoke. However, it was all downhill to the steamboat wharf and we made it there in high gear.

Somehow we found a bunch of empty barrels. Then we stole some crushed ice from the hold of a nearby fish-dragger. The barrels were packed and securely covered as they sat on freight dollies ready to be loaded aboard the outgoing steamer early next morning. When the freight office opened at daybreak, we nailed shipping tags addressed to a prominent New York fish buyer — two tags per barrel. The fish barrels went on a C.O.D. consignment basis, except that we had to pay the shipment costs to Woods Hole, a strain on our finances.

We had visions of those fine fat fish, many of them full of roe, bringing us a handsome paycheck after shipping expenses. Instead, to our complete surprise, we received a business-sized letter that contained a bill for the cost of having shipped several barrels of unwanted alewives. That was a learning experience and another reminder of Chester Robinson's "poor fisherman."

To try to offset the herring misadventure, I had to find a job that would provide a reliable income. A few days earlier the schooner *ALICE S. WENTWORTH* under Capt. Zeb Tilton had arrived at the wharf with a full cargo of road oil in barrels. The product originated at Providence, and had been consigned to the Vineyard Haven branch of the Standard Oil Company, soon to be known as Mobil Oil.

The oil was being trucked to a sandpit at a side road near the top of Tashmoo Hill. Fred Vincent, a town selectman, was also the manager of Mobil with his office and storage tanks on Beach Road. Joe Campbell was his assistant. There was rumor of an available job at the sandpit. I inquired about the opportunity. Mr. Vincent explained that he had a contract with the state Highway Department to resurface the main roads of the island. A huge tank, brought over on a barge, was about to be located at the sandpit. An attached furnace heated internal coils that made the sticky oil flow. Tank trucks would be there to load the hot oil and discharge it on the roads through spray racks at the rear of the specially-designed vehicles. Their own heaters maintained the necessary liquidity of the cargo. Sanding trucks followed the oilers. Cars that followed too closely picked up an undercoating of liquid tar.

A sloping ramp with a platform near the open hatch at the top of the tank constructed of heavy planking and timbers was promptly put in place. My job was to roll the barrels out of the sandpit with enough momentum to get them up the ramp to the platform. Once there, I had to up-end the barrel, grab a nearby pickaxe and punch a big hole in the thin metal. The next step was to tip the barrel toward the rim of the hatch and, as the oil plop-plopped into the tank, raise the bottom high enough to completely drain the contents. It was really a two-man job, but I soon discovered that it was a one-man take-it-or-leave-it situation. Later I learned that a dozen other applicants had refused to do it without a helper. Apparently I didn't know any better!

The road oil project was completed by June 1st, coinciding with the 30-day State Highway contract. My part of the program consisted of 12-hour days at 50 cents an hour, six days a week over a period of five weeks. My responsibility began each day with firing up the tank heater at five A.M. By the time that the trucks arrived at seven, the storage tank full of liquid asphalt would be up to a flowable temperature. The barrels had to be kept rolling until noon, at which time I was allowed a half-hour lunch break. The truck drivers grabbed a sandwich while their tanks were being relocated. By the end of the day, a big heap of empty oil drums lay under the ramp ready to be trucked to the town dump before dark, providing space for the following day's accumulation. What a relief it was to turn off that roaring oil burner at the end of each day.

My uniform-of-the-day consisted of a floppy hat, goggles (spattered with tar) and tar-coated coveralls, wet with sweat, and gooey gloves. My clean clothes were draped over my recently-acquired Indian Scout motorcycle parked in the shade of the nearby trees. The 15-minute ride home was a cooling delight. A rag soaked in kerosene helped to remove most of the road oil from my face and hands. After a bath and a good supper, it was time to be on the way to Oak Bluffs, where a mild form of beer had become available, 3.2 percent alcohol.

The Boston House on Circuit Avenue became the island oasis with Prohibition now a thing of the past. All brands of beer soon became much more potent. The drinking-and-driving era became an immediate reality. However, after a long hot day wrestling heavy barrels in that sandpit, beer proved to be a great thirst-quencher. Former schoolmates and shipmates appeared during the evening to drink, smoke cigarettes and listen to thundering jukebox entertainment. The atmosphere helped to counteract the gloom of the Depression years.

After the road oil ordeal ended, it was time to line up a chance to go fishing during favorable summer weather. However, I met Hollis Smith in the post office and he said, "How would you like an easy job for a change?" Hollis normally was a professional land surveyor, but he went on to say, "The Bigelow family at West Chop (I vaguely remember that section of West Chop being known as "Mink Meadows") has put me in charge of building a golf course there in the middle of the best forest land anywhere on the island. Four lanes will be cleared to form a rectangle while leaving a square section of trees in the center." He had hired a crew of wood-choppers armed with axes and two-man saws to destroy hundreds of big, beautiful trees. Chainsaws were not then in existence to speed the destruction. However, in those days, we did not have the sense to be concerned or sentimental about it. Trees were firewood!

Hollis needed an operator for a big Cleatrac tractor, the forerunner of Caterpillar tractors and bulldozers. The tractor would be used to haul logs and to pull stumps. So, I took the job. Five days a week, eight hours a day for a week's pay of 25 dollars. We could not work on weekends because our commotion would disturb the peace of the area residents.

The Cleatrac was a jouncing, bucking mode of locomotion that caused the driver to have the appearance of a Wild West rodeo rider. The exhaust pipe extended vertically about four feet above the engine and almost the same distance in front of my position on the driver's seat. The result was that the driver inhaled a rich mixture of air and carbon monoxide. Along with exhaust fumes, a constant cloud of dust was usually generated by the clattering tractor treads.

The motorcycle ride out to the job was a ten-minute trip. I tried to be there a half-hour early in order to service the tractor. In addition to routine maintenance, the Cleatrac had dozens of fittings where the grease gun needed to be applied. My two assistants were Winnie Norton and Melvin Sears. It was noisy, dirty work but we had a good time, especially during the lunch hour when we talked philosophy and told dirty jokes.

When all four stretches of the rectangular areas had been cleared of trees, bushes and stumps, the bare ground required leveling. A road grader was brought in for the preliminary work, but the tractor was kept busy towing equipment like a disc harrow cultivator or a heavy wooden sled, upon which we loaded rocks and boulders. By mid-August, the preliminary work was done.

The next phase of the project consisted of bringing in truckloads of loam that had to be spread evenly over the entire cleared area, except on what would be sand-traps. Other work, such as creating greens, laying pipe for irrigation and spreading tons of grass seed would occupy the crew for the balance of the warm weather season.

Norton and Sears stayed on the payroll for the duration, but it soon became time for me to leave the job. I needed to satisfy my urge to go boating. I would miss Winnie, who was a clown, and Mel, with his intellectual observations. (Among other subjects, Mel had studied the life of Michelangelo.) He and our good-natured boss, Hollis Smith, entertained us during our lunch hour with a series of discussions on many subjects of historical interest.

At that time, Tom Tilton and his son, Leslie, nicknamed "Kizer," were fishing in a 40-foot dragger known as the *ARTEMISIA B.* (Later he owned the *QUEST* and finally, the larger *THREE BELLS)*. Anyhow, they were making five-day trips dragging for fluke south of Nantucket. A third man was needed as a mastheader for daytime swordfishing. At night, the net was towed two hours at a stretch to catch jumbo fluke, big skates, stingrays, and squid spawn, a gelatin-like substance containing squid eggs that was vigorously shaken out of the suspended net before setting out again. Squid spawn is favorite food for flounders and other bottom feeders.

During the night one man did the steering and tried to stay awake while the other two snoozed for about two hours, stretched out on pipe berths in the hot smoky atmosphere of the cabin. We rotated until a new day dawned. Then it was time to flake the net on the port-side rail where it would dry (cotton netting in those days). The nighttime fluke-dragging was done at depths that ranged from 10 to 15 fathoms. We then headed offshore in a southerly direction, cruising leisurely until we could see boats on the horizon.

Most of the active inshore fleet consisted of Provincetown sloops. Actually, they were huge catboats, 40 to 50 feet in length with lofty topmasts and five or six-men crews. One of those P-towners, the sloop *JESSE DUTRA*, joined us as we circled a big underwater swordfish. We did not move fast enough. The *DUTRA* whirled around while their striker nailed the fish, put a man in the dory and went on their way as we rode the glassy swells and loudly shouted obscenities at the "P-towners" for stealing our fish!

Later that day, as we headed inshore, we sighted a finning swordfish at a distance, when our engine suddenly slowed to a stop thanks to the combination of an empty fuel tank and dirty fuel filters. By the time the engine came to life again, the fish was gone.

After another long night of fluke-dragging, we proceeded toward Woods Hole, where the next day we sold about 2,500 pounds of fluke and one moderate-sized swordfish. That was a typical summertime fishing trip. Expenses included several hundred gallons of gasoline, a hold full of crushed ice and a week's supply of food. The net crew share averaged something like 50 dollars.

The changeover from summer to winter fishing usually happened by mid-October each year. Extra crew members generally depended on the bay scalloping during the weeks of early winter. My summer of fishing with the Tiltons had been a satisfactory activity. But, like other similar boats, they went "two-handed" during the winter.

Chapter 32

Dredging Drudgery

By mid-December that year, bay scallops were getting scarce. About that time, there was news of a channel-dredging job at Menemsha. A big outfit, Bay State Dredging Company, had arrived from Boston with all the required equipment. The Boston tug *VENUS* took advantage of good weather to tow the entire combination to an anchorage outside the Menemsha jetties. Then a smaller tug, the *DONKEY*, was utilized at slack tide to bring in the dredge, the big houseboat and finally, two bargeloads of pipeline. Menemsha Basin was crowded with dredging equipment. A quarter-mile length of pipeline pontoons completed the complex combination.

Among others who applied for a job were Ted Yates, whose family maintained West Chop Lighthouse, and myself. We were rated as deckhands and were "privileged" to work the midnight to 8 A.M. shift, our part of the around-the-clock activity. However, the day crew did most of the heavy work of shifting pipeline as the dredge slowly chewed its way forward while creating a wider and deeper channel all the way into Menemsha Pond.

It soon became evident that the wear and tear involved in such dredging was impressive. The steel blades of the rotary cutter suspended from the forward end of the swinging dredge required constant replacement. The huge centrifugal pump, driven by a massive diesel engine, often broke down because of the huge volume of sand, gravel and rocks that mixed with the water it forced through a quarter-mile of 12" pipe line. That mixture was discharged in an area previously approved by the Corp of Army Engineers and town authorities.

Winter weather gave us a rough time. Pipe joints leaked and had to be repaired in a spray of freezing salt water. Such nighttime work could be readily classified as hardship. After an hour or so of such miserable activity, we returned to the noisy dredge to soak up the warmth and swig a mug of hot coffee. When the day crew arrived at 8 A.M., we eagerly leapt on board the *DONKEY,* skippered by Walter Manning of Gay Head, for the return trip to Menemsha. From there, we traveled the North Road back to Vineyard Haven in a well-ventilated Studebaker touring car. When the Menemsha channel dredging work was completed sometime in January 1934, the dredge and pipeline were moved across Menemsha Pond where we dug a new channel into Quitsa Pond. A week later, the dredging contract was completed. All the equipment was taken back to Menemsha Basin where everything was made ready to be towed to the next contract at Bass River in the town of Yarmouth on Cape Cod.

Yates and I were invited to go along but we decided to stay on the island and look for a more comfortable way to make a living. Soon after, Ted joined the Coast Guard and wound up making a career of it. I finished the winter as a crew member of the 60-foot Nantucket dragger *NATIVE* operating out of Vineyard Haven. I joined Capt. Manuel Canha, his father-in-law and cook Joseph Authier, and Jimmy Fortin, owner and engineer, as their mate and deckhand. The three-masted Maine schooner *DAWN WILKIE* was at anchor in the outer harbor waiting for a fair wind to the westward. We were offered a chance to tow the vessel to City Island, New York. However, we refused, opting instead for a rough five-day trip dragging for yellowtail flounders on Nantucket shoals. A strong nor'wester finally drove us into Nantucket Harbor. Between fishing trips, I kept occupied by shucking bay scallops in a nearby shanty at the going rate of 50 cents a gallon.

Sometime in March, I managed somehow to acquire the Point Judith dragger *RELIANCE*, an unusually able craft, a western rig about 38 feet long powered with a big, heavy-duty Palmer engine. Blackback flounders along with scup and sea bass provided the inshore dragger fleet with steady production during their early spring migration.

Chapter 33

Flashes of Memory

What follows is a series of random "flashes of memory," recollections of activities that took place over many years but arranged in a haphazard sequence with no reference to any specific period of time.

At a very young age, my favorite hangout was at Jimmy Vincent's boatyard in Vineyard Haven. (Now the Martha's Vineyard Shipyard.) There was always the powerful aroma of copper paint in the cluttered workshop. A romantic atmosphere. The yard's work skiff, a battered old relic, was beached near the marine railway. I learned to row that thing with two unmatched oars that caused some directional difficulties. When Jimmy Vincent retired, the yard operation was taken over by Jim Look and Carl Magnusen of West Tisbury.

Winter weather during my youth was severe when compared to conditions since 1945, with northwest gales and freezing temperatures the normal conditions. Through the mid-winter months, we occasionally had to endure a typical northeast gale and snowstorm that roared constantly for 48 hours or more. Deep snow covered the island. Horse-drawn plows and crews of shovelers gradually cleared the roads until travel could be resumed.

The crews of many coasting schooners anchored in the mouth of Vineyard Haven Harbor generally tried to escape the fury of those northeast storms by hoisting their anchors and a few sails as the tide turned to the west in order to make their way over to Tarpaulin Cove and safety in the lee of Naushon Island. For many years, running a mariner's mail station was part of the lighthouse keeper's duty at Tarpaulin Cove, a favorite anchorage.

In Vineyard Haven, after a big snowstorm, the town roads were coated with hard-packed snow. Nighttime sledding was a very popular activity, especially when Police Chief Flaherty officially closed a particular hillside road to traffic at sundown. The intersection of State Road and Edgartown Road was established as the top of the hill. The lower end of the ride was at the intersection now known as Five Corners. Steerable Flexible Flyer sleds were everyone's favorite.

A concrete traffic dummy stood in mid-highway near the entrance of Main Street on the corner where the old Mansion House Hotel was located. Usually the chief would have a garage tow truck remove the dangerous dummy as part of the open-to-sledding procedure. Usually. One very cold and slippery night, someone provided us with a super sled that could carry six passengers. Somehow, I managed to get the pilot's job — up front with my feet on the steering bars. Away we went, whizzing down the hill until unbelievably, the dummy, which for unknown reasons had not been removed, loomed directly in our path. Manuel Coutino sat directly behind me. We both shouted, "Get ready to roll off the sled!" Fortunately, with the steering bar pushed hard over, we just clipped the menace and were able to complete the fast trip safely.

Ice harvesting was usually done in mid January, when the ice on the Vineyard's fresh-water ponds had reached a thickness of eight to ten inches. Occasionally, a snowstorm or a January thaw would delay the cutting.

When conditions were right, Harry Peakes, the cold-storage mogul of Vineyard Haven, would round up all the available outdoor characters, including me, instructing them, if they wanted work, to show up at his Lambert's Cove ice house on the northern shore of a large pond (Old House Pond). A crew of 15 or 20 of us characters, with long handsaws, would start in front of the ice-house conveyor and cut a narrow channel toward the center of the pond. The ice in that first cut, only about three feet long with long-handled ice chisels. Those cakes were then pushed with iron-tipped poles into the upward-moving conveyor, providing open water along which the rest of the harvest was floated.

The ice house, a huge building, its double walls packed full of sawdust for insulation, was filled to capacity with several hundred tons of block ice. The 300-pound blocks sat on a layer of sawdust that prevented them from freezing solidly together.

A gasoline engine, probably an old low-geared truck motor, powered the conveyor mechanism. My memory of the operation has faded, like the enclosed snapshot which shows the scene when one year's harvest, probably 1925, was nearly completed.

Harry Peakes also owned and operated a freezer plant on Beach Road in Vineyard Haven between the Boatyard and the Socony-Mobil Oil storage tanks. Ice for retail delivery to homes was hauled from the Lambert's Cove ice house and kept in a small cold-storage building near the present Benjamin-Gannon boatyard. A two-man team, Pete and Burgess (I've forgotten their last names), delivered ice in REO trucks that carried a ton or more of block ice in their rear-mounted insulated boxes, to any residence displaying a big card with the word "ICE" prominently displayed in a front window. Ice picks, ice tongs and waterproof shoulder pads were the tools of the trade.

"That's the way it was" in the 1920's and 1930's, to quote Vineyarder Walter Cronkite.

✶

In those days, there were two competitive daily New Bedford newspapers: the *Standard* and the *Times*. Eventually they combined to become the *Standard-Times*. The bundles arrived at the steamboat wharf and like many other paperboys, I had a designated delivery route, mostly uphill on a bicycle. In time, I became the island circulation manager for the *New Bedford Times*. My position required the transport of bundled newspapers to each island town all the way to Gay Head. I bought a much used Studebaker touring car from an Oak Bluffs dealer known as "Doc Chic." Usually one or two schoolkids went along for the ride as volunteer helpers.

That Studebaker was a troublesome car that required continuous repair work. The car featured "disc" wheels which somehow had a tendency to wear out tires at an alarming rate. Finally, one night at the Gay Head end of the newspaper delivery, I'd had enough and decided to get rid of the car. I remembered a road that paralleled the downward sloping eastern end of the Gay Head cliffs. I swerved the car at a speed slow enough so that I could safely jump out and watched the poor old Studebaker disappear over the edge. The headlights illuminated the scene as the car plunged and rolled its way down to the beach, where it finally came to rest on a bunch of boulders. Maybe some of it is still there. A customer, Napoleon Madison, gave me a ride home.

By the following morning, I was in a state of remorse about having deliberately wrecked the Studebaker. It was such a quirky thing to do. I could have sold it or given it away. It was a sudden senseless impulse. As I stood at the top of the cliff that night, I looked down at my former companion and observed that it had landed right side up on the boulders with the engine running and both headlights brightly focused on the rocky shoreline. A permanent painful memory.

But I needed the replacement car immediately. The William G. Manter

Buick Agency on Beach Street was a convenient source of used cars. The sales manager, Manuel Campbell, greeted me by saying, "I have news that you need a car right away! I have something special for you." In the storage garage nearby we walked past several standard Buicks and Chevys until we came to a super-sized open touring car, a huge dark green Stutz with a tan cloth top. Manuel said, "Just what you need; imagine the number of bundles of newspapers that you could stack in that back seat!" He went on to explain that the Stutz had been previously owned by a wealthy family from Philadelphia who had recently acquired a secluded summer residence somewhere in the hills of Chilmark. They soon realized that the Stutz was too cumbersome to negotiate the narrow rutted road leading to their new estate and they'd traded the big car for a more practical station wagon. Manuel was a good salesman who knew that it would be an easy deal with me as a prospective buyer. After a demonstration ride we began to talk about the price. I could own the magnificent Stutz for $250: only $50 as a down payment and the balance to be paid at the rate of $25 a month. A full gas tank made the deal complete.

The Stutz transport service was an adventurous experience but it ended with the merger of the two New Bedford newspapers. Besides, it was springtime and the urge to go fishing prevailed. I sold the Stutz to a college student — an island visitor whose name I do not remember. A Model T Roadster replaced the Stutz as a more practical form of island transportation.

✶

Bartlet "Bart" Mayhew was the proprietor of a Vineyard Haven taxi business with headquarters on Main Street in Vineyard Haven. His one limousine was a huge Pierce-Arrow sedan with Dana Baxter as chauffeur, in uniform. The pair was reserved for wealthy passengers and special occasions. Bart favored Buick touring cars and sedans for his taxi service. Most of his passengers originated at the steamboat docks at Vineyard Haven and Oak Bluffs.

Bart Mayhew also had a repair shop that was located about a mile out of town near the State Road. The building was of fieldstone construction and was known as "The Crystal Palace." Oscar Flanders was Bart's most important employee. (He was married to one of Bart's daughters.) He served as chief mechanic and as a truck driver who carried most of the up-island freight. In his spare time, he created a special six-wheeled vehicle constructed of two Model T Fords joined by a swiveling feature in the center. This enabled the strange contraption to bend around corners gracefully. The long, boxy car, known as "The Caterpillar," was adaptable for the transport of passengers forward with mailbags and freight aft. The quaint vehicle was a special photo attraction for island visitors. It served a useful purpose for a few years.

✶

Soon after high school graduation in 1931, the year that the new school was opened, I became intrigued with aviation. The military required at least two years of college education in order to qualify for flight training. The alternative was to hang around the original Island airfield at Katama. A Southerner, Bill Seward, had established a summertime business of sightseeing flights and student instruction. He owned two aircraft: a Bird biplane with an OX-5 Curtis V-type water cooled engine and a Stearman Biplane powered with a five-cylinder, radial, air-cooled Kinner engine. A mechanic or volunteer began the engine starting process by rotating the propeller for several revolutions until the pilot yelled "Contact!"

The pilot, sitting in the aft cockpit, knew exactly how many turns of the propeller were necessary to prime the engine for starting. The shout, "Contact!", meant that he had turned on the ignition switches. The next move required a special, all-out yank on a propeller blade and a quick leap backward out of the way when the engine came to life. If the engine sputtered and stalled, the process had to be repeated, but usually the first effort was sufficient. The forward cockpit was for a passenger or a student pilot.

One particular summer, I had become employed by Marshall MacDonough, proprietor of the Tashmoo Springs Bottling Company. The plant was located about a mile beyond Vineyard Haven near the state highway. Bill Figuerido had the monotonous job of operating the bottling machine-filling and capping endless bottles of Coca-Cola, two dozen bottles per case, all of which had to be inspected before delivery. On occasion he would switch over to other flavors of soda pop. My basic job was to pick up and invert the full bottles (two in each hand) and watch carefully for any slivers of broken glass settling in the liquid that would be revealed by a bright light in the background. About twenty cases worth of that activity produced a combination of eyestrain and sore fingers. It was always a relief to load the company truck with those bottled beverages for delivery to stores, yacht clubs and tennis clubs that were down island, mainly Vineyard Haven, Oak Bluffs and Edgartown. Five gallon jugs of Tashmoo Springs drinking water were special orders on the delivery route. It was a pleasant experience through which I met people of an entirely different social background than the native islanders of my type.

My favorite delivery was to the Katama Airport to refill the Coca-Cola cooler in Bill Seward's office, an end-of-the-day stop. There I had a deal to work for a couple of hours at cleaning spark plugs or washing an airplane in order to earn some "flying time" instruction.

My reward was a weekly opportunity for twenty minutes of flying instruction. It was an early evening performance given when the regular students or sightseeing customers had vanished. By that time, the prevailing southerly breezes began delivering the customary layer of fog inland over the cooling landscape. After two or three wide circles over the village of Edgartown, Bill Seward would yell, "Time to head back; I can barely see the water tower!" Then we would drop until we could see the sandy road. We would follow it until we could locate the wind sock on the roof of the hangar building and glide in for a safe landing on the grassy Katama Airfield runway.

In clear weather, with a wind velocity of thirty miles an hour or more, Seward would engage in his favorite sport of flying "backwards." He would throttle back the engine while holding the plane at an upward angle. Gradually, we drifted backwards like a kite, but slowly lose altitude until it became necessary to restore engine power and climb to a thousand feet or higher. Biplanes were such wonderful flying machines.

The most exciting feature about learning to fly was the "tailspin" exercise. Occasionally, in clear sunny weather, we would take off and climb to an altitude of 5000 feet or more. Bill Seward would shout, "Here we go! I'll give you three minutes to get us out of the spin!" Up went the nose until we stalled. Then the plane fell into a dive with the tail rotating above us. To come out of that dangerous maneuver required full engine power with control stick and rudder pedals in opposition to the plane's rotation. Instant awareness of the spin rotation right or left was urgent. Experience and quick judgment were the requirements for survival. In early practice. the pilot completely controlled the gyrating aircraft while the student learned the procedure by gently following the rapid action of the control system. A rather sweaty experience for both participants, I must admit.

The pilot had to be prepared for the possibility of the student "freezing" at the controls during a spin. In such an emergency, the pilot used his handy wooden club to reach over and "zonk" the petrified student in order to cause instant relaxation. It was an understandable necessity. Several students became disenchanted with learning to fly. Others were simply disqualified for further instruction. By the time I was ready for my first solo flight, the summer season had officially ended with the arrival of Labor Day. Most of the students and sightseers had returned to their mainland homes. Vacations ended as the school year began.

Bill Seward decided to move his flying service to Roosevelt field at Port Washington, Long Island, NY. His slowpoke mechanic, whose nickname was "Lightnin'", would fly the OX-5 Bird in company with Seward in the Stearman. I could have stayed and gone with them as an employee, but problems at home prevented such an adventurous opportunity. My father had become an invalid and was bedridden with rheumatoid arthritis. My mother had to serve as his nurse for many years, along with being our housekeeper and cook. She also, in her spare time, did housecleaning for several neighbors at 50 cents an hour. She was busy from 6 AM until midnight every day of the week.

Fortunately, brother Tad was employed by H.C. Hancock as a carpenter and cabinet maker. A good worker with a reliable income.

On the other hand, I was not very responsible, jumping around from one occupation to another and having fun with cars and motorcycles!

Shameful behavior and no excuse for it during that era of our family life.

The following summer, a new aviation school was established at the Katama Airport. The Curtis-Wright Aviation School arrived with several Stearman and Travel-Air biplanes. The pilots were former military flyers and they loved to perform all sorts of stunts in those orange aircraft. Every day was an air show with parachute jumps as part of the activity.

One of my outstanding memories in learning to fly was the exhaust smell of aviation gasoline and watching the open-valve rocker arms of the OX-5 eight-cylinder engine all dancing in rhythm while sending spatters of oil back onto the windshield. Our leather helmets and glass goggles became likewise spattered, which created the problem of trying to maintain sufficient visibility to make a smooth landing on the grassy pasture that served as an airport. The early days of general aviation proved to be a wonderfully adventurous era. The memories are extraordinary.

Chapter 34

The Fishing Schooner Era

The history of the Gloucester fishing schooners is available in the form of an excellent book entitled "Fast and Able" by Gordon W. Thomas.

Nearly all the vessels of that era were built at the nearby Essex Shipyards. Arthur D. Story was a famous builder. They were built to withstand the roughest sort of use. The hulls were substantially constructed of seasoned white oak: double-sawn frames, close together. The planking was generally "trunnel" or "trenail" fastened with long hickory pegs with a wedge slot on the outer ends.

Many of the smaller vessels were planked with long leaf yellow pine, known simply as hard pine. It contained resin that made it practically worm proof. Some of those pine planked craft survived for 50 years or more. Hard pine became the desired planking for workboats of all types and sizes.

Fifty years ago the offshore fishing fleet consisted mostly of schooners/two-masted sailing vessels with diesel engine auxiliary power. By that time, many of the big dory trawlers were being re-rigged as draggers. Their original old Fairbanks-Morse engines were replaced with more powerful modern machinery. The main sails were generally eliminated in favor of a big three-cornered riding sail. The foresail and one jib were furled when fishing but were ready to hoist when it came time to ride out a storm.

The newer vessels were designed with wider, bulkier stern sections in order to carry the considerable weight of a big diesel engine and large fuel tanks. The two masts were shortened but ruggedly rigged with the purpose of being capable of handling huge cod-end hoists of cod and haddock brought in over the rail. A suitable riding sail was utilized on the mainmast to minimize the rolling action of the vessel.

Captain Ben Pine, famous Gloucester racing skipper (*GERTRUDE L. THEBEAUD* vs the Canadian schooner "BLUENOSE", Captain Angus Walters) had a series of three such vessels built, two at Thomaston, Maine and one at Ipswich, Massachusetts during 1943 and 1944. They were the *COLUMBIA*, the *PURITAN* and the *PILGRIM.* For many years the *COLUMBIA,* with Capt. Mike Sears, was a consistent Gloucester High-Liner.

These buoyant vessels were great fish producers. They could continue to operate in raging winter gales on Georges Bank, when the big steel Boston trawlers were forced to lay drifting for long periods all awash. The schooners were known as wonderful seaboats.

In my youth on Martha's Vineyard, boats of all sizes and shapes were a way of life. Lobster boats, catboats and small draggers, gasoline-powered, were common. However, there were five island-owned schooners. Four of them hailed from Edgartown, the other from one, Vineyard Haven.

The Edgartown schooners were the *HAZEL M. JACKSON* (Captain Bob Jackson); *THE LIBERTY* (Captain Claude Wagner); the *MALVINA B.* (Captain Isaac (Ike) Norton). Captain Ike later had the schooner-rigged dragger *CATHERINE AND MARY*, as well. Can't forget the schooner *B. T. HILLMAN*, or Captain Horace Hillman, its owner and master. All were relatively small vessels, in the 65 foot to 70 foot range. They went swordfishing all summer, but became draggers for the winter season.

The other Vineyard schooner was the "3 & 1 & 1", a handsome craft built by the Morse Shipyard in Thomaston, Maine for Captain John Salvadore. Sea scalloping was Captain John's principal occupation. Vineyard Haven was his homeport. In those days, there were only three or four vessels in the sea scallop industry on Georges Bank. The sandy bottom was paved with huge scallops, with shells the size of dinner plates! There were no union rules or sensible watches at that time.

After the first tow with two ten foot rakes, or dredges (one from each side), the deck was piled high with scallops, a few fish and plenty of trash. Every half-hour the rakes had to be "hauled back" as they were solid full again.

Captain John, who was known as a "driver," and his whole crew of ten men would work for 30 hours or more at a stretch! Then they'd anchored for about four hours before repeating the seemingly endless process.

This endurance contest went on for nearly two weeks, or until the food, fuel and ice were consumed. The shucking activity continued all the way into the market at Woods Hole. An average trip of 2,800 gallons of sea scallops represented a crew share of between 75 and 100 dollars.

Many of the crew squandered their hard earned money in the nearest barroom. Their thirst was unquenchable!

When winter weather arrived, Salvadore would remove the scallop gear and replace it with fish-dragging equipment: nets and trawl doors instead of dredges. The "3 & 1 & 1" with a smaller crew, five fishermen, would proceed to Cape May, New Jersey, where winter fishing conditions were generally much more favorable.

When the swordfishing season ended, by late September, the Edgartown schooners also went through a transition. Topmasts and bowsprits came ashore to be stored for the winter. Then the winter fish-dragging gear was brought aboard. In those days, yellow-tail flounders were plentiful in 20 to 30 fathoms, south of the Vineyard. Usually, they could get in a three or four-day trip between winter gales. Cold work for a modest week's pay!

Early in the spring of 1935, I had an urge to try a summer of offshore sword-fishing. To that end, I visited with Captain Bob Jackson and requested a "site", preferably as the wheelsman. I had been told by former crewmen that being up in the topmast hoops looking for swordfish all day was not very comfortable. Georges Bank is noted for wet weather, dense fog in particular. Being up on that gyrating topmast required boots and "oilers" in order to keep dry and reasonably warm. Also, newcomers to the masthead job, some 75 feet above the deck, usually suffered sea-sickness during the first few days of the cruise.

Eventually, I learned that there were some minor hazards about the steering job, which will be mentioned in due course.

The privilege of being "hired" as a crew member required nearly a month's work in getting the vessel cleaned, rigged and painted, inside and outside (at no pay!).

The *JACKSON* was docked on the south side of the "Steamboat Wharf". The pilothouse was unbolted and hoisted ashore out of the way. Then the scraping, sanding and painting went on every day through the month of May. Finally, we cast off and steamed over to Fairhaven, where we hauled out on the marine railway for the semi-annual bottom cleaning and painting. Afloat again a few days later, we headed toward Woods Hole.

The *HAZEL M. JACKSON* was now in a yacht-like condition. We tied up at Sam Cahoon's fish pier where we loaded 18 tons of ice in 300 pound blocks. The fish hold was solid full of ice. Wrestling those blocks into position was a very sweaty project. Then, after filling the fuel oil tanks, we proceeded back to Edgartown. Next day, a truckload of groceries arrived for us. The cook, George Paul, needed help to stow it all in the galley refrigerator and lockers, except for a barrel full of corned beef, which was "iced down" in the fish hold. The wooden water tank (cypress), located under the galley floor, was filled to capacity — 500 gallons. As reserve water supply, about two dozen swordfish kegs were also filled with town water and tightly corked. At dawn next morning, the diesel engine came alive, rumbling at low R.P.M. and pouring dense clouds of smoke through the water cooled stern exhaust. A flock of seagulls circled overhead, squawking at the disturbance.

We were soon underway on our first trip of the season, a warm sunny June morning. (The for'sl and riding sails were hoisted.) We rounded Cape Pogue and took advantage of a favorable southerly tide out through Muskeget Channel. Captain Bob said to me at the wheel, "Let her go south by west for a while. Maybe we will see a few sharks today". The weather was nice, with a light WSW breeze. Steaming along at about eight knots, we crossed the steamer track (ship-traffic between Nantucket Lightship and Ambrose Lightship off New York Harbor) by mid-afternoon.

An hour or so later, we saw the first shark, a hammerhead. By sundown, we had seen several blue sharks, or their dorsal fins, in the distance. Also an occasional whale.

At dusk, we "hove to" for the night. A 14-pound sounding-lead attached to 100 fathoms of tarred cotton line was coiled neatly in a tub near the starboard rail, aft. The line was marked in fathoms. It was my sideline job as wheelsman to heave and haul the sounding lead. Before we made the first sounding, Captain Bob secured a typical outdoor thermometer to the leadline about a fathom above the sounding lead. He tossed the lead and the line whizzed over the rail until it went slack. The skipper said, "See if you can haul that lead back faster than I can coil the line in the tub". With a "nipper" on each hand, I barely made it! The water was 65 fathoms deep. The thermometer read 62 degrees. He said, "Swordfish like it a few degrees warmer than that."

Another day dawned with fine calm weather. After breakfast, we were underway headed due east toward deeper, warmer water. Captain Bob shouted, "Time to go aloft, boys, and remember, look underwater, I can see fins from the bowsprit". Five men went up the rigging; Bill O'Neill was the chosen "mastheader". He stood on the smallest spreader and was held in place by a half-circle steel band and a safety belt fashioned from a piece of fire hose, attached to eye bolts. At the top of the mast was a sizeable horn button which, in turn, was wired to a big old style car horn bolted to the engine room cabin house, where the wheelsman could hear the signals above the heavy rumble of the engine exhaust. One long toot conveyed "steer to starboard", a short toot indicated "steady as you go". Two short toots meant "steer to port", followed by the usual short toot for "steady". These signals served to direct the vessel toward the swordfish seen from aloft. Sometimes the fish would be finning a mile away, or an underwater fish could very well be within a few hundred yards in any direction. When horn signals ceased, the wheelsman watched Captain Bob, the harpooner, who, standing in the pulpit out on the bowsprit, would point the harpoon pole in the direction to steer the schooner. Once the pole was thrown, the wheel was rolled hard-a-starboard, in order to keep the buoy-line away from the propeller.

"Old Glory" out of Gloucester.

George, the cook, would be on deck during this action, where he would watch the buoy-line uncoil at high speed until it was time to pick up the keg buoy and fling it over the side. One of the crew came down on deck where, with the vessel moving slowly in a starboard circle, he would bring the dory we had been towing alongside and jump into it. Then we would tow him along until he could grab the keg, which was boiling along toward deeper water. Then we were underway again to circle the dory at a distance. Usually there would be a chance to "iron" other fish in the general vicinity. However, on this trip the first swordfish came by surprise . . . underwater and directly ahead.

Crew members of the "hazel M. Jackson. (Athearn in round hat

The crew aloft overlooked it; Captain Bob saw the fish first and barely had time to harpoon the streamlined creature at a depth of several feet! By mid-afternoon, we had four fish on deck. A good start on the trip. While we were "jogging" during the night, we maintained a watch on deck. Each of us, including the Captain and cook, stood a one-hour watch on the lookout for other craft of the fishing fleet. However, big ships (we called them steamers) were our main concern. It was mostly our problem to keep out of their way. Big ships generally stay on course.

Usually there was a light breeze during the night. With the steering wheel tied, the schooner was on a port tack until midnight, then on a starboard tack until dawn. The man on watch had to keep a sharp lookout for other vessels in the fleet, especially those that had anchored.

The close-hauled fores'l served as a wind scoop and a source of ventilation for the crew's quarters below. Getting up on deck for an hour's watch, a crew member would gradually realize that the impressive breeze came from the sail and not from a change in weather conditions. However, there were nights when we had a flat calm. The fores'l became noisy with the slatting motion of the gaff, and had to be lowered in order for the men below to snooze undisturbed. A moderate breeze made the vessel behave as she should and kept us comfortable.

The following three days were unfavorable for us. A moderate northeast breeze brought with it fog and showers. We sailed around with a few of the crew standing in the lower rigging or on the lantern boards. Only two underwater fish were brought aboard during that period. Easterly weather is a problem in this activity, since marine life stays well below the surface during it.

Two small schooners, the *ALVA* and the *BETHLEHEM,* Portuguese craft hailing from New Bedford, cruised in our vicinity.

After ten days of swordfishing, we were about 75 miles East of Montauk, Long Island. We had 35 fish iced in the hold. Captain Bob decided that it was time to be on our way to market. The first trip of swordfish to arrive at the Boston Fish Pier could expect to receive the best price per pound for the season. We had a strong southwest wind in our favor all the way to the Vineyard Lightship and the Cape Cod Canal.

The following morning, the fish were unloaded. In the course of the day, we loaded ice and refilled the fuel tanks. Next day we returned to our Edgartown homeport. The crew's share for that first trip was 185 dollars per man, considerable money in those days! Three days later, after loading a fresh supply of groceries, we sailed on the second trip. This time to the southeast part of Georges Bank.

The Gloucester fleet was there ahead of us, big vessels with sharp crews and lofty topmasts that reached up into the sky. Names like *AMERICAN, OLIVIA BROWN, ALPAR, OLD GLORY,* and *MILDRED SILVIA* come to mind.

Here is an overlooked ancient news item dated August 27, 1924 that hints at the full story of that trip:

"The new schooner *HAZEL M. JACKSON* was among the swordfishing vessels that was caught offshore in the recent hurricane. Fortunately, Captain Bob Jackson had navigated his schooner into deeper water after leaving Georges Bank.

The full fury of the storm came out of the northwest. Sails had been securely furled, hatches and gangways made water tight.

Captain Jackson and his seven-man crew had lashed themselves to the main boom by straddling the gaff and the furled mainsail.

Huge breaking waves swept over the vessel as she scudded to leeward under `bare poles'. Swordfish kegs and buoy lines went overboard. When the storm subsided, they were able to get under way and jog slowly to windward. There was no serious damage.

Next day, the *HAZEL M. JACKSON* arrived at her home-port in Edgartown, where a crowd of townspeople were waiting on the steamboat wharf to celebrate their safe return.

The Vineyard fishing fleet was accounted for and all were safely in port."

Thirty years later, almost to the day, the 90 foot schooner *MARJORIE PARKER*, owned by the writer, was demolished by Hurricane "CAROL" at Union Wharf, Fairhaven, Massachusetts on August 31, 1954. The vessel had just been overhauled and refitted for a special offshore charter project.

There was a stranger among the fleet. A new vessel with the name *SKILLIGOLEE.* She had two huge tall masts of equal height. No topmast. The forward mast was so high that a topmast was not necessary. There were no hoops, but instead, a pair of comfortable wicker chairs, complete with footrests, was bolted to the spreaders, one on each side of the mast. The two mastheaders, secured by safety belts, relaxed while they gazed out over their ocean perimeter on lookout for the elusive swordfish.

It was flat calm with a southeast groundswell. Late in the afternoon, we stopped the engine and laid to with the new schooner nearby. Captain Bob pulled our dory in alongside and said to me, "Come on, let's go aboard there." I jumped in with him, grabbed the oars and rowed a few hundred yards over to the newcomer. We were greeted by Captain Jimmy Abbott. He took our bowline and said, "Come aboard!"

Jimmy, a veteran skipper of Gloucester fishing schooners, had known Bob Jackson for years. He introduced us to the owner, whose name was Quincy Adams Shaw. The *SKILLIGOLEE,* a Gloucester design, recently built at the Story shipyard in Essex, was a seagoing yacht. Crews quarters forward, Owner and guest accommodations amidship (the space normally known as the fish hold), a fancy engine room aft and a small cabin for the engineer. The big Atlas Imperial diesel engine was especially impressive.

We soon learned that the owner, Mr. Shaw,had a taste for spirits and was seldom sober. He insisted on serving as harpooner and would ride around on the bowsprit pulpit for hours while sipping on a bottle of Scotch. One of the crew quietly told us that as "striker" (harpooner) Shaw "couldn't hit a bull on the ass with a bass fiddle!" He went on to say that during a recent rough day, while steaming to windward, the vessel plunged into a big wave, whereby Shaw was washed out of the pulpit, disappearing under the schooner, only to pop up in the wake astern a few minutes later. The man at the wheel had quickly cast the dory adrift. Shaw was able to swim over and hold onto the dory gunwale until they picked him up. He was hauled aboard unhurt, luckily, no propeller gashes and in a more sober condition! An hour later, Shaw was back out on the bowsprit, ready for more adventures, we were told.

A week later the *SKILLIGOLEE* was homeward bound toward Gloucester. They had twelve swordfish aboard, which were iced in insulated boxes on deck. A day or two before that, during a brief spell of clear weather, we had seen those two very tall masts on the distant horizon.

We encountered a southeast storm one night while we jogged on the offshore side of Georges Bank. Sometime before daylight, we had to put a reef in the fore'sl. At dawn, while we sailed on a starboard tack, the crew member on watch shouted down the gangway, "Get on deck quick — a big ship is coming right at us!" We scrambled up there, half dressed, getting soaked by the driving rain and flying salt spray. The 40-knot "breeze" had kicked up a rough breaking sea. The huge ship, now within a half mile, seemed intent on running us down. All our decklights were turned on. The engineer was trying to start the engine, but there wasn't time. The ship was nearly upon us! Our sails saved us. As we jogged to windward, the colossal passenger ship crossed our wake, probably within a hundred yards! No one appeared on the wing of the bridge or anywhere on deck. Rivets on the black steel hull were plainly visible. Our dory, on a long tether astern, disappeared on the other side of the ship. The bow wave came toward us in the form of a rushing mountainous breaker. The skipper yelled, "Get up in the riggin!" The ship, going at more than twenty knots, passed by in a welter of foam, but we had a glance at the stern where we read the name COLUMBUS, and under that, in smaller white letters, the homeport, *BREMEN*. A. German ship evidently.

Then the boiling bow wave caught up with us and tumbled in on deck. The great volume and velocity of so much water swept all the way forward, taking every unsecured thing with it, most of which went overboard. We were lucky. No serious damage. Mostly a bad scare. The storm soon went by. The weather cleared as sea conditions improved. In the course of the day we got underway and diligently gathered up the things that had gone overboard . . . oars, kegs, pen boards, etc. By good fortune we found the missing dory, half sunk and damaged but still useable.

Many years later, in the early stages of World War II, there was a newspaper report that the German liner *COLUMBUS* had departed the safety of a South American port with the hope of reaching Germany. Somewhere in mid-ocean they were intercepted by a British battleship, and the magnificent *COLUMBUS* was torpedoed and sunk. Such is the futility of war.

Now, to resume the swordfishing story, we had several other close calls. During periods of thick fog, especially at night, the foghorns of approaching ships would be answered by our old style Lothrop portable horn that was activated by pumping a handle vigorously. The man on watch would generate a long blast from our wheezy air-horn. Those of us in our bunks below could hear the steady swish-swish-swish of a slow turning propeller as the ship drew closer. The interval of the horn blasts became more frequent, collision seemed imminent. By this time our anxiety was great, until the horn and propeller sounds began to diminish while we felt the effect of the passing ship's wake. We seldom saw a ship in clear weather.

We had the luxury of a crate of oranges that was lashed to the focs'tle gangway shelter. While on deck watch at night we looked forward to the special treat of peeling and eating an orange. They lasted for about ten days, the average trip two weeks. However, our fourth trip stretched to three weeks. We managed on slim rations, finally resorting to swordfish steaks for supper. Incidentally, the meal schedule was breakfast 6 A.M., dinner at 11 A.M. and supper at 4 P.M. Most of us needed a "mug-up" or maybe a sandwich by 8 or 9 P.M. After supper, the cook would shake down the coal fire in order to allow the stove to cool off, which made for more tolerable sleeping conditions at night.

At 6 A.M. the cook would shout, "On the table, boys!" We tumbled out of the bunks to sit on the lockers and gaze at a huge platter of fried eggs, bacon and ham. Also, a pan of biscuits and a big pot of coffee. When the weather was rough, a damp blanket was spread over the table to keep the crockery in place. The coffee pot was then kept safely on the stove and cups were refilled from there.

By mid-day we resumed fishing in calm weather with a confused lumpy swell. With five men aloft, the *JACKSON* was very lively. Sea water sloshed in through the scuppers with every long roll. In fact, when underway, deeply laden with a hold full of ice, the main deck was continually wet. By this time, on the third trip of the season, green moss had formed on the deck, a slippery dangerous condition. Finally we resorted to coal ashes from the galley stove and scrubbing brushes to reduce that hazard.

Now about that other hazard (mentioned before) that was sometimes a problem for the man at the wheel. To be blunt about it, there was, on unpredictable occasions, a shower of puke or tobacco juice, but the most frequent annoyance was piddle! Seasickness from the masthead occurred mostly during the first two or three days of the voyage. Tobacco juice was a more constant menace because wind and dampness prevented customary smoking! But the piddle problem was something else! The five mastheaders, high above the deck could, each one in turn, at fairly frequent unpredictable intervals, produce an alarming quantity of chemical spray! Consequently, it was necessary for the man at the wheel to be dressed for wet weather on sunny days, too!

An experienced mastheader, although dressed in woolen clothes and waterproof "oilers" would try to be artistic about it. The first essential was to be positioned so as to piddle to leeward. Done properly, hardly a drop would spatter the sails or land on deck. With the cooperation of the top mastheader, a signal would be sent to the wheelsman who would promptly put the vessel on a tack that would allow the piddler a clear shot to leeward. An expert could form a series of figure eights and sometimes, in bright sunshine, create miniature rainbows. One or two crew members seemed psychologically unable to perform from that altitude while clinging to the swaying mast. They would have to come down on deck. Usually, that provided time to go below for another cup of coffee, etc.

The skipper, perched in the bowsprit pulpit, tried to ignore those maneuvers as a necessary nuisance. However, during one of those brief impromptu side trips, we came upon a series of underwater swordfish, of which we captured four. A profitable detour!

Early in September, on the fifth and last cruise of the summer, we went directly to the northern edge of Georges Bank. The skipper wanted a sounding frequently after we arrived there. The object was to locate a deep gully between Georges and Browns Bank to the north. Finally, after a series of soundings that resulted in "No bottom!" It was a relief to quit hauling that lead out of a hundred fathoms of water. A tiresome job! (A sounding lead had a hollow bottom that was filled with hard grease which would collect a sample of the bottom material for examination and to also provide information about our location on the navigation charts).

The top mastheader, Billy O'Neil, volunteered to swap jobs for a few days. It was quite an experience. It was fun to push the horn button, then watch the vessel quickly change course. On clear days, we generally managed to hoist several fish aboard, all big ones, too. Sometimes we had all four of our dorys in action at once. When the doryman had his fish secured to the dory gunwale, he would up-end an oar, a signal to come and pick him up. After a day as masthead-er, especially in rough weather, coming down on deck provided a great contrast, since the deck seemed nearly stationary. Hardly any motion!

At the end of the day, after supper, while there was daylight, the whole crew was busy cleaning the day's catch. The fish were allowed to stay on deck all night to "harden up". Next morning, after breakfast, two or three of us worked in the hold digging holes with a chipper down into the block ice in order to place each fish carefully. Heavy, sweaty exercise!

Then, one evening, the radio news broadcast mentioned that a hurricane was brewing somewhere east of Cape Hatteras. We got underway immediately. Captain Bob said, "Let her go nor'west — we'll fetch *AMERICA* somewhere!"

ASTERIAS entering Woods Hole Harbor.

With 78 fish in the hold, it was time to be on the way to market.

The fishing schooner era provided us "old timers" with many marvelous memories.

✶

In reference to the Edgartown fishing schooner *HAZEL M. JACKSON*: the owner, Capt. Bob Jackson, experienced a sudden flash fire in the Fo'c'sle (forward living quarters) during the annual cleaning and painting a few years previous to my being a crew member.

Paint remover fumes somehow ignited, causing an inferno. Capt. Bob and other workers managed to escape up the gangway to the deck. The men all had serious burns, but Capt. Bob, the last one to reach the deck was badly scorched over his face and neck. After a long healing process his face was permanently scarred and his eyes were bloodshot, but fortunately, his vision was unaffected. The Fire Department quickly extinguished the blaze while Dr. Nevin treated the men's burns and rushed them to the Vineyard Hospital for complete care.

Chapter 35

R/V Asterias

Early in 1939 Ed Athearn, a Martha's Vineyard native, was busy during the winter months operating his fishing dragger *ELMARDO* as a ferry service between Vineyard Haven and Woods Hole. Steamer service, for economy reasons, had been reduced to one vessel and one round trip daily between New Bedford and the Islands. Winter storms or dense fog would keep the ferry steamer in port, usually at Nantucket. At such times, the *ELMARDO* was in great demand.

Capacity loads of passengers, baggage, and food supplies were safely transported. Many emergency trips were made for medical specialists required by the Vineyard hospital, generally at night.

Among notable people who utilized this service were Stephen C. Luce, influential Island banker and Columbus O. Iselin, director and cofounder of the Woods Hole Oceanographic Institution. Mr. Iselin was a daily commuter. The genial director, impressed with Athearn's abilities, offered him a job as Captain with W.H.O.I. World War was brewing. The Navy was in the process of taking over W.H.O.I. in order to supplement its limited knowledge of oceanography.

A short time later, the U.S.A. declared war on Germany. The Oceanographic Research vessel *ATLANTIS,* the world's largest ketch-rigged sailing craft, was cruising in the Caribbean. The world-famous ship would present an easy target for an enemy submarine. Therefore, she was ordered into Mobile, Alabama where she was mothballed for the duration.

Meanwhile, a quaint 73 foot double-ender, the *ANTON DOHRN*, had been delivered to W.H.O.I. by the marine biology division of the Carnegie Institution.

A separate story could be written about this strange craft and her eventual wartime activities. A decision was made to proceed with rejuvenating the *DOHRN* — a complete repowering and reconditioning project on the chance that the vessel would be made ready for wartime sea duty.

There was urgency to get the Navy work started. The *DOHRN* would not be available for a long time.

We had only one boat ready and able to begin the Navy program — the 42 foot utility boat *ASTERIAS,* a husky little vessel built for W.H.O.I. in 1931 by Major Casey at his Fairhaven, Massachusetts shipyard (at about the same time that *ATLANTIS* was enroute from the Copenhagen shipyard where she was built). *ASTERIAS* was intended for inshore biological work. She is similar to commercial fishing boats of that era . . . very substantially built of white oak and Southern hard pine. Fastenings were galvanized iron wedge-shaped hatch nails known as "button head spikes". Keel bolts and drift rods are 3/4" galvanized iron — very durable. The engine, at that time, was as a slow-turning heavy-duty gasoline masterpiece.

ASTERIAS was promptly pressed into service with Athearn as skipper. Orders were to rendezvous with a Navy ship at a position in the Gulf Stream some 200 miles ESE of Montauk, New York. As it was midsummer, the weather was mostly ideal except for a huge swell created by a hurricane that went by far to the East. Several barrels of reserve gasoline were secured on deck. At required intervals, gasoline was siphoned into the main tanks.

Rather than broadcast secret activities, *ASTERIAS* converged with the Navy ship late in the working day. At this time the scientific personnel carried on a shouting conversation concerning their cooperative venture. During this operation, *ASTERIAS* would be eased in close enough to receive rations, pots of beef stew and such that were extended in a long-handled dip net. It was a tricky maneuver, nicely done — a daily adventure.

Over a ten-day period, the vessels drifted steadily northeast on the deep blue waters of the Gulf Stream. Underwater acoustics were the expedition's purpose. A supply of prepackaged explosives was made ready for use. In the course of the day, a series of "shots" were lowered and fired at variable depths. Sonic equipment on the distant Navy ship recorded the pattern of small explosions. Water temperatures were continually recorded at all depths.

The expedition was trying to determine the location of "cold layers" of water under which

German submarines were known to hide. The enemy was aware that U.S. Navy sonar signals would deflect from a cold plateau in the deep ocean. It was time to perfect a new sonar system which the escort Navy ship was in the process of testing. Convoy Destroyer Escorts, DES, would henceforth be modernized with the best sonar search equipment available at that time. Convoys of troop and supply ships would soon be directed toward European ports.

ASTERIAS continued to carry out a variety of technical projects. One job was to study wave action along the south shore of Martha's Vineyard. The height and frequency of breaking waves was recorded during changeable weather conditions. — information that was needed for future military beach landings.

Another adventurous directive was to proceed seaward in prevailing winter gales. Various types of oils were pumped overboard to test the soothing effect upon the angry, breaking waves. Peanut oil proved to be the most effective. The sharp seas became big swells under a layer of congealed peanut oil. Acres of it later washed ashore; gulls and other seabirds had a banquet! But the Navy had found a way to calm the troubled waters.

It was during these rough water projects that Athearn became very much aware of the seagoing qualities inherent with *ASTERIAS.* In the wildest sea conditions, she rode like a duck, with an easy comfortable behavior — a special advantage for the men who worked on deck. Whether going to windward or at any angle to wave conditions, she handled with ease. A riding sail did not seem necessary — *ASTERIAS,* a rare combination of excellent design and construction . . . the natural seaboat!

When the 73 foot *ANTON DOHRN* was finally ready for sea duty, Athearn made the transfer to the rehabilitated double-ender with considerable reluctance. However, between wartime cruises, which were sometimes of several weeks duration, it was always a special pleasure to commute to Vineyard Haven with other Island crew members in the ever reliable *ASTERIAS.*

When the war ended, she continued to do whatever oceanographic work that was required. Each skipper took good care of her. A G.M. diesel replaced the original gas engine. A flying bridge atop the wheelhouse was a modern feature. A new, larger combination wheelhouse and deck lab had been built before the era of the flying bridge control station. These improvements were a distinct advantage to the scientific personnel and the boat crew.

Captain Dick Colburn kept *ASTERIAS* active and in yacht-like condition until she was replaced in 1980 by the new somewhat larger fiberglass version. Modern progress.

W.H.O.I. offered *ASTERIAS* for sale on a sealed bid procedure. Athearn was among the bidders, but Ocean Research (O.R.E.) at Falmouth won the contest. She was operated out of MacDougal's boatyard, testing instruments (with a minimum of maintenance) through 1985. At that time O.R.E. was sold to another company, which came along with their own futuristic version of a boat.

With all useable equipment removed, *ASTERIAS* was hauled out and stored. After six months of sitting on blocks, the veteran seaboat had taken on a rather weatherbeaten appearance. There was a common attitude that the boat had served her time. She was too much of a contrast to the shiny new playthings surrounding her. The yard management pondered her future.

By chance, Athearn wandered into the yard one day. To come upon his favorite boat in such deplorable circumstances was a complete surprise. It was time for action. At the nearby O.R.E. office, Bill Eagan was encouraging. Ownership of the *ASTERIAS* had been transferred to MacDougal's boatyard. He would check with them regarding the status of the boat. The answer came by phone the following day — *ASTERIAS* was available! The next step was to negotiate with Fred Metel, yard manager, to have his crew prepare the classic vessel for launching.

David Lewis, a resident of Osterville and a former shipmate, agreed to join the project as a working partner. He proved to be invaluable. The boatyard crew became too busy to give the *ASTERIAS* their attention. With management permission, Dave Lewis did practically all the work on the hull exterior — power sanding, caulking and painting. Plenty of sweaty, tiring work.

The target date for launching was June 30. At 5:00 p.m. on that date, the R/V *ASTERIAS* was picked by the Travel-Lift crew and set afloat in Falmouth Harbor! Athearn celebrated her prospective new career by splashing a cup of coffee over her stem as a christening gesture!

Rays of late afternoon sunlight glistened on the new two-tone gray and blue paint along her topsides. Free of the suspending straps, she was moved and secured at a nearby pier. There were a few trickly leaks coming mostly from dried-out seams under the oak ice sheathing.

By good fortune and the yard manager's tolerance, the boat was allowed to sit quietly at the pier for several days. Thereby, she resumed her natural posture while the leaks slowly tightened. During that interlude, the complex wiring system was studied. The batteries proved to be in excellent condition. The long-idled diesel engine, to their amazement, started instantly and functioned smoothly!

Dave Lewis and some friends delivered the *ASTERIAS* to her new mooring in Cotuit. It was a beautiful bright July day with a strong tide in their favor. Since that time, the two partners have made every effort to get *ASTERIAS* in a state of first-class operating condition. The summer weekends were reserved for family "yachting" in a character boat that cruised leisurely along with scores of expensive cocktail craft. The partners agree that they have a sense of special satisfaction to be on board one of the most experienced seagoing vessels of her size in existence!

During winter months of the future they expect to proceed with whatever repairs or refastening seem necessary — all part of the worthwhile project of a complete restoration. The quality and strength of construction in *ASTERIAS* could very well keep her profitably active for several more decades. She is considered to be adaptable for a variety of practical uses.

There is every reason to believe she will have a pleasant and successful future!

Chapter 36

The Treacherous Hurricane of September 21st, 1938!

One morning in the month of May, 1938, a new power boat arrived in Vineyard Haven harbor, delivered by a two-man crew from a shipyard in Boothbay, Maine. I learned that much by rowing out while the boat was being secured to a mooring. Being inquisitive, I inquired; further conversation with the crew revealed that the 46 foot power yacht *QUAMPACHE* had been designed by William H. Hand and built to the specifications of Mr. Howard S. Hart. Mr. Hart, the patriarch of the Harthaven colony in Oak Bluffs, had recently married Helen Howland of Vineyard Haven and changed his homeport.

Before I rowed the Maine boys ashore, they invited me to go on board and inspect the layout of the boat. The pilot house was forward and the spacious engine room was under a trunk cabin directly aft. The boat was powered with a big, shiny, six-cylinder Hall-Scott gasoline engine which I was told would propel the boat at twelve knots. The fo'c'sle living quarters were comfortably complete. Shipmate stove, storage lockers, four built-in bunks and proper bathroom facilities. Outside, teak decks and brass hardware were typical yacht-like features.

When I put the Maine boys ashore, they advised me to contact Mr. Hart right away in regard to a job as skipper of the *QUAMPACHE.* In about an hour, with the cooperation and influence of Captain Ralph M. Packer, I was introduced to Mr. and Mrs. Hart and was promptly hired to maintain and captain their new boat. It was such a marvelous opportunity and I was so pleased to get such a perfect job at the time that I still can not recollect what wages were involved.

During the course of the summer, we made many day cruises to Menemsha, Cuttyhunk and Tarpaulin Cove, for beach parties. Once or twice a week we made a trip to Woods Hole to pick up family members or friends who had arrived there by train. Usually those ferry trips coincided with periods of thick fog in Vineyard Sound.

While at breakfast on the morning of September 21st, 1938, my Atwater-Kent radio was, as usual, tuned to a Boston news and weather station. The weather forecaster suggested that the Cape Cod area would probably experience an increasing northeast wind during the day.

A short time later, I was at the Park Beach and out aboard the *QUAMPACHE.* The harbor was perfectly calm, but the sky was overcast and bunches of dark fleecy clouds at a lower level drifted slowly from an easterly direction. There was something strange about the atmosphere.

Before doing the usual morning chores, I decided to get out an anchor to windward. A mooring has its limitations in rough northeast weather conditions. With about 50 fathoms of anchor line (one-inch Manilla) shackled to a hundred-pound kedge anchor, all neatly arranged in the bottom of the skiff, I rowed toward the northeast and with all the rope uncoiled, dumped the big clumsy anchor over the side. I felt a sense of satisfaction.

Along about at 11 that morning I rowed ashore and went home to have an early lunch. Then a light southeast breeze had kicked up and I could feel a few sprinkles of rain.

An hour or so later, the wind had swelled into a southeast gale. Before going back to Owens Park, I rode out to West Chop to see if any boats were in sight. It was a wild scene. A small double-ended power boat just in from a fishing trip on nearby Middleground shoal was bouncing to windward in showers of spray behind the bell-buoy, waging a losing battle against the wind and steep waves. As the boat turned quickly and came in close to the West Chop shore, I recognized George Dolby at the tiller. I thought he would anchor in the lee, but he kept heading westward. Then I realized that he was intent on reaching Lambert's Cove.

On the way back to Owens Park, I came upon a series of fallen branches that I had to drag out of the way if I were to reach Main Street. By the time I made it to Owens Park, the pier was nearly submerged and the tide was flowing over the beach area. I parked my Model A Ford in the Havenside driveway near the top of the hill. It was a struggle to get to the shore against the howling wind. My skiff was one of many floating amidst the beach grass.

The *QUAMPACHE* was moored only about 300 yards from the shore. I pushed the skiff beyond the surf, leaped in, grabbed the oars and rowed like mad. Between heavy gusts of wind, I made some headway, probably getting within a hundred feet of my goal at times. But each time, a roaring blast of wet wind forced the boat back. The oars lifted out of the rowlocks, flapping in the air until I could work them back into the rowlocks. After several attempts to control the problem, I said to hell with it and allowed the skiff to quickly drift stern-first up over the sand dunes to the hillside of the shoreline. Determined to get on board the *QUAMPACHE*, I hiked alongshore against wind and tide until I came upon a rowboat with oars tucked under the seats. In a matter of minutes rowing downwind, I arrived alongside the *QUAMPACHE*, stowed the oars and made a flying leap over the rail with the bowline in hand, which I rapidly secured to a stern cleat.

I managed to open the starboard pilothouse door. A glance out over the breakwater revealed the monstrous ferry steamer *NAUSHON,* approaching inbound from Nantucket. I couldn't believe it. The wharf was underwater except for the tops of a few pilings. However, Captain Sandsbury, who in normal weather would have docked at Oak Bluffs, demonstrated his great skill in maneuvering the *NAUSHON* across the end of the wharf. Despite his effort, the big ferry had to move out of there. Pilings cracked and hawsers parted. The powerful twin-screw steamer worked astern around the corner of the wharf until she pointed directly into the hurricane-force wind. The *NAUSHON* moved ahead slowly until Sandsbury gave the order to drop both anchors, just about where Zeb Tilton usually anchored his schooner *ALICE S. WENTWORTH*, by good fortune happened to be in the lee of a coalyard pier in New Bedford harbor where Capt. Zeb and his crew had secured the vessel with docklines tied to loaded railway coal cars and caplog bollards where they safely survived the raging storm. Otherwise the New Bedford and Fairhaven waterfronts were in shambles. (Nowadays the *SHENANDOAH* is moored there.)

The *NAUSHON* drifted rapidly to leeward, nearly sideways, until she was suddenly fetched up by her anchors about two hundred yards to windward. For a few minutes the *NAUSHON* had threatened to wipe out most of the fleet of small craft at moorings behind the breakwater — those that had not yet been blown ashore. I started the *QUAMPACHE*'s engine and stood on the bow with a sharp knife ready to cut loose from the mooring rope and anchor line. Fortunately, it was not necessary.

The intense wind soon diminished as it hauled around to a southwesterly direction. At the same time, the storm tide gradually lowered to a normal level. Eventually we learned about the terrible devastation the unpredicted hurricane had caused along the Eastern Seaboard.

Martha's Vineyard and Nantucket happened to be on the northeast fringes of the hurricane. Menemsha and Edgartown harbors suffered the greatest damage from wind and water. Incidentally, George Dolby finally arrived in Menemsha, saved, he said, by water flowing into his live well instead of sinking his able double-ender.

The two local vessels, the B & E and the 3 & 1 & 1, both schooner-rigged scallop-draggers, arrived at Vineyard Haven as the hurricane ended after a 24-hour run from Georges Bank. Both skippers — John Salvador and Louis Sears — reported having had good weather until they reached Great Point at Nantucket and entered Nantucket Sound. From there, they were buffeted by a strong south-to-southwest wind, the retreating tail-end of that unbelievably disastrous hurricane.

The *New Bedford Standard* and other mainland newspapers soon provided front-page news and pictures of the huge catastrophe. Everett S. Allen, a neighbor, began his career as a journalist on that fateful day of the '38 hurricane, his first assignment covering the New Bedford waterfront. After serving for many years as editor of the same newspaper, he became the author of several unusually good books, one of which *The Wind That Shook the World,* most graphically describes the widespread events resulting from that utterly devastating hurricane.

Chapter 37

The ELMARDO boat service. The winter of 1938 and 1939

The yachting season ended by mid-October. The *QUAMPACHE* was put into winter storage at Mr. Hart's Oak Bluffs boat basin.

Rather than return to commercial fishing, I thought about starting a passenger service between Vineyard Haven and Woods Hole. At that time, the New Haven Railroad owned the island ferry steamers. My idea came from a Vineyard newspaper report that revealed for reasons of economy, only one steamer would be kept in operation during the coming winter. Home base would be Vineyard Haven. The steamer *NOBSKA* would leave there every day at six AM, stop at Woods Hole and New Bedford, return to Woods Hole and then head over to Oak Bluffs prior to the long run to Nantucket. Such limited service plus weather problems presented an opportunity for supplementary service between the Vineyard and the mainland.

Winter time passenger service between Vineyard Haven and Woods Hole required a seaworthy boat in excellent condition. Those qualifications brought to mind a 38 foot seagoing boat by the name of *ELMARDO.* The owner, Winslow "Coot" Hall operated the boat only during the summer months for offshore lobstering and swordfishing from the Island of Cuttyhunk. The *ELMARDO* was built by a Maine shipyard on the style of a western-type dragger, with the Pilot house forward. The Palmer engine, slow-turning at 350 R.P.M. with three separate cylinders, was as smooth, quiet and powerful as a steam engine. The boat was solidly built and always well-maintained: my version of the perfect boat for the transport project.

Captain Coot Hall was quite famous as a fishing guide. In his other boat, a MacKenzie bass boat, he was noted for his ability to prowl around the big boulders of "Sow and Pigs" ledge in darkness while trolling for those huge striped bass, a sportfisherman's ideal adventure.

Somehow, I managed to make a deal with Coot to acquire the *ELMARDO.* The boat was idle and moored for the winter. My experience in having operated the former Cuttyhunk boat *MILDRED* as an island freighter probably served as a reference for my boating capability.

As I remember, the agreement was that I would pay Captain Hall 50 percent of my weekly earnings after operating expenses were deducted until I would eventually own the boat at a price that would be satisfactory to both of us. The actual sale price is a blank in my memory.

After a verbal agreement and a handshake, I was promptly underway and had a nice cruise to Vineyard Haven where the *ELMARDO* was secured to the south side of Owens Park Pier, my headquarters for the new supplementary transport service between Vineyard Haven and Woods Hole.

A campaign of advertising for the proposed *ELMARDO* boat service began. Eye-catching newspaper ads and cardboard posters in prominent public places produced immediate attention.

The eight o'clock departure time appealed to island travelers who had a spare car stored in the Woods Hole Garage. Probably the most prominent passenger (in good weather) was Steven C. Luce, an island banker who was generally known by his middle name "Carey." He seemed to be intrigued by the idea of an independent island boat service despite his involvement with the steamboat ferry service. Toward the end of the winter season, he talked seriously about finding a much larger vessel for me to operate on a year-round basis.

Before starting the service, I had rigged a pipe-framed canvas dodger as protection between the pilot house and the starboard rigging. The boat was equipped with outside steering and controls. In cold weather, several passengers could squeeze into the pilot house, but when the windows were plastered with slushy ice, properly-dressed passengers usually stood outside and kept me company while we crossed Vineyard Sound.

Along with the required Coast Guard equipment, the *ELMARDO* carried a new 16-foot fisherman's dory (18 foot O.A.) secured in chocks on deck for potential use as a lifeboat. During some extremely rough passages that winter, with plenty of water on deck, the dory strained her lashings while afloat.

My steadiest passenger was Columbus O.D. Iselin, the genial director and co-founder of the Woods Hole Oceanographic Institution, whom I saw five days a week. He became a volunteer crew man and would take over the steering whenever I went below to check on conditions in the engine room.

On one of his commutes, he brought up the subject of potential employment at the Institute. He would need a skipper for the 40-foot Casey boat *ASTERIAS* in order to proceed with some inshore oceanography while the ketch *ATLANTIS* was being built by a shipyard in Copenhagen, Denmark. This opportunity became more attractive as I thought about it.

In the meantime the *ELMARDO* was being kept busy with two round-trips between Vineyard Haven and Woods Hole every day except during severe weather, when I'd head over in the morning and return in the late afternoon.

The *ELMARDO* was called upon for special trips on many occasions. People stranded at Woods Hole were often anxious to return home to the island. On quite a number of occasions, an emergency at Martha's Vineyard Hospital required an urgent trip to Woods Hole in order to transport a medical specialist, usually a surgeon, for an immediate operation. As a rule, those night trips were tough and miserable. I often wondered how the doctors managed to perform their skilled work after such an uncomfortable experience.

A newly married couple, Norman and Jane Downs Burt, had made a reservation for a night-time voyage to Woods Hole as a start on their planned mainland honeymoon. Jane and Norman proved to be quite adventurous. Their wedding took place during a typical northeast snow storm. Having returned from the mainland in that wild weather, I secured the *ELMARDO* with extra docklines and fenders with the notion that no one in his or her right mind would consider crossing Vineyard Sound that night. Still, I waited until the appointed hour of eight o'clock, believing that they would cancel their trip. At that moment, a car with bright headlights came down the hill and the two honeymooners arrived on the pier in the wind and swirling snow.

They jumped on board with their baggage. Janie shouted, "Let's go, Ed! It's a great night for a boat ride." Rather than disagree, I quickly decided to give them a demonstration. We cast off and were soon plunging to windward in the open harbor. I said to myself that fifteen or twenty minutes of such activity would be plenty and we would return to the pier. No such thing. Snuggled with Norman in the warmth of the pilot house, Jane yelled, "Keep going! It's wonderful!" The new husband was probably not so enthused!

Two factors were in our favor. Fortunately, the storm was howling from the east-northeast, which gave us somewhat of a lee along the East Chop shoreline. The other advantage was the west tide in our favor as we headed toward Woods Hole. The seas were easier to ride, especially with the three-cornered riding sail rigged between the *ELMARDO* mast and boom. The power of wind and tide, along with impressive following sea conditions, provided a quick passage toward the main channel at Woods Hole.

Nobska Light was a dim glow in the flying snow as the sound of the booming foghorn grew louder. Conditions improved as we entered the ship channel with a clanging bell buoy and a flashing lighted buoy for guidance. As I steered a due north compass course, the channel range lights gradually became visible. We were soon tied up at the Forbes' private pier, where the newlyweds hustled ashore. They had a car waiting for their honeymoon to be continued inland.

After a peaceful overnight stay at the Woods Hole private pier, I made an early start with the *ELMARDO* for a return to Vineyard Haven in order to resume the scheduled morning departure. The weather had cleared, the easterly storm was moderating, and another experience was completed.

By the way, one-way passenger fare was a dollar. The charge for a special trip was ten dollars in daylight and fifteen dollars at night.

Before ending this rambling series of memorable adventure, I must mention a particularly rough trip to Woods Hole in the *ELMARDO.* It came about on a bright and sunny but very cold Saturday in early February. A westerly gale was blowing full force, although in the lee of West Chop, Vineyard Haven Harbor was deceptively placid.

Three men, all ministers, came on board and spoke about a nice day for a boatride. No other passengers appeared. The religious gentlemen advised that they would be attending a church convention in Middleboro and that one of their brethren would be available with his car upon their arrival at Woods Hole.

A full moon ebb tide was boiling to the westward in opposition to the full scale westerly gale. I tried to explain that phenomenon to the ministers, but they couldn't believe it.

Until we went past the bell buoy off West Chop.

Vineyard Sound was a raging mass of wildly breaking seas that truly appeared to be unbelievable. The waves looked to be about ten feet high and maybe fifteen feet apart. It was a dreadful sight. I turned the boat around and yelled to the ministers that we would have to cancel the trip. Their reply: "Oh, no, we simply must get to Woods Hole for a most important meeting!"

"Okay," I said, "we'll try it. You fellows stay in the pilot house and keep the door closed." Before getting underway, I secured the hatch covers with locking iron bars.

An ordinary winter gale out of the northwest would be a normal condition. We would be in the lee of Naushon Island for a relatively comfortable cruise. But on this particular day it seemed that all the wind in the world was being funnelled into Vineyard Sound from the west with no lee anywhere. A very unusual situation.

Proceeding slowly, we entered a tide rip at the eastern end of the Middleground Shoal. A series of breaking waves, each with a deep gully between, nearly overwhelmed us. At times we were briefly submerged as water poured over the bow and filled the deck to the railcaps. The plate-glass pilot house windows fortunately stayed intact.

Gradually the *ELMARDO* worked her way to windward, leaping from one foaming breaker to another. Controlling the boat kept me busy, steering on a slant toward Tarpaulin Cove and frequently disengaging the propeller to prevent *ELMARDO* from diving out of sight. I nearly forgot about the ministers after they disappeared into the cabin below.

Finally, we reached a point where it was practical to make a turn to starboard and run to leeward in a northeasterly direction toward Woods Hole.

By the time we entered the harbor, I realized that we had spent three very active hours in getting across Vineyard Sound. A normal trip would average about an hour and fifteen minutes.

After securing the boat at Forbes Landing, I expected the ministers to appear. A look below revealed three very messy-looking men huddled together on the cabin floor in the clutches of extreme seasickness. A man waiting there to meet them helped me to haul them up on deck into the fresh cold air. Afterward, I was told that they suffered motion sickness in the car going to Middleboro. My next job was to clean the cabin, but I will avoid the details about that.

By departure time at four PM, the condition of Vineyard Sound had greatly improved. The cargo hold was filled with urgently-needed food supplies and a truckload of bundled newspapers. About a dozen passengers stood around on deck. The westerly gale had begun to moderate and the tide had turned and was flooding to the eastward. The return trip to Vineyard Haven, made in the record time of one hour, proved an enjoyable interlude for the skipper and his group of passengers. The day had provided remarkable contrast of events.

✶

Dr. Charles F. Lane was one of the most legendary of Vineyard characters, was the "up-island" doctor. He was in attendance when I was born.

Dr. Lane, a tall and skinny man, was noted for his outdoor costume of a long black coat and a tall hat (like Abraham Lincoln's). He combined his medical activities with the operation of the Island's first telephone service: for the benefit of his clientele, he said. Between visits to patients, he could be seen climbing a telephone pole in his black coat and tall hat to repair an electrical connection.

He lived in Vineyard Haven at the Mansion House and had an office on Main Street, near the post office, where he was available at certain hours. His telephone office was located in Cottage City, before it became Oak Bluffs, and was above the post office with an entrance from a place known as Arcade. Dr. Lane's pioneer telephone business was eventually sold to the New England Telephone Company. Service was soon expanded to all the Island towns.

During that part of his career, Dr. Lane became the owner of a large building on the corner of Main and Union Street with stores on the ground floor. The building continues to be known as "Lane's Block."

Dr. Lane was noted for his medical capabilities, his energy and his brevity of speech. He was an important part of Martha's Vineyard history.

Chapter 38

World War II Activities

The Research Vessel —***ANTON DOHRN***

As we entered Woods Hole harbor aboard our commuter boat *RISK,* we noticed a strange craft at the Woods Hole Oceanographic Institute wharf. On this bright summer morning, June 29, 1940, we were about due for a surprise. Columbus Iselin, our director, had mentioned that the Carnegie Institute vessel, *ANTON DOHRN,* was en route from Florida and due at any time.

As we drew closer, the *DOHRN* appeared to be a curious combination of features — a tired-looking, old double-ender with no sheer and a row of large, closely-spaced oval-shaped portholes along each side. A canvas canopy stretched tightly over a pipe framework, and covering the entire length of the quaint craft. The steering station, located amid-ships, consisted of an elevated wooden grating, an antique binnacle and a large, elaborate wooden steering wheel with engine pedestal-type controls, one on each side of the platform (the original center console!)

The layout was unique: crew's quarters forward, engine room amidships, main cabin with galley aft, hinged skylights over each section and no spars. The Carnegie people were finished with the *DOHRN* and now it was a matter of an official decision being made regarding its adaptability for future use.

There we were, studying this weird craft, which for several decades had served as a platform for towing fine mesh plankton nets around the Florida Keys, not a promising prospect for conversion to North Atlantic oceanography. It soon became known, however, that W.H.O.I. officials had already made the decision to try to utilize their gift. A contract was drawn up with the MacDougal Boatyard at nearby Falmouth Harbor to proceed with an extensive refurbishing project. We, the potential crew, were rightly dubious about it.

Data obtain from W.H.O..I. archives relating to the *DOHRN* is as follows:

Built in Miami, Florida, 1911
Dimensions: 78' x 16'8" x 6'
Planking: 2" hard pine
Keel and Keelson: hard pine
Frames: 5" x 6" Madeira 8" apart
Floor timbers, clamps and shelves: hard pine
Hull fastenings: 3/8" x 6" square bronze nails (spikes)

Decking, covering boards and rail caps: all hard pine - three watertight compartments
Two Globe gasoline engines (original) direct drive at 350 RPM
Fuel, 1300 gals; Water, 1200 gals.
Copper, tin-lined tanks

Included in the data copies was a long list of outmoded general equipment

Eventually we were advised that the renovation of R/V *ANTON DOHRN* was complete. The next day we departed the MacDougal's boatyard amidst a background of loud horns and whistles. A great send-off!

Once outside Falmouth Harbor, we took advantage of a strong northeast wind to test the *DOHRN's* behavior. On Vineyard Sound a flood tide was bucking the wind, creating dangerously rough conditions. We steered at all angles to wind and sea and then stopped the engines, allowing the vessel to drift. Water gushed across the deck as the wallowing motion built up momentum. As the cook, recently hired, was stowing dishes in the galley, a boxful flew off the counter and landed with a crash on the floor. We could hear him swearing in at least two languages.

Underway again, we rounded Nobska Point, and soon eased the *DOHRN* into a predetermined berth at the western end of the W.H.O.I. pier. A crowd of shore employees came running out to greet us. We heard all sorts of remarks about the transformed appearance of the new *ANTON DOHRN*. In the midst of all this activity, the cook appeared on deck with his sea bag and the announcement that he had quit. He wasn't about to serve on a "vessel that would continually roll like a barrel!"

The *DOHRN* now appeared to be some sort of seagoing craft — a ketch rig with sizeable three-cornered riding sails on both masts. There was a spacious combination pilot house and deck lab aft with room to stow an eighteen-foot fisherman's dory in chocks on the stern. There was enough space under the dory, between the chocks, to coil a hundred fathoms of three-inch manila rope. That rope proved to be invaluable, an investment in safety at sea in the form of a drouge, or sea anchor.

Fleet in port: ATLANTIS, ANTON DOHRN, ASTERIAS, and RISK (commuter boat)

Ed Athearn and cook in dinghy somehere in the Atlantic. (Photo taken from ship)

"ANTON DOHRN" - "Hove to" in Gulf Stream waiting to rendezvous with Navy Ship. Photo from dinghy.

Ed Athearn, "ANTON DOHRN" skipper

Ensign Bauer taking noon sunsight with aircraft-type sextant.

"ANTHON DOHRN" diving into head sea

"ANTON DOHRN" entering New York Harbor January, 1943 with Manhattan ahead.

Ed Athearn & scientist McCrary in postside doorway aboard "ANTON DOHRN"

View of Oceanographic fleet in port - July 21, 1945. Photo taken from roof cupola by Val Worthington. (ANTON DOHRN behind small building, upper right.)

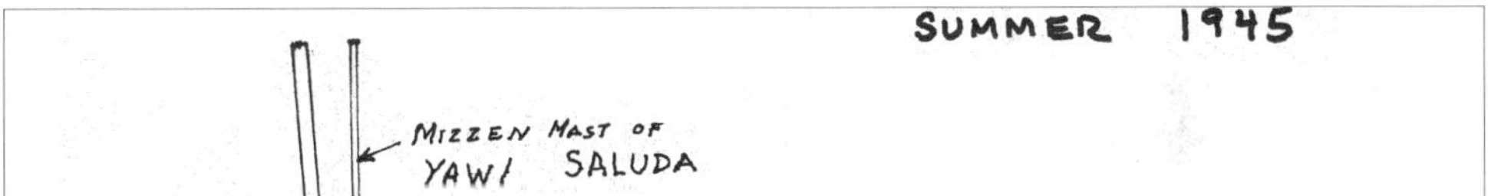

We encountered another kind of celebration upon arriving at our W.H.O.I. pier. Nearly everyone on the waterfront came along to inspect the new *ANTON DOHRN*! Technicians appeared with electronics to be installed: the radio-telephone, a deep-ranging depth recorder, oscillographs and a maze of other electrical equipment for the lab section of the deck house, the scientific nerve center. Radar and Loran were not yet available for small vessels. While the installation work was progressing for several days, Stanley Poole, the mate, and I were subjected to an intensive course of instruction in celestial navigation. On clear nights we practiced star sights with our aircraft-type sextants while standing on the nearby wharf. Later, at sea, we had to learn the knack of trying to get an accurate sight from the pitching and rolling deck of the ancient double-ender.

During that period of high-pressure activity, there came a temporary diversion. A Navy lieutenant, with W.H.O.I. cooperation, was testing smoke screen equipment for future beach landings. A special oil-fired furnace had been secured on the aft deck of a leased fishing boat. In order to try to create a dense, dark blanket of smoke, lamp black was being mixed with clean new SAE 30 lube oil. The results of burning that mixture were not satisfactory. I suggested a stunt I had seen rum-runners use while being pursued by Coast Guard patrol boats off Noman's Land. It was simply a matter of using a supply of dirty black drain oil which was piped into the fiery hot exhaust manifolds at high speeds. I offered to demonstrate the idea.

With a borrowed speedboat, we used a five-gallon can piped into the exhaust manifold with a shut-off valve. We filled the can with jet-black drain oil and proceeded to circle the harbor at full speed. There was a light southwest breeze as we roared around the demonstration area in front of W.H.O.I. With the engine temperature at peak, I opened the oil valve. What a sight! In ten minutes, we had generated a huge volume of unbelievably thick, black smoke! It rolled ashore and shut off visibility along the entire waterfront. Gulls and other seabirds, along with some nearby landbirds, were seen landing to avoid the dense, black atmosphere.

It seemed like the answer for the military. In the South Pacific, where smoke screen protection was required for beach landings, there was a fleet of high powered P.T. boats on patrol. They created a continuous supply of black drain oil and the big engines, like those of the early rum-runners, were ideally suited for laying heavy smoke instantly over wide areas. This evidently was considered too simple, too practical, too cost-effective for the Navy brass. They seemed unable to comprehend such elementary procedure.

Returning to her original assignment, the *DOHRN* was at long last considered ready for sea duty: scientific equipment installed and tested; short trial runs in Vineyard Sound completed; all necessary supplies taken on. Five Vineyarders made up the crew: Athearn, Skipper; Stanley Poole, Mate; Nelson Bryant, Engineer; John MacEachren, Cook; and Royal Daggett, Electrician and Radio Operator. Three scientists, graduates of Columbia University, completed our roster. Six of the crew would be required to maintain an alternate six and six watch while at sea. In other words, three men would be on duty for six hours to be relieved by three others for a similar period of duty: one man steering, one man on lookout for other vessels, the third man in charge of the complex electronics, frequent bathythermograph (BT) lowerings (down to 100 fathoms) and the continuous logging of water temperatures. That was to be the round-the-clock routine beginning with Cruise #2.

Recently, while searching my files for *DOHRN* information, I discovered a bundle of sailing orders, issued by Columbus Iselin, relating to 30 consecutive cruises. Cruise #1 (see attached letter dated June 17, 1941), involved the *ATLANTIS*. In the *ASTERIAS* story, I mentioned that the *ATLANTIS* was mothballed in Mobile, Alabama, early in the war program. That was incorrect. The first voyage in the *ANTON DOHRN* was made in company with the *ATLANTIS* and a chartered schooner by the name of *BLUE DOLPHIN*. Our instructions were to proceed eastward to latitude 39o30o and longitude 70o30o, where we would spend several days conducting underwater sound transmission tests. The Coast Guard *ARGO* was ordered to rendezvous with us with Dr. Maurice Ewing in charge of the expedition. It must have been several weeks after this initial combined cruise with the *ATLANTIS* in the Caribbean, and with German submarines closing in on the Eastern Seaboard, that the *ATLANTIS* was ordered into Mobile for the duration of World War II.

Cruise #1 proved to be satisfactory and successful. Fog inshore, but clear and calm east of the 100 fathom curve. In company with *ATLANTIS,* we returned to Woods Hole on schedule, mission accomplished.

The *DOHRN* went on with a continuous series of bathythermograph survey cruises. We operated between Cape Sable, Nova Scotia and Cape Hatteras, North Carolina. We zigzagged a pattern of lines on special hydrographic charts over depths ranging from fifty to a thousand fathoms. A BT lowering was made at twenty-minute intervals around the clock in all kinds of weather to make an accurate record of water temperatures. It was tiresome and hazardous. We had to maintain a steady eight knots in order to comply with orders from the Navy. Thick fog inshore and on Georges Bank all summer made the job most difficult. We were running blacked out, as were all other vessels subject to the rules of war. We had, no doubt, dozens of close calls.

Once, at dusk, a glint of sunshine appeared in the fog. Standing at the chart table, I happened to glance through the starboard window. The bow of a huge ship was headed on a collision course with us! I shouted, “FULL AHEAD!” to the man on wheel watch. The ship passed astern within a hundred yards!

On another foggy BT cruise we were working parallel courses with the destroyer *SEMMES.* That was Cruise #4, with Fritz Fuglister in charge of the scientific work. We maintained our relative positions by radio-telephone-coded conversation. Those hundreds of low visibility miles in the *DOHRN* were especially hard on the nerves, because of the loud roar of the twin-diesel dry exhausts directly forward of the pilot house. The bow lookout could barely hear whistle or foghorn signals from other craft. A real hit or miss situation! Those of us with bunks in the aft cabin would try to get an hour’s snooze while listening to the swishing rumble of the propellors and the variable whine of the shafts as they rotated in their water-cooled bearings. The rumble of the engines was constant and bearable, but the BT electric-driven winch created its own discordant music. From overhead, at regular intervals, came an orchestration of moans, groans and harassing squeals! All that distraction, however, gradually became routine for most of us. The water temperature recordings continued around the clock. We logged thousands of miles on that project during the first year of operation.

Following seventeen consecutive cruises, this seemingly endless BT project was almost completed by the latter part of November, 1941. After Cruise #12, a series of Navy Ensigns sailed with us, usually three new men on each cruise. These were young fellows fresh out of college with but three months of Navy indoctrination, known as “90-Day Wonders.” Many of them had never even seen the ocean before! They were required to act as crew members in order to learn basic seamanship, especially the art of taking constant bathythermograph recordings.

Fritz Fuglister of W.H.O.I. was the scientist in charge of most of the early BT cruises. Capt. Gilbert Oakley, our navigation teacher, made an occasional voyage with us. Dr. Maurice Ewing was usually the chief oceanographer, in charge of all the long-range offshore expeditions.

With reference to sailing orders numbers 18 to 30, I will record only the more notable features of the *ANTON DOHRN* wartime adventures.

Chapter 39

ANTON DOHRN Highlights

Cruise #18 - sailed December 13, 1941. Early in the month of December we began a new era of underwater photography with camera equipment developed by Doctors Maurice Ewing and Alan Vine. A new scientific crew came on board: Joseph L. Worzel in charge, along with Texans John Ewing (Doc Ewing's younger brother) and George Tirey.

Cruise #19 - sailed February 25, 1942. For the following weeks of winter weather, we had the privilege of learning underwater photographic techniques by operating in the bays and harbors of New England. At each camera station BT temperatures were recorded. It was a luxury to be in the lee of the land while winter storms roared past.

Cruise #20 - sailed March 6, 1942. After a stop at Mystic, Connecticut, to have some service work done on the diesel engines, we proceeded with instructions to conduct a photographic survey of Narraganset Bay and New London harbor and submarine base. The Navy Department wanted to know about water transparency conditions. At each designated station a twelve by twelve section of the harbor bottom was photographed by technicians Ewing and Tirey. Lambert Knight was in charge of BT recordings at each location. It was a daylight project dependent upon land ranges. The shoreline and background were on wartime blackout after dark. March winds whistled through the rigging!

Cruise #21 - sailed March 17, 1942. A continuation of the previous cruise: a survey of New Bedford harbor, then on to Portsmouth, New Hampshire, and finally to Casco Bay and Portland, Maine. Joe Worzel was the scientist in charge of this cruise, with the same crew as Cruise #20.

We learned that the Navy was concerned abut the possibility of German mines being planted in ship channels. They were particularly uneasy about the area near the Portsmouth Navy Yard and submarine base. We worked the river currents and side eddies, making hundreds of close-together bottom pictures. All sorts of clutter was seen but fortunately, not an enemy mine.

Upon returning to our Woods Hole base, we learned that the smooth-water winter interlude was ended. Cruise #22 would prove to be much more adventurous. Sailing orders from Director Iselin were in the form of two closely-spaced pages of detailed instructions for a particularly complex cruise. Operating headquarters would be at Norfolk, Virginia. Dr. C.S. Piggot of the Bureau of Ordnance, Washington, D.C. was to supervise our activities. Joe Worzel was once more in charge of the scientific work. We were to stop at New York and Cape May on our way south. Systematic BT recordings and transparency measurements were to be made, especially in harbor approaches. We were requested to survey Delaware Bay, including the ports of Baltimore, Wilmington and Philadelphia. Lambert Knight was in charge of the BT Program. We soon learned that these activities were part of gathering preliminary knowledge relating to the formations of convoys in protected areas, i.e. protection from enemy mines and submarines.

The sailing instructions, however, clearly revealed that our principal objective would be an intense survey (BT recording and transparency measurements) of the approaches to Chesapeake Bay followed by a similar investigation of the lower bay, particularly in the Norfolk and Hampton Roads area. We had heard rumors about an extensive minefield seaward of Chesapeake Bay.

On that clear sunny day, several miles away, we could see a lightship stationed at the Bay entrance. We had received no instructions about avoiding that danger. The lightship did not respond to our radio-phone call for advice. We had a secret I.D. code to use in special situations of that sort. With no response, we steamed merrily along at eight knots in a straight line toward the lightship. I went aloft and stood a lookout for anything underwater in our path that resembled a mine. It was a useless gesture on my part, for had we encountered a mine, we would have been instantly disintegrated!

When we arrived alongside the guardian lightship, the skipper and visible crew were all wiping their brows. We had made it across the mined territory by the greatest of good fortune. Evidently the *DOHRN,* being a small wooden vessel, was a neutral element for those hazardous magnetic mines. Before proceeding into port, we were provided with a special chart showing the zigzag channel we would henceforth have to learn to navigate with great care.

Our instructions were to proceed into the Norfolk Navy Yard where we were directed by the commandant of the 5th Naval District to tie up alongside one of the smaller aircraft carriers. A Jacob's ladder was lowered from the deck of the carrier so that we could get ashore and wander around the Section Base. The cook went directly to the commissary where he ordered a truckload of supplies. We wandered around the base, a sloppy-looking bunch of civilians amidst the neatly-uniformed Navy personnel. Each of us had a special I.D. card that allowed us the necessary freedom to roam in and out of American military areas anywhere.

Sometime after midnight, those of us asleep in the aft cabin were suddenly awakened by a loud torrent of water pouring down the cabin stairs from the pilothouse. The four of us scrambled for the stairway, virtually swimming up the stairs like a bunch of fish trying to climb a waterfall. In the glare of the decklights we were amazed to learn that we had tied up directly under an 18-inch discharge outlet and in such a position that the full force of the stream came right in the opened starboard-side pilothouse door. We were lucky that the port door was also open, allowing the greater part of the deluge to flow through and over the side, but the volume of water flowing into the aft cabin was still sinking the *DOHRN.* Tie-up lines were quickly cast off amidst much shouting. With engines full ahead we moved out of danger and secured to a nearby pier for the remainder of the night.

There was water more than a foot deep over the cabin floor. By dawn we were pumped out and things were once again near normal, even the deckhouse electronics. All wet clothing stored in lockers under our bunks were strung out to dry in the breeze next day — more colorful informality in that starchy Naval atmosphere. Later we learned that the discharged water had come from one of the carrier's freshwater ballast tanks. The engineer on watch had been unaware that we'd tied up alongside.

Weather conditions were typical Southern discomfort — very hot and humid. The following day, we received new sailing orders to patrol offshore in company with a British Navy vessel, which would serve as our escort. The British vessel proved to be a former long-range fishing trawler, steam-powered and ideally suited for hunting submarines. Its silent machinery improved the capability of its underwater echo reception.

According to the sailing orders, the main objective during this cruise would be "to photograph certain large objects on the bottom off-shore from Chesapeake Bay." German submarines lurking along the Eastern seaboard had torpedoed a series of fully-laden oil tankers that were trying to reach the safety of northern ports. Navy ships were randomly depth-charging every target they could locate on the chance that an occasional enemy sub was quietly sitting down there, waiting to surface at night. Our job, therefore, was to locate each object using our sonar in concert with the "pinging" scanner on the escort vessel.

We discovered both new and old wrecks, each of which was carefully photographed and catalogued by exact position, etc. The special waterproof underwater camera we were using, the creation of Drs. Alan Vine and Maurice Ewing, along with a cluster of flash bulbs, was mounted at the upper end of a 10 foot by 3 inch pipe. The device was lowered from the B.T. winch on a quarter-inch steel cable and was so designed that when the lower end of the pipe struck bottom or an object, a triggering device would fire the flash bulbs and release the camera shutter simultaneously. This simple rig could photograph an area measuring about twelve square feet. Working over a wreck, we could, after a series of shots, put together a mosaic of pictures that would tell us the size, type and, in a general way, the age of the wrecked ship.

Our immediate problem was to learn how to navigate the tricky channel through the mined area. It was a surprise to find that the mines were spread in a wide territory extending 25 miles off-shore from the approaches to Chesapeake Bay and southward to Cape Hatteras! A "clear" band of safe travel could be established only within one mile of the beach.

The first run-out through the mines was made by closely following the zigzag course of our British trawler escort. outside the danger limit and in a safe depth, we began the sonar search for large objects on the bottom. The success of this project eventually led to a series of cruises ordered by the Commandant of the Eastern Sea Frontier, during which we tried to locate every wreck from south of Cape Hatteras to the outer edges of Georges Bank. Every sunken vessel was carefully positioned on our charts; latitude, longitude and depth of water. As a result of these expectations, the Hydrographic Office in Washington, D.C. produced an entirely new chart entitled "Identified wrecks of the Atlantic Coast within a depth of 100 fathoms as recorded by the Research Vessel *ANTON DOHRN*." We were proud to receive a copy of that special chart.

Cruise #24 - locating wrecks east of Norfolk was scheduled to last three weeks. Locating an object, we would anchor a buoy over it. The *DOHRN* either drifted or anchored at night, but the trawler escort continued its round-the-clock search for a live target. One day we saw a periscope nearby, but it quickly vanished. Herr Kapitan apparently concluded that we were not a worthwhile target. The escort returned to Norfolk for supplies but we tracked the sub on our sonar until it went out of our range in deep water.

The real purpose of locating wrecks, we soon learned, was to find enemy submarines that Navy ships had immobilized by depth-charge explosives. If we could have found one, they hoped to raise it with salvage equipment and bring it into port to study its technical equipment.

In the late afternoon of the last day of this cruise, we were invited on board the British Escort for tea. The sea was calm, with a gentle swell, so we tied alongside, with some big rubber fenders between the two vessels. While we visited an alarm signaled that a target had come within range. We breathed more easily when a pod of whales surfaced. We cast off and headed into port, with the big trawler following about a mile astern. Partway through the mine field, we heard a tremendous explosion. The steam-powered trawler had struck a stray mine which, in turn, had exploded the boilers. The terrible tragedy spared only a few badly-injured survivors, who were rescued by a nearby Navy craft. Our friends were gone. The sadness was devastating.

We later learned that three explosions had apparently destroyed the trawler. The mine concussion caused the steam boilers to explode, which in turn must have detonated the two racks of twenty depth charges that were located on deck at the stern.

Our next mission brought us new adventures during a 24-hour cruise eastward of Cape Charles, where we could rendezvous with a convoy of cargo ships bound for European ports. The *DOHRN's* newly-developed sonar submarine detector was to be kept in constant operation until the huge convoy caught up with us. We had hoped that the fleet of ships would arrive during daylight hours. Destroyer escorts fanned out ahead of the convoy. Sometime after midnight a voice came in on our standby radiophone frequency: "A-D, A-D . . . your code number, please.

Royal Daggett, on watch, quickly responded with the correct number.

"OK A-D. "We have you on radar. You look like a surfaced submarine! Now get the hell out of there before you are run down!"

Sailing instructions after this contact with the #1 destroyer escort were for us to proceed at full speed in a northerly direction for at least two hours in order to avoid the huge fleet of ships that spread out in formation over an area 20 miles wide and in length beyond the horizon!

We were hardly underway, however, when the dark shadow of an oncoming, blacked-out ship was seen by an alert bow watch sailor. At first he thought it was a breaking wave in the moderate northeast conditions, but quickly proved to be the phosphorescent bow wave of an approaching ship. In a hard-a-port turn to the west, we were able to parallel the course of the ship as she "swooshed" past our port side, no further than a hundred yards away, at the convoy formation speech of 8 - 10 knots!

With the whole crew on watch (except the cook) and with our two B.T. boys on the spreaders at the masthead, we kept very busy dodging ships coming at us. Finally at dawn, we could once again safely head to the north and away from the stragglers at the tail end of the massive convoy.

It had been a harrowing and exhausting experience. What a relief it was to unstrap our life jackets and resume the normal sea routine!

During the course of that summer, we were involved with two other convoy expeditions, but on both occasions they were completed during daylight hours and in good weather. We had plenty of advance notice and were well out of the way before the zigzagging destroyer escorts and an immense fleet of camouflaged ships came over the horizon.

Once relieved of convoy projects, we were ordered to return to the Norfolk Navy Base. A minesweeper had picked up and disarmed a German mine, and the next step was to deliver it to the Quantico Marine Base where experts in demolition would take it apart for study. The mine was evidently considered too hazardous to transport over land. Orders came from Navy headquarters for us to take on the responsibility. The Navy boys carefully lowered the big bad ball and secured it on deck. Away we went up the Bay and into the winding, muddy Potomac River. With the mine safely unloaded, two of us had the pleasure of a jeep ride into Washington, D.C. for a visit with Navy officials. There was talk about formalizing the *DOHRN* personnel with ratings and uniforms, but nothing ever came of it. We continued to function in our usual ragtag attire and routine.

The following day happened to be Sunday — clear, bright and sunny with a brisk northwest breeze. As we rounded a bend in the river, one of the crew watching the shoreline scenery shouted, "There is Mt. Vernon, residence of George Washington back in the colonial days!" Here was a real patriotic inspiration. We swung around, nosed into the river current and dropped anchor. The two 18 foot dorys were lowered and made ready for a sailing race to the shore a half-mile away. With the cook volunteering to stay on board, the crew divided between the two boats, the sails were quickly rigged and away we went with a fair wind, steering with a 10 foot oar with an action similar to sculling. Lambert Knight and his crew were winners by about a boat length.

We wandered up the sloping green meadow enjoying our freedom and the pleasant summertime scenery. We were met by caretakers of the historic estate and, after explaining our presence, we were escorted in and around the beautiful, historic home. The day was a most memorable experience for all of us, in great contrast to our months of arduous sea-going duty.

We returned to the Norfolk Section Base to await further orders. The next day we were ordered to proceed to Cape May, New Jersey where we would work with Navy blimps that were based at Lakehurst on a submarine-hunting project that would keep us busy for several weeks. By this time the Atlantic war had begun to wane. The Pacific war, however, raged in full force on land and sea, particularly in the South Pacific.

After a series of offshore patrols working with Navy PBY seaplanes, or "flying boats," the submarine campaign was declared over and an armistice with Germany was cause for a worldwide rejoicing! With orders to return to Woods Hole, we stopped for a night of celebrating in the barrooms of Point Pleasant, New Jersey.

To best capture the flavor of the *ANTON DOHRN*'s World War II saga a number of incidents and anecdotes are worth recording.

Sometime during the second year of the *DOHRN*'s new career, we needed to find a solution to the extreme rolling action of this peculiar craft. We returned to the MacDougal drydock where "rolling chocks" were designed and installed. These wooden fins were about 18 feet long and 12 inches wide, but tapered at the ends. They were secured by bolts through the planking and frames about five feet below the water line. On our next cruise we soon learned that the new chocks provided a comfortable stabilizing effect in average sea conditions. As wave action increased, however, the ancient double-ender behaved in an unmanageable fashion, lurching and squirming like a slow-motion earthquake. Sleeping crew members were tossed out of their bunks, while those on watch had to perform acrobatics and grab for handrails to stay on their feet.

Another disadvantage became apparent. When underway, the *DOHRN* had always leaked, but in moderation. Now, with the anti-rolling devices, it was evident that new strains were affecting the hull structure. The pumps could barely keep up with the incoming water. Our engineer, Nelson Bryant, was a busy man during rough weather. We would look down the engine-room hatch and watch him opening and closing gate valves, while water a foot deep sloshed over the floor between the pair of laboring diesel engines. Often during these extreme conditions, we had to turn and run slowly before wind and sea to get rid of the excess of bilge water. Nelson did a great job of keeping us afloat through many long hours of rough seafaring conditions. The "rolling chocks" were modified, then finally removed altogether when regular dry-docking was scheduled.

In the early stages of the war we were engaged in testing a new, experimental explosive of tremendous destructive power. The mixture was compounded in a small building located across the harbor at Woods Hole on the little island of Nonamessett, near the eastern end of Naushon Island. A special crew of demolition engineers was in charge of production. Our job was to take the hazardous stuff offshore for deep water testing. Joe Worzel, a protegé of Dr. Maurice Ewing, ran these experiments. Six 55 gallon oil barrels, with the heads removed, were two-thirds filled with the bluish, yellowish, waxy mixture. The barrels were securely lashed together with wire, cables and turnbuckles. The *DOHRN* was equipped with a special winch and hoisting boom for the job. The six drums were placed on deck and clamped to the starboard rail. A special five-foot reel, containing 1,200 feet of 5/8 inch firing cable was bolted to the deck on the portside. The bunch of barrels and their dangerous contents weighed 1,500 pounds.

Away we went offshore to a point some 20 miles east of the 100 fathom curve. We had calm weather fortunately and carefully eased the barrels over the side where they lay against the rubber-tire fenders. The trick was to get underway, release the barrels, go full steam ahead and watch the firing cable rapidly unwind. The winch cable, also attached to the barrel-lifting cables, was likewise unwinding. Down to the last few turns of firing cable, the winch operator applied the brake. Joe, in the deckhouse, at my hand signal, slammed the firing plunger down. Nothing happened.

We had to wind in the bundle of barrels and, once again, they hung alongside. The dynamite firing caps had failed. Joe brought out his test set and, with me holding it steady in the rail, he probed all the electrical connections. I kept him informed of the dial readings, and he soon discovered the bad contact: a loose wire. He installed a new set of firing caps as he balanced on the wallowing barrels. We recall his saying, "Don't worry; if this charge explodes alongside now, we won't know a thing about it!"

Once again the big bundle was released, the cables ran out and at the given signal, an unbelievable explosion occurred! VAROOM!! A column of spray and black smoke erupted upward one hundred feet or more! The poor old *DOHRN* seemed to lift a foot or so above the normal displacement. The concussion was tremendous! In the galley, dishes shattered and coffee mugs jumped off their hooks. Nelson Bryant searched the engine room for broken pipes or seacocks. That huge explosion was the cause of most of the *DOHRN's* future leaking problems, but the project was otherwise a success. We returned to our home base where we were congratulated both for our survival and the scientific results obtained. Whatever doubts we, the crew of the *ANTON DOHRN* had harbored regarding the vessel's seaworthiness were multiplied after experiencing the big blast. The hull probably needed to be completely refastened and recaulked. We were told that further testing of explosives was to be continued on a smaller scale in Vineyard Sound.

Now was the time to find a replacement for the *DOHRN.* Another winter was approaching and we really needed a vessel suitable for off-shore work.

Dr. Paul M. Fye was appointed supervisor of the explosives program. We appealed to him to take over the *DOHRN* for his local project. Dr. Iselin granted me a period of ten days to locate an available schooner or motor-sailer, a vessel that could "lay to" safely in offshore winter gales. As this was early in World War II, however, we soon learned that the Navy or the Coast Guard had grabbed every seagoing craft fit for coastal patrol work.

The only exception was the 73 foot fishing schooner *RELIANCE,* owned by a friend of mine, Captain Ephraim, "Jack" Eldredge, whose home port was Noank, Connecticut. War restrictions had convinced Jack to retire. He had always maintained the vessel properly and the canvas sails were nearly new. As the *RELIANCE* seemed an ideal solution to our future sea activities, W.H.O.I. promptly purchased her, and Captain Eldredge delivered the schooner to her new homeport at Woods Hole.

Our elation quickly turned to unbelievable disappointment, however, when we learned that a decision had been made to use the schooner for Dr. Fye's inshore explosives experiments. We couldn't believe it! Stanley Poole, the *ANTON DOHRN's* mate, was promoted to captain of the *RELIANCE.*

With more offshore work scheduled, the entire *ANTON DOHRN* crew had to be convinced that we would not be called upon to take risks similar to those of previous cruises. Of course, we did on occasion. An interlude of repair work had immediate priority. The necessary caulking and refastening was done at the convenient MacDougal's marine railway.

Gradually we realized that the *DOHRN,* with its maze of complicated electrical systems so carefully installed, was indispensable for the foreseeable future. We continued to follow orders and, by good fortune, survived the Atlantic version of World War II.

In late August, 1943, before the "rolling chock era," we received orders to proceed across the Gulf Stream. The object was to locate the eastern edge of the Stream. Dr. Maurice Ewing was on board and in charge of the expedition. Eventually we recorded a sudden change in water temperature. There we discovered the "edge" of the clear blue water as it contrasted with the cloudy greenish color of the Atlantic Ocean — a wavy distinct line separating the two areas of salt water. We had of course seen this same sudden contrast many times when entering the Stream beyond the continental shelf. The Gulf Stream current generally overlaps the standard ocean water in variations of wind and weather.

Speaking of weather, we were encountering ocean swells of ever-increasing size. Soon we received a radio report advising us to stay at our location for at least 36 hours, as we were in between two powerful hurricanes, one close to Bermuda, the other about a hundred miles east of our position. Both storms were traveling in a northeasterly direction. Within a few hours mountainous swells from the two parallel storms converged around us, creating a confusion of motion that is difficult to describe. The poor old *DOHRN* rolled violently, making steering nearly impossible. Dr. Ewing caught a heavy storage battery that tumbled out of its container. At that moment, the boat was knocked to starboard on a beam-end roll. As sea water gushed in the doorway, he had to let the battery go overboard, thereby saving himself from doing likewise. When conditions improved, we decided to get underway in a northwesterly direction toward the United States.

Back on soundings, we encountered dense fog all the way into Woods Hole. Director Columbus Iselin was on the wharf to greet us. His sense of urgency was evident: "The Navy has an emergency in the vicinity of outer Nantucket Shoals. They are depth charging a probable enemy submarine. Refuel and get supplies quickly. They want you there at daybreak tomorrow morning to photograph the target for verification."

A new scientific group was ready to come on board. As it was late in the day and most of us in the crew were native Vineyarders, we decided to head for Vineyard Haven. There, while loading supplies, our families brought us clean clothes. Oscar Flanders and other island characters were spectators on the wharf. Before dark we were past Cape Poge and on the way seaward via Muskeget Channel.

We were steering toward a rendezvous with new adventures. Visibility was improving with an increasing northeast wind. At dawn we came upon four Navy ships patrolling the area. With a sloppy northeast sea running, and a mixture of fog and drizzle limiting visibility, we eased up to an anchored rubber buoy, which marked the "target" location. An oil slick was spreading to leeward by tide and wind.

Our depth recorder provided us with an outline of an object as we maneuvered to lower the special camera equipment. The winch whined and squealed as the camera rig came to the surface. A cluster of new flashbulbs was replaced before each lowering. A dozen shots were quickly processed and developed in the makeshift darkroom — a former clothes closet!

My original suspicions were taking shape. The target was an old wreck which was nearly hidden by marine growth. One picture clearly showed the shapes of several large portholes. Large schools of fish were visible in each picture. We had photographed a section of the sunken Nantucket lightship! Navy explosives had blown open the hull and ruptured the fuel tanks. Many years before World War II the lightship had been sliced in two during dense fog by the British liner *OLYMPIC.*

In order to prove this theory to our Navy escorts, we went in search of the other section of the lightship. An hour later, after circling and sounding, we discovered the other part of the wrecked lightship about a half mile to the southwest. Another series of underwater pictures proved the situation conclusively.

The Navy boys had bombed both of these sections of the wreck for the previous 24 hours, with the notion that they had a pair of crippled enemy submarines! What an embarrassment for Navy experts and their technological resources! Two more wreck locations were added to the special *ANTON DOHRN* chart.

We promptly returned to our Woods Hole base for further orders. Soon after the lightship episode, we were proud to receive a commendation from the Commandant of the Eastern Sea Frontier for our useful activities, especially our ability to distinguish old wrecks from possible recently-sunken enemy submarines.

R.V. ANTON DOHRN was widely known for broadcasting a super powerful radio-telephone output. When we went on the air, our big high-powered Halicrafter radio-phone would blank out nearby conversations completely. Commercial fishermen were annoyed with us, except for the fleet of Gloucester mackerel seiners. En route offshore during daylight hours, we were steaming through huge schools of mackerel. Many of those seiners were converted World War I submarine chasers. We kept the fishermen informed about mackerel activities and locations and undoubtedly contributed considerably to seafood production during that time.

Whenever we came in sight of any vessel that had listened to our booming radio voice, its crew was astounded to learn that the *ANTON DOHRN* was just a quaint little old double-ender — not at all the ocean liner that they had imagined!

The peculiar appearance of the *DOHRN* was a source of amusement to us crew members. Some of us gradually developed a sense of sentimental faith about this strange craft. After many harrowing adventures on the high seas, the old veteran always brought us safely back to port. On several occasions we were caught offshore in gale wind conditions. In cold weather it was usually a sudden nor'wester. Cold air made for rougher, sharper seas. The waves were also closer together. In such conditions the *DOHRN* would refuse to go to windward. Being of sharp design forward, the poor old vessel would dive into a big wave and become temporarily submerged!

We soon learned that the way to go was downhill. That 100 fathom coil of 3 inch manila was our salvation. The outer end had a series of knots tied in it to create more drag. The inner end was a spliced loop secured to the big oak towing post in the stern. The sails were furled and with both engines on slow ahead, we rode comfortably, with never a sea breaking over the pointed stern, despite breaking seas all around us! Usually after about 24 hours or so, the wind and sea would moderate. We would winch in the long hawser and turn toward the northwest for the long cruise back to our original position. Survival was the name of the game!

While searching the file cabinet for any overlooked envelopes containing sailing orders, I came upon two more: Cruise #13, on September 22, 1941 and Cruise #24, on May 18, 1942. Columbus Iselin came on board with sealed orders for Cruise #13 on the morning of September 22, 1941. He casually explained that this would be a bathythermograph cruise of special significance. A sizeable hurricane was located somewhere southeast of Cape Hatteras and moving steadily in a northerly direction. Our mission would be to proceed toward Nova Scotia immediately, making a continual series of B.T. water temperature recordings. Then we were to turn around and retrace our course for a comparison of water temperatures after the anticipated turbulence created by the hurricane. We were to try to reach Lurcher Shoal in the Bay of Fundy before the big storm caught up with us.

Fritz Fuglister was in charge of the project. His two assistants were Dr. Pierce and Mr. Couper. An alternate course was to head for Cashes Ledge buoy in the Gulf of Maine, then to head northward, for a hoped-for safe harbor on the coat of Maine. Away we went to the eastward on a flat calm sea with heavy dark clouds overhead that indicated threatening weather.

As we crossed Great South Channel, we counted the number of in-bound vessels. An armada of trawlers and other craft stretched across the horizon, all headed at full speed for their homeports. The big trawler *NOTRE DAME* crossed our bow. The captain, a Newfoundlander known as "the High Priest," came on the radio with this advice: "Old Son, you better turn that canoe around and get into a harbor before it's too late!" We had our orders, however, and by dusk had received radio reports that the hurricane had intensified and was moving at 50 mph toward the south shore of Long Island. Its ETA was around dawn of the following day. Thus, by the time we came on the Whistle buoy near Cashes Ledge, it seemed prudent to lay a course toward Maine. Northeast Harbor was our goal. We arrived there at noon the following day in bright, sunny weather with a fresh northwest wind. Evidently a high pressure atmosphere had moved down from Canada and pushed the hurricane offshore: the big storm had veered northeast and gone on its way more than a hundred miles east of the New England coast.

To counteract the tensions of the previous 24 hours, we went on a leisurely cruise into the far reaches of Sommes Sound, a nearly land-locked fiord blazing with the brilliant colors of fall foliage on the surrounding mountain slopes.

By sundown, were viewing the mountains from our outward-bound, offshore position as we steered a course for Boon Island Lighthouse, a checkpoint on our way toward the Cape Cod Canal en route to the home base at Woods Hole. What had begun as a bold adventure ended as a yachting cruise.

The purpose of Cruise #24 was to test a newly-developed B.T. — a sophisticated torpedo-shaped instrument with photographic capabilities and better temperature recording qualities. The added size and weight made the tired old electric winch complain in a chorus of greatly amplified groans and squeals.

Lambert Knight was responsible for the testing of this new instrument. The recordings were to begin at the Nomans Land whistle buoy and from there out to the hundred-fathom curve which we would follow southward until we reached Diamond Shoals off Cape Hatteras. That was all provided, of course, that the new B.T. continued to function properly. A special objective of this cruise was to try to complete the run south and back to the starting point with no interruption in the scheduled recordings.

Our intentions were good until somewhere east of Hudson Canyon, where we came upon some interesting floating wreckage. Objects of all sorts were spread over miles of the glassy calm ocean — the residue of a recently torpedoed ship. Two splintered wooden lifeboats drifted in the midst of a mile-long oil slick along with debris of every type. But the real excitement was the sight of hundreds of shiny square metal cans that glinted in the sunlight. When we scooped one on board, it proved to be a container of about five gallons capacity with the stamped legend "Cashew Nuts, Product of India!"

Lambert Knight was anxious to continue our recording routine without interruption, but temptation prevailed. We promptly became salvagers, like most Islanders. Here was a chance to "cash in" on acres of canned cashew nuts. We talked about lowering the dories but we had a long-handled scoop net on board, which proved workable. Maneuvering around the area, we soon had a deckload of the big square cans, probably over 200 of them, stacked in available spaces from bow to stern. Square bundles of compressed green leaves also were awash in the variety of clutter. We managed to strap one and hoist it on board. The mysterious object was as heavy as lead.

We had dallied long enough. It was time to resume the B.T. recording project. A decision had to be made about our valuable cargo. The cans were showing signs of rust and had to be washed in fresh water, dried and stored somewhere. By dark we were abreast of Atlantic City. There lay the answer to disposing of our cargo. The boardwalk vendors might be prospective buyers. During daylight hours the famous beach was busy. At night the shoreline was blacked out. There were no lighted buoys along the entrance channel. We proceeded westward slowly through the night, keeping an eye on the depth indicator. By dawn, land was in sight, with the outer buoy ahead. Absecon Inlet was buoyed on both sides of the channel to guide us between the shoals. Boiling white breakers were quite impressive.

We tied up in a basin where much of the fishing fleet was located and we went ashore as wartime tourists. We rotated the watch, leaving two men on board for security. With a sample can of cashew nuts, we taxied over to the boardwalk. An hour later, we had sold the entire deckload except for a dozen cans we'd held onto for the crew to take home.

We were advised to ship the soggy bale of leaves to a New Jersey laboratory for analysis. A letter from the lab eventually appeared at our W.H.O.I. base stating that we had rescued a bale of senna leaves, one of the ingredients used in the manufacture of laxative products! There was no mention of value.

After our one-day "vacation" on the boardwalk and beach at Atlantic City, we were on our way and past the sea buoy before sunset. We returned to the position of the "Salvage

Project," and resumed the B.T. recordings along the hundred-fathom depth in a southerly direction. By the time we reached the outer edges of Diamond Shoals, we received radio instructions to proceed into the harbor at Ocrakoke, North Carolina, below Cape Hatteras.

During the next two weeks we made runs offshore at night, usually in company with either a Navy patrol boat or one of the Coast Guard's 83 foot cutters, searching for submarines and taking B.T. recordings. Off Moorhead City we located, photographed and identified several large objects, all of which proved to be recently torpedoed oil tankers. In a few of the pictures, the ships' names were clearly visible.

By the time the project was completed, weather had become a problem. Strong northeast winds prevailed with particularly rough conditions around Cape Hatteras. Orders came to return to the navy base at Norfolk. We made our way across a bay near Moorhead City to take advantage of the inland waterway. Except for crossing choppy Pamlico Sound, we had an easy cruise in smooth water for a change.

A few days later we were escorted out through the minefield to the relative safety of the open sea. The voyage back to Woods Hole was uneventful.

The *DOHRN* continued to make a series of short cruises, mostly to test newly-developed electronics.

A humorous aside: during previous months, one of our occasional radio contacts was the Moore-McCormack cargo ship *ARGENTINA*. Her captain, Terry Keogh, was one of my former shipmates. After being "hove to" for several hours waiting for a hurricane to subside, he called us to announce, "The storm was so intense that it blew the stars down out of the sky and changed the days of the week!"

Finally the W.H.O.I. Board of Directors decided to decommission the ancient vessel. The *DOHRN* had served her purpose. Electronic and scientific equipment was removed. Newspaper display advertising declared the vessel for sale.

A marine contractor in New Bedford bought the *DOHRN*. We soon heard that the engines had been discarded and replaced with modern versions with three times the original horsepower.

One day the *DOHRN* appeared in Woods Hole Channel towing a huge barge loaded with gravel. Somebody commented, "That's the worst possible use for that worn-out old hull." A few months later we learned that the *ANTON DOHRN* had been abandoned and was sinking somewhere south of Cuttyhunk Island.

In review, it has since seemed nearly miraculous that the *DOHRN* managed to accomplish all those wartime missions. A weird, basically unseaworthy craft, she gave us plenty of scares and much apprehension, but proved a faithful craft with the necessary integrity to do what had to be done.

Chapter 40

Surviving the 1944 Hurricane

At Sea in the Eye of a Hurricane

September 14, 1944. Several days after that wartime hurricane had gone by, a brief item appeared in the local newspaper. "The fishing dragger GLADIATOR arrived in port last night. The vessel was severely damaged as the result of being at sea during the recent hurricane."

Only two lines! Sometime later, the skipper and some of the crew members told the following complete story. A quotation from Patrick Sullivan, engineer on the GLADIATOR, says it all: "I didn't pray to be saved . . . I prayed for me soul!"

GLADIATOR was a new, heavily-built, wooden Eastern-type vessel, rigged on both sides and completing her first fishing trip — 30,000 pounds of ground fish were iced down in the fishhold pens.

The rhythm of the slow turning, heavy-duty diesel engine was comforting. Thick fog had persisted since leaving port. Frequent blasts of the foghorn were getting on the crew's nerves. Three men were on watch; Tom, at the wheel, steered a south-southeast course. Jake, the skipper, at an open pilothouse window, was depending on Mike, atop the bow whaleback, on lookout for other vessels and occasionally pointing to indicate a distant foghorn in that direction. After 10 days of around-the-clock fishing, trying to stay alert was becoming very tiresome. The other five crew members were asleep in their bunks down forward.

An hour earlier, on the mate's watch, they had encountered a steadily increasing groundswell from the southeast. Jake turned to beam a flashlight on the nearby barometer. "Dropped two-tenths in the last hour," he said. "Something is brewing! We should have waited for the radiophone to be installed!" Wartime regulations had delayed the installation. A depth recorder was their only navigational instrument and it was flashing on the 12-fathom mark.

Pat, the engineer, appeared in the fo'c'sle gangway with a mug of coffee, which he balanced over the obstructions on the lurching deck as he made his way aft. Suddenly the fog cleared. Then all hell broke loose — a terrific blast of wind along with thunder and lightning. There was a rain squall mixed with hail the size of marbles. Pat, with his coffee mug, scrambled up the steps into the wheelhouse shouting, "What the hell is this — the end of the world?!" Jake turned on the deck lights as Mike hustled down off the whaleback and took shelter in the forward gangway.

The swells became cresting waves as Jake yelled, "Hatch covers!" Two crew members quickly lifted the steel covers onto both hatches. That's all they had time for. A gust of wind struck, followed by another blast of wind and spray from the southeast.

The big swells quickly became huge cresting waves as the wind increased to hurricane force . . . a great roaring sound in a smother of stinging sea spray . . . barometer below 29 and dropping!

In a matter of minutes, it was impossible to steam to windward. With every plunge of the bow, the whaleback submerged and solid seawater flowed aft, quickly filling the main deck to the rail caps. The trawl nets normally lashed to the rails, were being swept across the deck as the overloaded vessel rolled heavily, spilling much of the deck load of seawater over the rails.

Now the new danger was evident; one or both nets would soon go overboard where they would quickly be gathered around the propeller. Jake shouted, "Shut her off!" Pat grabbed the engine control levers, slowed the engine and brought it to a stop. The *GLADIATOR,* now at the mercy of wind and sea, unable to make headway, swung off to starboard and lay-to with her port quarter taking the brunt of the onrushing, breaking waves. It was a bad situation . . . with the treacherous Nantucket Shoals directly to leeward!

"For God's sake, Pat," Jake shouted to the engineer, "start the Lister and see how things are in the engine room!" Pat quickly disappeared down the engine room ladder. Soon the reassuring sound of the auxiliary engine's exhaust could be heard above the turmoil of the storm. The Lister served to drive a five KW generator, but was also ready to belt-drive a centrifugal bilge pump or an air compressor.

The force of the hurricane rapidly increased to a howling fury. Each breaking sea swept the vessel closer to the shoals. The sounder became useless, with flashes all around the dial.

One of those ever-bigger breaking waves knocked the vessel on her beam ends and swept her along for quite a distance. Before the *GLADIATOR* could right herself, another great wave caught her, whereupon she struck bottom with a shuddering *whump*! The vessel was hove down on her port side. On her beam ends, while struggling to right herself, she was then picked up by another huge breaker and swept to leeward. The port side trawl net had washed overboard. The drogue effect at first brought the bow to windward for a few moments, until the next cresting wave swung the vessel to starboard, thereby creating a more hazardous situation. The floats on the mouth of the net had tangled with the forward gallows frame, but soon parted, allowing the net to disappear.

About that time a monstrous breaker carried the vessel to leeward some distance. Again she struck the hard, sandy bottom. In those deep valleys, between seas, the roar of the storm was greatly diminished. In contrast, emerging upward on another wave crest, the noise was deafening! Conversation was impossible!

Then the starboard net went overboard. The drogue effect once again brought the vessel's bow to windward. The trawl towing cables were seen unwinding from the double drum winch. The brakes were not properly tightened. A helpless situation. No way for a crew member to reach the brake wheels in that situation! Each drum contained 300 fathoms of one inch wire cable. Soon, the cables had unwound, the ends yanked out of their clamps and whipped out through the hanging blocks of the starboard side gallows frames.

At that moment, another towering wave tumbled the *GLADIATOR* into a deep trough. This time, just as the vessel struck bottom, a great wall of seawater crashed aboard. The damage was devastating. Both dories were torn loose. The top of the engine room deckhouse was gone entirely. Tons of water had flooded the engine room. Engineer Pat, waist-deep in water when the lights went out, used a flashlight to find the switchboard and turn off all the electrical circuits.

At this stage of the nightmare, there were two fortunate events. The faithful Lister two-cylinder air-cooled auxiliary diesel, located above the sloshing water, kept pounding along . . . belt-driving a three-inch centrifugal bilge pump. At the same time, it was becoming evident that the vessel was being carried into deeper water. The motion was easier, the waves farther apart.

Captain Jake appeared in the engine room to make sure that Pat had survived. The vessel had developed a severe starboard list. Jake lost his balance, struck his head on something in the dark and knocked himself unconscious. He would have drowned but Pat lifted him upright and lashed him to an engine rocker arm with an electrical extension wire. By the time Jake regained consciousness, the weather and sea conditions were definitely improving.

The vessel's motion became more tolerable as the interval of the waves lengthened. Now, in deeper water, there was a much better chance to survive. Then came a brief interlude of calm . . . no wind at all . . . the eye of the storm. They were on the western side of the eye of the hurricane. Suddenly, the wind returned, screeching out of the northwest, creating another force of chaotic sea conditions. With the tide flowing northerly, driven by huge southeast swells, the opposing northwest gale tossed the crippled vessel in all directions.

After a while — probably about an hour — the wind abruptly diminished. Sea conditions were improving. The vessel was in darkness. The batteries and the entire electrical system were ruined by salt water. Pat, with his precious flashlight, kept the Lister diesel operational on the bilge pump. Gradually, the engine room water level became noticeably lower.

Jake climbed the ladder up into the wheelhouse. There he found Tom standing braced between the chart table and the skipper's bunk in the small stateroom adjoining the pilothouse. Tom's first words were, "Pat was right, this must be the end of the world!" He had found a workable flashlight. Jake opened a pilothouse window frame . . . the glass had shattered. He beamed the light forward. There, huddled together at the top of the gangway, were the other five crew members. Five faces with the blank look of despair. However, Big Sam, the cook, shouted in a hoarse voice, "Hey, you guys, how about ham and eggs?"

Jake proceeded to work his way forward over the cluttered, sloping deck. The crewmen came out and took a look around. It was the dawn of a new day . . . a new lease on life. The foc's'cle contained seawater several feet deep—a hell of a mess! The big oil-burning galley stove had torn loose and was lying upside down on the floor.

Jake shouted, "Come on boys, let's get her pumped out!"

There were two old-fashioned Edison diaphragm hand-operated pumps located on deck in front of the winch. The handles were put into position. The salvage began. One pump took care of the engine room and the other, the fishhold. Off came the forward hatch covers. What a sight! When the vessel lay on her beam ends to starboard,the pen boards on the port side fishpens had broken, and all the fish on that side had tumbled down onto the starboard pens. No wonder the vessel had a severe starboard list! There was work to be done!

Four men were on deck working the hand pumps. The other four were in the hold pitchforking fish back over to the port side pens. Tons of fish and ice were transferred until the vessel was back on "even keel." By the way, they were encouraged to find that no seawater had reached the fishhold. Although the vessel had taken a terrible pounding, the bulkheads fore and aft had remained watertight.

Jake remarked that the heavy list to starboard had been a condition in their favor when the vessel struck several times on such hard, sandy bottom. The *GLADIATOR,* being new and of extremely rugged construction, was bounced around on her beam ends, a more resilient position with much shoaler draft. Had she been in an upright, normal mode, she would have struck bottom with a violence that could have cruushed the keel and related framewowrk.

At the end of day one after the hurricane, the vessel was all pumped out. The water in the foc's'cle was drained aft through an opened valve in the bottom of the forward bulkhead, where it could be pumped overboard.

Canned food stored in lockers was brought up and opened. Things like cold baked beans tasted real good Pat reactivited the engine room blow-torch in order to produce a pot of boiling hot coffee—a royal treat!

By this time the vessel was drifting slowly in a general northeasterly direction. There was a gentle southwest breeze ruffling the subsiding swells. As they were in South Channel, an occasional ship, inbound or outbound, was seen in the disstance.

At this stage, the engine room was the principal scene of activity—getting the big diesel dried out after the base was flushed of salt, water and a new supply of oil in required quantity applied.

Finally, when they were somewhere in the Guolf of Maine, the engine was ready to start. The faithful Lister auxiliary had been belted to the two-stage air compressor. With the gauge showing 150 pounds of compressed air, Pat said, "Okay, now we will give her a try!" He pulled the air-starting lever, anad the Atlas-Imperial diesel came to life. All six o f the big cylinders were soon making the familiar slow rhythmic, rumbling sound.

It was time to get underway. Jake headed the vessel in a westerly direction. Fortunately, an hour or so later, they came upon the dragger *INVADER* outbound. The skipper hailed Jake, "Where in the hell were you in the big breeze?" Then he noticed the missing dories and the wrecked engine house. "Hey, you guys must have had a bad time," he shouted.

"We're lucky to be here at all," Jake yelled back. "Where are we to?"

As they drifted closer, the skipper provided the necessaary information to Jake: their present position and a compass course to the entrance of Pollock Rip Channel, their destination being the homeport of New Bedford.

Sometime after midnight that night, the *GLADIATOR* ws docked at Pier 3. Eight very weary fishermen were ready to step ashore. Alex, the youngest of the crew, grabbed the bow line and leaped onto the pier. He turned and said, "No more fishing for me!" He took a few steps and promptly disappeared. There was a loud splash. The storm had ripped up wharf planking, and there were several big, open gaps. Alex was quicky rescued. With the vessel secured, the weary fishermen holding flashlights, carefully made their way ashore.

Chapter 41

Origin of the Vineyard Black Dog

The name ***Black Dog*** on the island of Martha's Vineyard seems to be subject to plenty of attention lately. It is generally known that the image of this square-nosed canine was in the form of a sign that established the popular beach front restaurant and bakery by that name.

Some time ago the ***Black Dog*** design was utilized as a T-shirt logo, supplementary enterprise. Gradually, the magic logo was adapted to a catalog full of articles for the mail-order trade as an expansion of the worldwide T-shirt demand.

Now, to get away from the above preamble, it is time to reflect on the main subject: The origin of the Vineyard ***Black Dog*** phenomenon.

From 1962-63, the writer was employed as a rigger at the Mystic Seaport Museum in Connecticut. It was a welcome change from seafaring and selling commercial fishing boats. My first job there involved wire-splicing and rigging for the newly installed masts and other spars on board the former Gloucester fishing schooner *L.A. DUNTON*. From there, I was put aboard the famous whaler *CHARLES W. MORGAN*, a full-time rigger. The *Morgan,* the last survivor of square-rigged whale ships, has special significance for my family. My grandfather, for whom I was named, sailed on several long voyages in that ship. In fact, he spent most of his adult life cruising the oceans of the world as a whale hunter, a test of human endurance relieved only by occasionally reaching a tropical paradise such as Honolulu. There water casks would be refilled and supplies of fresh meat and a variety of fruits and vegetables stored on board, providing a welcome change from salt meat and stale biscuits.

The period of my service at Mystic Seaport was quite special. The curator of the entire Marine Museum at that time was Eduord Stackpole, who hailed from Nantucket. My place of residence during a year of occupation at the Seaport was in a house at nearby Noank, located on a high bluff overlooking Fisher's Island Sound. The house was owned by a good friend, Capt. Adrian Lane, who was at sea on the R/V *ATLANTIS.* His family lived in a nearby house. Upon moving into that vacant house, I developed a sense of loneliness. After a vigorous day's work at the Seaport, I avoided the Main Street gin mills in favor of getting "early to bed".

About that time I began to think about a dog as a companion . . . a genuine pal. I wrote a notice that read, "Wanted — a puppy or young dog, retriever-type", and tacked it to the Seaport bulletin board with my name and phone number. Ben Gamsby, a *MORGAN* co-worker, saw the ad and said to me, "Follow me home after work and I will show you a choice of seven puppies."

We arrived at his house in the Thames River town of Gales Ferry in the late daylight of a June evening. The mother dog, Patsy, and her newly-weaned pups greeted us through the wire mesh of their doghouse yard. Ben told me that Patsy was part boxer and part black Lab. The father, a neighbor's dog, was a black Lab of mixed ancestry. The pups, only five (two had found homes earlier that day) were a comical variety of character, color and boundless energy.

One pup ran circles around the others, yipping and yapping all the while. He was a black male with white feet and a white patch on his chest. His nose was nearly as square as his mother's and his lower lip protruded, a feature that accentuated his personality. He also had a stubby tail like his mother. I said to Ben, "That's the one I want!" Ben replied, "You would! He's the pup we'd like to keep! When he had his shots, we had the vet nip off some of his long tail". Ben went on to say, "My family is having a contest to think up a suitable name for this pup so that we can start a new breed which would be known as *black boxers."*

It was a touchy situation. I declined an invitation to stay for supper. Ben decided that he would need to talk with his family regarding my insistence about adopting the lively black puppy. He would have a decision overnight.

The following morning when Ben parked his pick-up truck next to my car, he beckoned me to come and take a look. As he lowered the window, there was my prize puppy standing on his hind legs with only his head in sight. "He's all yours!" was Ben's greeting. A memorable moment. I reached over, picked him up and held him with his white front feet on my shoulder while he squirmed and busily licked my face and ear.

We were off to a good start. Ben had supplied a collar for the pup with a length of clothesline attached. He had also brought along a water dish, a bottle of milk and a box of puppy biscuits. He refused any payment for the extras and advised that, after much discussion the night before, he and his family had concluded that their little "black rascal" would have a good home with me. I thanked him for such special consideration.

We boarded the *MORGAN* and I took my new pal forward where we found some loose lumber that served as an enclosure near the anchor windlass. We stretched a piece of canvas over a corner of the fence to provide a sheltered, shaded area. When we went aft to start the day's work, "Poochy" complained for a while, whining and also learning to bark. However, I returned quite often to reassure him that everything was okay.

Before the day was over, I had decided to name my new pal "Toby". Somehow the name seemed to be entirely suitable. He adapted readily to riding on a blanket in the back seat of my big sedan. That night at the Noank house I put a folded blanket on the bedroom floor for the pup's bed, but he whined until I lifted him up on my bed where he curled into a comfortable spot, no longer lonesome. In the morning, I hustled him outside after finding wet spots on my blanket. Over a period of ten days my chum, Toby, achieved the status of being basically "housebroken", a process requiring patience and persistence, as always.

By the end of that summer, the Seaport rigging work was completed. My friend Toby was nearly full grown. He was intelligent and attentive. We worked together on a program of training that he seemed to enjoy. Our Seaport friends gave us a farewell party with Toby as the center of attention. The Mystic interlude was a very pleasant experience.

A new era began when we reached Cape Cod and rented an apartment in West Falmouth. My trade name, Athearn Marine Agency, was reactivated and when the advertising appeared in commercial fishing magazines, my telephone began to ring with calls from prospective boat buyers and sellers. That resulted in plenty of travel to coastal fishing ports from Camden, Maine to Cape May, New Jersey. In the course of that year, Toby and I rolled up an impressive thirty thousand miles!

One day, as we travelled along a Point Judith, Rhode Island highway, a state trooper waved us to a stop. While he was writing out a speeding ticket, I decided to take Toby for a short walk. I opened the rear door and let him out. Toby promptly lifted his leg on the Trooper's feet. Leather puttees provided limited protection, but the liquid stream quickly overflowed the shoe on his right foot. The cop was so intent on his ticket pad as he leaned on the hood of the car that he was not aware of Toby's contribution until it was about all over. He then turned to me and said, "The speeding ticket fine is fifteen dollars, but I will not add ten dollars to it because of your dog's indiscretion. The fine is payable immediately at the courthouse in this town of Wakefield!" The clerk at the office where we paid the fine said, "That state cop is having a field day by stopping only cars with out-of-state plates."

We had an otherwise successful day as we continued on past the town of Westerly to New London in order to examine a trawler that was dry-docked at the Thames Shipyard. The submarine base, located about three miles south of the village of Gales Ferry where Toby was born, was visible directly across the river. Every day provided us with a new adventure.

My pal Toby developed a peculiar characteristic during his first year. When the month of March rolled around, he became hyperactive and couldn't seem to relax, day *or* night. I walked him as usual but his behavior was erratic. I called the vet and he advised, "Don't worry about his actions, it's the mating season. He's ready for his first sexual exploit!"

At the first opportunity Toby bolted out the door and was gone for several days. I searched in vain all around town trying to follow reports of where he had been seen recently. On his first expedition, a friend caught him and brought him home. After further escapades he would return home in a gaunt and exhausted condition.

Capt. Bob Douglas of Vineyard Haven was a frequent visitor at my West Falmouth headquarters. Bob and Toby always greeted each other with great enthusiasm. Capt. Bob always used the name Tobias when talking to Toby. Whenever we visited the Vineyard, we had an invitation to stay for a while at the Douglas residence overlooking Vineyard Haven harbor. We rowed a skiff around the harbor with Toby sitting on the stern seat. On several occasions, we sailed to Nantucket on board the topsail schooner *SHENANDOAH*. Capt. Bob was delighted to have Toby as a special guest — the ship's mascot, a genuine seafaring dog.

Now we come to the object of this report. Toby had a girlfriend, Goldie, a beautiful young Golden Retriever, at a nearby neighbor's house. During the times she was "in season" she was confined in the back yard with an oversized doghouse, enclosed by a wire fence high enough — about eight feet — and strong enough to restrain a horse.

Goldie was due to be introduced to a male Golden Retriever, also of pure pedigree, during her next cycle to thereby produce a litter of proper puppies. However, Toby happened to pick up Goldie's scent at the crucial time and flew into action. He dashed across the neighbor's yard and scrambled up and over that high wire fence. I made haste to the scene, but before I could get inside the gate to separate them, the deed had been done. The neighbor, a temperamental lady observing the whole performance, was outraged! She yelled at length about my careless indifference regarding Toby's wild behavior.

The puppies were born on a cold, rainy November day, late in the waning light. My arrival home at that particular time seemed to be a miraculous coincidence. The neighbor waved to me from her doorway calling, "Come and get the puppies before they all die!" It was nearly too late. A total of nine tiny black puppies — some with white markings or white feet — huddled together below the doorway of Goldie's shelter, a pathetic sight, an ultimate inhuman disaster.

I phoned Dr. Jenson, the town vet, at his home. He told me, "Bring them right over and we will try to save them." He used all his skills and did all he could, feeding them a special formula with a medicine dropper, but finally there were only two survivors — one all black male and one little black female with white feet, just like her daddy, Toby.

Three months later, the two survivors had developed into a pair of healthy young dogs, thanks to the attention of my kind-hearted landlady who took care of them whenever I was away.

In the meantime, Capt. Bob Douglas was waiting for the news that the puppies were ready for adoption. After several phone conversations, he said to me — in his rapid mode of talking — "Come on over to the island with those two pups. I will take one or both of them." He greeted us, the pups and me, with the excitement of such a special occasion.

The following day he called to tell me that he had decided to keep the female because she closely resembled my pal, Toby. He went on to say, "I've already named her Black Dog." My reply was, "You didn't have to strain your imagination very much! Maybe, after a while, you will dream up a more suitable name for such an exceptional dog!" Of course, the name stayed with her and now it has become famous everywhere.

Capt. Bob informed me that an Oak Bluffs woman had taken the black male. Several months later I learned that she did not have the patience to train the dog, with the result that she had him "put away". Sad news.

Black Dog became the lone survivor of the nine puppies born to Goldie, that beautiful Golden Retriever. Now, the name has become legendary. The logo design bears a remarkable resemblance to both Black Dog and her father, Toby. That is how it all came about, and the key factor was my seagoing shipmate, Toby.

The writer, with his 90' Schooner MARJORIE PARKER at Mullins Wharf in Fairhaven, Mass. in July 1954—ready to leave for an expedition to Georges Bank on a special contract to establish the original "Texas Tower"—a U.S. Government project:—known as the first "Eary Warning System" relating to the Russian "Cold War."

Incidentally, in the early days of the schooner *SHENANDOAH,* Capt. Douglas proceeded to have a new tugboat built, a beamy sixty foot steel vessel powered by twin diesel engines. Roy Campbell, as skipper, maintained the tug in yacht-like condition while on emergency standby. The black-hulled towboat was known by the name *WHITEFOOT,* in big white letters on bow and stern. Another score for Black Dog and Toby. A new Black Dog promotion could be generated by producing bales of black T-shirts bearing the name "Whitefoot," underlined by four white paws under the name — a stunt that could well develop into another bonanza for its producers as well as for the Chamber of Commerce on the wonderful island of Martha's Vineyard.

Chapter 42

The Transition of Boating: Before and After World War II

The following story is generated mostly from clear memories of the marine scene during the 1930's in comparison to developments after World War II ended.

My early experiences were basically as a commercial fisherman with a coastwise operating range between Camden, Maine and Cape May, New Jersey. My ancestry and origin was on the island of Martha's Vineyard. My home port was Vineyard Haven, Massachusetts. Nearly all the native islanders kept their boats in use year round. Auxiliary catboats were the most popular and therefore outnumbered other types. Mostly they were built for commercial activity. Centerboard boats contained a "live well" compartment built to contain fish and lobsters. The motorboats, generally known as launches, were commonly used to haul and set lobster traps. The older boats were "double enders" but gradually the transom stern designs became more popular because they provided more deck space; thus, lobster traps could be stacked, ready to be tumbled overboard.

Marine engines with the company name Lathrop or Palmer were best known for their reliability. They were slow-turning, heavy-duty two or three cylinder models (separate cylinders). Because they were salt water-cooled, they developed rust problems long before any serious wear became evident. Nearly all marine gasoline engines of that era were equipped with two systems of ignition: battery-powered distributor on one side and a gear-driven magneto on the other side which served as the main source of spark plug ignition. It was quite reassuring to have two spark plugs for each cylinder.

The old style open flywheel engines were gradually replaced by solid-block four cylinder models, such as the Redwing Thoroughbred, that were rated forty to fifty horsepower at 1800 RPM direct drive. Engine companies with names such as Scripps, Kermath and Hall-Scott became popular, especially for use in the larger yachts of that period.

Inshore fishing draggers of the forty-foot size usually were powered with four cylinder 40 hp or six cylinder 65 hp (at rpm) gasoline engines produced by the Lathrop Engine Company at Mystic, Connecticut. Offshore fishing vessels — sloop or schooner — rigged in the 1920-30 era — depended on their Fairbanks-Morse diesel engines that were rated about 15 hp per cylinder. They were big clumsy engines known as CO's (crude oil) that belched a trail of dense black smoke. Those two-cycle monsters were gradually replaced by four cycle machinery such as Wolverine, Atlas Imperial, Cooper Bessemer and Superior which were much more powerful and efficient.

Eventually, General Motors and Caterpillar dominated the commercial marine engine market. The really big steel trawlers operating out of the Boston Fish Pier were re-powered with newly designed opposed-piston Fairbanks-Morse diesel engines, powerful engines that provided a remarkable durability of thirty years or more. The development of enclosed freshwater cooling systems including heat exchangers was a revolutionary improvement for all marine engines, an engineering feature that came into use during the late 1930's. From that time on, electrolysis was recognized as a major problem. The combination of stray electrical currents, salty bilge water and a variety of metals such as iron, steel, brass and bronze produced many disintegrating conditions. Blocks of zinc were fastened at crucial locations on the bottoms of the vessels, which in turn were connected by a network of copper straps that kept the chemical problem under control.

The development of sophisticated electronic navigational equipment powered by engine room alternators and heavy-duty batteries created new requirements for properly installed electrical bonding systems.

Gradually, conventional wooden commercial vessels were replaced by steel construction of modern design and layout. However, steel hulls were much more vulnerable to electrolysis action that required a special system of protective devices necessitating constant maintenance.

Now back to the year 1935. The magazine Atlantic Fisherman contained a display of available fishing boats by the Knox Marine Exchange, Camden, Maine, Mr. John Bird, Proprietor. The picture of a forty foot dragger by the name of *WATER WITCH* caught my attention. The boat was powered by a Cummins six cylinder diesel engine. She was located at the Snow Shipyard in Rockland, Maine. A friend lent me the sale price, $3,500, and away I went by train and bus to buy the boat. It was early in the month of March and winter weather prevailed. The cabin reeked of diesel oil and the small Shipmate stove burned coal but produced little heat. Nights were long and cold as I tried to sleep on a pipe berth, rolled up in a blanket and a piece of canvas. The engine had problems. It was a former truck engine with high mileage installed in the boat without benefit of an overhaul. The starter-generator was a combined 32 volt unit. The engine was coupled to a huge Morse reduction gear which used a large percentage of the available horse power. That particular Cummins diesel may have been the first compact high-speed diesel engine to be installed in a fishing boat. At that time, Cummins diesel engines had just entered the marine engine market, mostly for pleasure boat use.

A shipyard mechanic tinkered with the engine fuel injection system until it performed on all six cylinders.

At dawn of the following day I was outward bound leaving the inland mountains astern and navigating the coastal "thoroughfares" along the rocky shoreline. All day the weather was flat calm with a dark gray overcLast sky. The engine ran smoothly with a smoky exhaust until mid-afternoon when, with the Portland Lightship insight, the rhythm changed to lower rpm's.

Looking offshore, I noticed a fleet of big trawlers all inbound toward Portland harbor. Evidently their barometers indicated an approaching storm. My intention was to pursue a course toward Boon Island Light, but common sense prevailed as I rolled the steering wheel to starboard and headed for Portland along with the incoming draggers.

It was nearly dark when I reached the O'Hara Fish Pier where there was space available to stay for the night.

Sometime before midnight, I went up on deck to check on the dock lines. Allowances had to be made for the twelve foot rise and fall of the tide. Snow flurries out of the northeast made for slippery walking on deck. An hour or so later, the wind arrived and it soon became a full scale northeast gale that continued to howl for more than twenty hours. The shore front and piers were buried in snowdrifts. The boat became a floating snowbank. A sufficient supply of food, water and cigarettes, along with some old magazines helped pass the time.

It is probable that the layover in Portland during such a wild northeaster would prove to be one of the greatest blessings of my life.

The *WATER WITCH* was top-heavy with a deck load of scallop dredges and other fishing gear. An unreliable engine and extremely rough sea conditions — a combination for unlikely survival.

When the weather cleared, I could not get the engine started; the batteries had to be recharged. I hailed an outbound lobsterman who came alongside. He advised that the nearest source of 32 volt power would be the new Portland fireboat at the nearby city pier. He said "Cast off your lines and I will tow you over there." The lobsterman was a good man and refused any payment. Arriving alongside the fireboat, I was introduced to the chief engineer. He surprised me by saying, "This vessel is powered with Cummins diesel machinery, two main engines and two pump engines!" He went on to say that he had just returned from the Cummins training center where he had received a complete course of instructions for the operation and maintenance of all types of Cummins diesel engines.

A pair of "jumper cables" was quickly connected to my batteries. In a matter of minutes, the old Cummins engine came to life. The chief observed the smoky exhaust and volunteered to correct the problem. He cleaned and repaired the entire fuel injection system and provided a complete new set of filters. As a parting gesture, he directed the fireboat crew to refill my fuel oil tanks. When I offered payment for such fortunate services, the chief said, "You are a guest of our city of Portland!"

My good fortune included meals and "mug-ups" on board the fireboat. It was a great interlude for which I will always be thankful. After listening to a radio weather forecast that predicted a calm night, but fresh to strong northwest winds for next day, I decided to get underway immediately. There was a round of handshakes with the crew and especially chief engineer Jack Kendrick. Of course, I made an effort to convey my sincere thanks for their hospitality and services as we parted company. My lines were tossed aboard while the fireboat skipper gave me a farewell salute with the ship's foghorn.

By midnight I was clear of Portland harbor and steering a course toward a flashing buoy outside the Isles of Shoals and in the direction of Cape Ann. The only traffic insight was a big tug towing three barges.

A new day had dawned by the time the *WATER WITCH* at a cruising speed of about seven knots, entered the Annisquam Canal and made the transit into Gloucester harbor. The famous racing schooner and dory trawler *GERTRUDE L. THEBEAUD*, owned by the legendary Captain

Ben Pine, had just returned from Georges Bank, so I followed the vessel to her berth and tied up alongside. The recent raging northeaster had caught them on the northern edge of Georges where they suffered for three days and nights while "jogging" under a "three-reefed" foresail. Ordeals of that nature never seemed to be included in the wholesale price of fish.

All day I roamed the waterfront looking at the fishing vessels and talking with an occasional acquaintance. By sundown, the brisk nor'wester was moderating. Early the following morning I was out of the harbor and headed for the Cape Cod Canal about sixty miles away. It was an exceptional day for the month of March: calm sunny weather.

I arrived at the eastern end of the canal by mid-afternoon. (This was the original old narrow canal, before it was dredged and widened prior to World War II.) A boiling headtide resulted in very slow progress to the westward.

By the time I had negotiated the narrow gaps of the three lift bridges (two highway and one railroad) and navigated the winding Wing's Neck channel, daylight had been replaced with darkness. The dense blackness of the overcast night was punctuated by flashing buoy lights and the distant glow of Cleveland Ledge Lighthouse.

On the way toward Woods Hole, the engine came to a stop. My first thought was, "I'm glad it happened here and now rather than somewhere in the narrows of Woods Hole Channel." Because the fuel tank supply was ample, the problem had to be in the oil filter system. The two filter containers, accessible on the forward bulkhead, had to be drained and new elements installed. When the air was pumped out of the fuel oil injectors, the old Cummins came to life again and the cruise continued. It was three AM when the *WATER WITCH*, the latest edition of the island fishing fleet, arrived at the Vineyard Haven Dock, the successful completion of an adventurous single-handed voyage.

The World War II era created many drastic changes in the maritime scene. A considerable number of fishing trawlers were taken by the Coast Guard and the Navy for special duty. Seagoing sailing yachts, mostly schooners, became gray ghosts as they cruised silently on offshore submarine patrol. Otherwise, yachting was in a state of hibernation during the war years.

However, when the war program came to an end, along with fuel rationing, the market for boats and automobiles became very lively.

By the time that my generation had survived World War II, we began to enjoy a whole new era, like bright sunshine after a long period of stormy weather. Many of us had the notion that the artificial prosperity of war would be replaced by another economic depression. But of course, we soon learned that we were entering a future of booming business conditions. While automobile assembly lines became reactivated, the market for boats, pleasure craft in particular, was immediately very busy. Boatyard sheds and yards were full of combination of sailing craft and power yachts, all in a state of suspense. Not many of them were for sale as the owners could hardly wait to get them ready to use again. There were exceptions among owners who had decided to take advantage of the brisk market for used boats while they waited for new boats to be built and made available.

One of the first substitutes in new boat construction was a 26 foot sheet-metal powerboat produced at Stamford, Connecticut — with the trade name of Steelcraft — a mass production attempt during 1947 that did not achieve popularity. Aside from the fact that they neither looked or behaved like boats, their main problem was noise. Engine and exhaust roar was amplified inside the metal hull, so that normal speech was nearly impossible and earmuffs a necessity.

Fortunately, by 1949 and into the 50's, many capable boatbuilders in coastal locations particularly between Maine and New Jersey, began to fill the demand for practical wooden boats of many types and sizes. Chris Craft resumed their volume production. There were many other familiar builders, like Matthews and Wheeler with their sizable cabin cruisers, and mass production builders of smaller sized lap-strake craft such as the Lyman Boat Company in Ohio. Custom-built sport fishing craft exemplified by Rybovich at West Palm Beach in Florida represented the Rolls Royce character of the marine world.

During the 1950's, the market for used boats became normal as a result of a variety of fine wooden boats that were displayed in boat shows and attractively advertised in so many marine publications.

The outstanding post-war event in mid-January every year was the famous New York Boat Show. Nearly all the boatbuilders of importance was there to represent and display their latest creations. The show contained everything in the form of marine equipment, including the latest examples of gasoline and diesel engines. Four floors of expansive but most entertaining confusion. The original marine convention.

It was at the 1949 New York Boat Show that I came upon an attractive design on display, a 28' craft that appeared to be a blend of a Maine lobster boat and a Jersey sea skiff. A trunk cabin model with a shelter wheelhouse and roomy cockpit, it was a practical boat with a six cylinder "flat-head" Chrysler Crown gasoline engine with a 2:1 reduction gear. It contained a salt water cooled engine rated at 110 HP when revved up to about 2500 RPM. The boat was substantially built with a white oak keel and framework, cedar planking, and a shiny black hull with contrasting white upper structure. The boat was known as an Egg Harbor 28; the builder's shop was located in a New Jersey village by that name.

My persuasive enthusiasm for the boat resulted in my becoming their top dealer, with an open territory from Maine to New York. Advertising with a picture of the 28' Egg Harbor boat was displayed in many marine magazines. The demand was immediate, with continuous inquiries by phone and the U.S. mail. An instant waiting list was established.

A series of Egg Harbor boats was promptly delivered by truck and trailer to my headquarters at MacDougal's Boatyard in Falmouth, Massachusetts. Each boat was sold at a price of $5,250.00, including delivery and standard equipment. My commission was 10% of the sale price. Some of the deals required taking a used boat in trade — a tricky business because of an undetermined market value. The volume of activity became too much for one dealer. Egg Harbor Boatbuilders expanded into greater production and larger designs so that it became necessary after the first year to appoint many other dealers in each state along the Eastern Seaboard.

This series of chapters conclude the first 50 years of Memories and Experiences. The ensuing thirty-one years would contain a more modern series of events that will hopefully be recorded in the near future.

Chapter 43

Radio Station WLW

Broadcasting from Cincinnati, Ohio during the nineteen thirties and in nineteen thirty-five, WLW became the most powerful station in the world with an output of 500,000 watts. The wire fences of the Western prairies were said to glow in the darkness of night.

Away out on George's Bank, fishing boat radios were turned to the evening programs, particularly a dreamy interlude entitled "Moon River", that consisted of poetry with a background of organ music, the station theme song. With the aerial wire strung aloft between the masts, the sound volume had to be carefully controlled in order to avoid a loud whine that was caused by the immense broadcast power.

The man who provided the commentary of the Moon River program had the most impressive voice—a deep, bass tone with perfect diction which he delivered in such a way as to create a religious reaction to the audience—something like a message directly from god.

His name, Peter Grant, became known to listeners around the world.

Many years later a modern version of Moon River was created by musician Henry Mancini.

(The following is reprinted from an article that appeared in the Enquirer Magazine on March 21, 1982)

Surely the most memorable of WLW's programs was "Moon River," that late night session of romantic poetry and organ mood music that became legendary among lovers from coast-to-coast. Little did they know that "Moon River" was conceived, so to speak, in a house of ill repute.

Eddie Byron, the brilliant writer-producer and creator of "Mr. District Attorney," was a producer at WLW in the early '30s when Powel Crosley called him into his office one day.

"Mr. Crosley said he would like to hear a nice program of poetry and soft organ music at midnight — beginning tomorrow night," Eddie told me years later. "When Mr. Crosley said he would like to hear a nice program of poetry and soft organ music beginning tomorrow night, that was what Mr. Crosley was going to hear."

Grant as he is today, spending some of his retiremant time horseback riding.

WLW
RADIO 7

(513) 241-9597

MOON RIVER

Moon River . . .
A lazy stream of dreams,
Where vain desires forget themselves
In the loveliness of sleep,
Moon River . . .
Enchanted white ribbon
Twined in the hair of the night,
Where nothing is but sleep.
Dream on . . . sleep on . . .
Care will not seek for thee.
Float on . . . Drift on . . .
Moon River, to the sea.

Down the valley of a thousand yesterdays
Flow the bright waters of Moon River.
On and down forever . . . forever waiting
To carry you down to the land of forgetfulness,
To the kingdom of sleep . . . to the realms of . . .
Moon River,
Where vain desires forget themselves
In the loveliness of sleep.
Moon River . . .
Enchanted white ribbon
Twined in the hair of night,
Where nothing is but sleep.
Dream on . . . sleep on . . .
Care will not seek for thee.
Float on . . . drift on . . .
Moon River, to the sea.

It so happened during those Prohibition days that there was a speakeasy on Court Street, run by a friendly madam, where Eddie and some of the musicians went from time to time after signing off the station. Eddie and Virginio Marucci, a staff violinist, headed for the speakeasy that night.

"I was sitting at the kitchen table of this joint, drinking and trying to write a theme for this damn program that had to be on the next night," Eddie remembered. "Somehow the name 'Moon River' popped into my head. After all, I grew up in Newport on the Ohio River and remembered moonlight on the river. It was pretty romantic."

Ladies in kimonos kept wandering in and out of the kitchen as Marucci played the violin.

"The more I drank, the better what I wrote sounded to me as I started off with 'Down the valley of a thousand yesterdays flow the bright waters of Moon River,'" said Eddie. "When I finished, the ladies were weeping, the madam was weeping, and I knew I had a winner."

Most of WLW's staff announcers narrated "Moon River" over the years, but it is Peter Grant whom everyone remembers. His deep, resonant voice and flair for reading poetry made him the favorite narrator.

WLW was 10 years old, and Pete was 26 when he came here from KMOX, St. Louis, to join the station as staff announcer. Pete began life as Melvin Maginn.

"'Moon River' was already on at midnight with Harry Holcombe as narrator," said Peter. "Harry, who now plays Grampa on those Country Time Lemonade commercials, was a staff actor and also appeared with a local theatrical company . . He was too busy to do 'Moon River,' which was why I took over."

The DeVore Sisters were the trio most closely associated with 'Moon River,' but later, other staff vocalists were heard — The Clooney Sisters (Rosemary and Betty), Anita Ellis, Ruby Wright, Doris Day, Lucille Norman and Jeannette Davis, to name a few.

Peter Grant during his early years as a staff announcer at WLW.

"When WLW's power was increased to 500,000 watts in 1935 on an experimental basis, 'Moon River' was heard all over the world," Peter recalled. "I got letters from everywhere — missionaries in China, people in England, Europe, South America and Africa."

A young song writer in Georgia, Johnny Mercer, also heard 'Moon River,' and many years later, he remembered it when he wrote the lyrics to a song by Henry Mancini and called it 'Moon River.'

Chapter 44

The Sloop Rigged Catboat - SUDDEN JERK

Now is the time to consider a somewhat different marine adventure. The subject "A big, bulky catboat known by the name *SUDDEN JERK*" that had been rerigged as a sloop and used for inshore fishing. Two island characters shared ownership. The "pardners" were Craig Kingsbury and Terry Keogh.

Craig's normal occupation was farming at his State Road location. His livestock included a pair of oxen which he used for heavy work instead of horses. A tall, rugged-looking character with a handlebar mustache, usually barefoot and chewing tobacco, he would have looked good in a typical Wild West movie production. But Craig seemed to have an urge for boating on occasion. He and I once sailed with Alton Tilton on the dragger, 3 & 1 on an expedition for yellow-tail flounders somewhere south of Noman's Land.

Terry Keogh was a Master Mariner with an unlimited ocean license. Although his preference was for sailing ships, he had commanded steam-powered passenger ships between U.S. and European seaports. He had been the navigating officer with Columbus Iselin when the ketch *ATLANTIS* was delivered from Copenhagen, Denmark, to the newly established Woods Hole Oceanographic Institution during the summer of 1931. By that time, Terry has developed a constant thirst for alcoholic beverages.

As captain of the *ATLANTIS* on the first scientific voyage, Keogh entered the port of Havana, Cuba for fresh water and supplies. While there, Terry and a few of his crewmade a tour of many barrooms. Thus fully fuelled, they took charge of a trolley car loaded with passengers for a wild ride through the city streets. Somehow, the electricity was turned off and the trolly car stopped before any damage was done. Terry and his crew were promptly arrested and jailed.

The American ambassador managed to bail them out, but Columbus Iselin finally had to journey to Havana to resolve the situation and to get the *ATLANTIS* underway and safely out to sea.

When the *ATLANTIS* returned to Woods hole, Keogh's professional seafaring career was suspended. He arrived at Vineyard Haven and soon became established as the town drunk. He was a comical sight in his battered felt hat and a stained pajama shirt, ragged khakis and worn-out shoes. One day, he followed us into Mrs. Luce's ice cream shop, where he observed himself in a full-length mirror. his reaction: “Is that really me, or someone else”?

He once shipped on a local dragger for a five-day fluke trip south of Nantucket, but when his supply of booze was gone, he began to talk bout draining the compass for thealcohol that it contained. The only solution was to land him in Edgartown to get him out of the way.

The *SUDDEN JERK* became Keogh's home afloat. He and Craig, along with another character, whose name escapes me, decided to rig the boat for swordfishing, complete with a long bowsprit and harpooner's pulpit.

The day came when they were ready to cruise over to Woods Hole for the necessary ice and other supplies for their proposed swordfishing trip. Part way across Vineyard Sound, the rusty old engine wheezed to a stop. After tinkering and cranking the engine for a while, Keogh shouted, "Let's sail this vessel somewhere? We have plenty of southwest wind and a strong east tide." The boat had no sail, but Keogh had a plan. There were four sizeable hatch covers on the main deck. hammers and spikes came from cabin lockers.

In a matter of minutes, two of the crew held the hatch covers in place while Keogh spiked them to the mast. The boat was moving toward the Falmouth shoreline. More lumber - cupboard doors and floor-boards - was brought up from the cabin. An impressive square-rigged catboat!

Keogh and Kingsbury claimed to have sailed the *SUDDEN JERK* straight into Falmouth Harbor - between the jetties and all the way up to MacDougal's boatyard. Keogh proudly proclaimed that never before had he used a hammer and a pinch bar to unrig a vessel's sails. Someone should have snapped some pictures of that unusual example of seamanship. The engine was repaired and they chugged their way safely into Woods Hole before sunset.

They docked the *SUDDEN JERK* at Dyer's coal wharf. The stores had closed for the day but of course the barrooms welcomed newcomers. By midnight, all three adventurers had become Loard the boat, but Craig Kingsbury tumbled into the fish hold; the hatch covers had not been replaced. Keogh dropped them into place as Craig lay spread out on a bunch of burlap bags.

Sometime before dawn Craig became conscious of his confinement. He crawled around trying to find a way out. Finally, he managed to stand up, whereupon he bumped his head and jarred a section of the hatch cover out of place. Fresh air greeted him as he crawled out on deck. His two shipmates snored peacefully in the cabin bunks.

While having breakfast at a nearby diner, they discovered a shortage of money, barely enough to pay the bill. The swordfishing trip had to be postponed and refinanced. They returned to Vineyard Haven.

It is possible that they managed to make a few day-trips swordfishing out of Menemsha, but I have no record of such activities.

The oversized sailboat *SUDDEN JERK* eventually reached such a stage of dilapidation that she would barely stay afloat. Somehow, she was hauled out and moved inland where she was permanently retired to Jim Adams' farm near South Road in Chilmark. She sat in a pasture there for years and served as a nautical landmark. Dozens of brown and white cows used her weathered planking daily to scratch their itchy hides.

All wooden boats have their own life story, but perhaps there is a Vineyard historian who could provide the information of the origin and history of that big catboat, which at the moment, is a complete mystery. it would be great to know the name of the builder, and where and when the boat was built. She probably had several proud owners who had sailed her with an original, romantic name.

While the old boat sat in the farmer's field for many years, she became a tourist attraction. Tour bus operators, en route to Gay Head via the South Road, always used their loud speakers to call attention to the boat with the explanation that the boat had been deposited there by a hurricane many years earlier. The visitors probably believed it!

Chapter 45

The Bay Scallop Season

A few hardy characters went tub trawling or handlining for codfish off Squibnocket and Noman's land, when the weather was favorable. Being a resident of Vineyard Haven, I had the opportunity to go scalloping in Lagoon Pond. i bought a 14 foot skiff with a culling board and two dredges from an old timer, Mr. Hamilton, who had become a patient at the Marine Hospital.

On November 1st, the opening day of the scallop season, an impressive fleet of rowboats engaged in a frenzy of activity, especially in the shallower areas between the bridge and Hines Point. The day's limit was five special burlap bags with drawstrings at the top, a big bushel of scallops in each bag. No mechanical power could be used – town conservation rules. Except for a few who used glass-bottom boxes and dip nets, most of us went at it the hard way with an anchor and about 300 feet of rope.

In order to get onto a good location, it was necessary to be out there at sunrise. When the anchor was set, the boat would drift with the prevailing breeze (usually from the northwest) the length of the coiled anchor rope. In calm conditions, or when it was necessary to change the towing angle, the oars had to be activated. The dredges were tossed overboard at the stern, with the proper length of towline secured to a cleat on each side. The next step was to climb over the culling board, a platform about three feet wide across the middle of the skiff extending over the gunwales, with edgeboards some four inches high, a necessary containment for the piles of seaweed, shells and scallops that were dumped after each tow of the dredges, which was accomplished by the operator pulling the boat and the dredges forward probably a length of 250 feet. Then we'd secure the anchorline on the bow cleat, go back over the culling board to the stern, pull first one dredge then the other, dump the contents on the platform, crawl over the heap to get forward and cast off the anchor rope.

The culling job was done as the boat drifted back, often bumping into the other craft likewise engaged. A few of the bigger skiffs carried a two-man crew, in some cases, a husband and wife team that could readily catch a double limit of ten bushel bags. One worked in the bow, the other in the stern, a most sensible arrangement. But many of us had to go it alone because of the limitations of space and carrying capacity.

The first two weeks of the scallop season were the most hectic. Most of us could catch our limit and be ashore by midday. The balance of the day was devoted to the tedious shucking process. Only the true fishermen continued after the initial "Klondike." As the winter progressed, with the fleet reduced to less than a dozen boats, it was a matter of sheer perseverance, until it became an all-day job to scrape up a single bag of bay scallops. Then, after supper, the shucking job was done on a bench near the back door (No scallop-opening was allowed – by parental rule – in the warm basement!) except in temperatures below freezing. A twelve-hour day with plenty of fresh air! Early in the following day the tasty scallops were delivered in a five gallon can to a buyer on the waterfront who paid an average of thirty-five cents a pound for the hard-earned product! Occasionally we saved a batch for a luxurious Sunday dinner.

Sometimes we had periods of severe cold weather when the ponds and the inner harbor became solidly frozen, putting a stop to the scallop business. if the cold continued long enough, the pond ice would get to be eight or ten inches thick. By that time Harry Peakes called us outdoor characters to help him cut ice at a big pond at Lambert's Cove. Large hand saws provided a warming exercise for some of the crew while others used slice-bars to cut the blocks to standard sizes and push them toward the conveyor belt that carried the 300 pound blocks up into the insulated icehouse on the pond shore. We had at least ten days of steady employment during which the ice storage building would be filled to capacity. Ten hour days at fifty cents an hour. A bonanza of cash!

After that the weather moderated, a period usually known as the January thaw. By that time only three or four of us regular fishermen tried to resume scalloping. My favorite place to work was up at the far end of Lagoon Pond in the lee of a high embankment, an area known as "Oklahoma." It was calm there. Underwater springs and sunshine soon dissolved the ice, creating a strip of open water that widened daily parallel to the shoreline.

My scallop boat and equipment were trucked overland and launched from an accessible beach. It was such a pleasure to be there. No competition. The water was crystal clear. The bottom sloped gradually to the depth of fifteen feet. The scallop crop was plentiful and of magnificent size. They could be seen all the way out to deep water. A short tow filled the dredges to capacity. Very little seaweed. The small scallops went quickly overboard, hopefully to become full-sized by the following year. The five-bag limit was easily achieved, a great contrast to previous production in the lower lagoon scallop grounds. It was an easy row back to the beach near the road where my Plymouth coupe was waiting. The rear seat cushions had been removed so that there was plenty of space to transport the five big bags of scallops over the roads to my backyard. After lunch I hired a neighbor, Joe Authier, to come over to help with the shucking process. The job was completed by sundown with the shell s dumped in a nearby cellar hole.

The upper lagoon shoreline provided good scalloping until the open season ended by April 1st. By then it was time to get ready for the blackback flounder season in Vineyard Sound. Many of the local draggers worked in the main channel close to Hedge Fence shoal. A lightship by that name was anchored at the east end of the shoal. At that time the smaller draggers were so underpowered that it was necessary to tow the net in the direction of the tide. We had about an hour of slack water between the six hour East or West flow of 3 knot current. At that stage, we managed to get in a one hour tow in both direction. The flounders were packed in wooden boxes that contained two bushels of fish along with a proper quantity of crushed ice. An easy unloading feature. After an hour of towing the net would usually produce anywhere from five to ten bushels of flounder, along with plenty of trash that we shoveled back overboard.

Later in the month of April the smaller draggers of the Vineyard fleet went to Hyannis and operated out of there through the month of May until the blackback flounder migration ended. Then it we time to return to our island homeport, at which time the boats were cleaned, hauled out on the marine railway and completely painted in readiness for the summer fluke and swordfishing season.

There was another profitable activity in that upper lagoon "Oklahoma" shoreline. Norman Benson provided me with a dozen eel pots complete with lines and buoys. He and his son Franklin were busy in September and October catching eels in West Tisbury Great Pond. He showed me how to seine bait, minnows of all sorts, in the late afternoon when they came into the warmer, shallow water near the beach. Then I was told to build a big crate about six feet square and four feet deep (known as a "car") that would be used to keep the eels alive for the forthcoming Italian market during the Christmas season. The vertical slats were about one-half inch apart, allowing a good circulation of water. The Bensons then advised me to anchor the "car" in Uncle Seth's Pond at Lambert's Cove. They lived nearby and kept their own eels there.

By that time, I had become the owner of a Franklin sedan, which had an air-cooled engine, a Dukes County Garage trade-in. With a makeshift trailer hitch, the big Franklin sedan easily towed my homemade utility trailer, upon which sat my fourteen-foot scalloping skiff.

The string of twelve eel pots was baited and set before sunset parallel to the "Oklahoma" shoreline in fifteen to twenty feet of water. Soon after sunrise the next morning, I was there to haul the pots for the first time. What a surprise! Every single pot was jammed solid full of large greenish colored eels! They were squeezed in so tight that the outer layer had the imprint of the square-wire mesh of the round pots on their skin. A door in the wooden end of the pot opened to let the eels slither out onto the bottom of the skiff. I bailed several buckets of water into the skiff so the eels could stay wet and alive. The pots would be hauled and rebaited at the end of the day. The eels had to be taken ashore and scoop-netted into a huge tup that sat on the trailer above the high-water mark. Then I made a fast trip up to Lambert's Cove to transfer the catch into the floating "car". Production continued at full capacity until late October when a sudden frost ended the season. When the Italian eel dealer arrived on the island about mid-December my collection of eels sold for something more than a thousand dollars, a fortune in those days! The total weight must have been considerable.